TEN PATHS TO
FREEDOM

TEN PATHS TO
FREEDOM

AWAKENING MADE SIMPLE

James Wood

James Wood Teachings, LLC
Tucson, Arizona

Book and cover design by Raven's Eye Design
ravenseyedesign.com

ISBN: 978-0615604404

For my students

There is a work to be done,
a teaching to be lived, and
no one is exempt.

—Richard Moss

CONTENTS

ACKNOWLEDGMENTS

Heartfelt thanks to the following:

Aly Waibel and Rebecca Weinstein for editing, suggestions, and inspiration, as well as many others who offered feedback.

Chad Bush at Raven's Eye Design for typesetting and graphics.

My students for growing, being, and living the Teaching.

My parents for their unflagging love and support.

My Teachers, without whom this book would have been impossible.

INTRODUCTION

*I am the cause of my suffering—but
only all of it.*
       —Byron Katie

Thou art That.
     —*Chandogya Upanishad*

WHAT IS THE PROBLEM?

Existence is agony.
Birth is painful, death is painful, and everything in between is painful: loss, failure, injury, disease, anger, loneliness, despair, heartache, *ad infinitum*. To exist is to be born, suffer, and die—a veritable *danse macabre*.

Of course, life has its moments of relief, respite, and pleasure—job promotions, island vacations, cocktail parties—but these experiences are temporary and incomplete. We are never completely fulfilled, or at least not permanently. No desire is ever fully satisfied, because within each satisfied desire is the seed of future craving. At the heart of life's pain is a profound *dissatisfaction,* a sense of incompleteness or fundamental insufficiency—a sense of *Is this all there is? This can't be it!*—that persists despite everything we do.

Think about it. No matter what you do, nothing lasts. No matter how much money you make, it is eventually lost. No matter how much you eat, you get hungry again. No matter how much sex you have, you need more of it. Nothing of this world satisfies completely. Even if you are materially wealthy and surrounded by luxury, you get sick or have accidents. Even with the best doctors, you eventually die. No matter what you have, no matter who you are, no matter what you do—you lose it all at death.

This sounds like a bad nightmare, and it is.

To be free of it, you must awaken from it.

Spiritual awakening—not religion, not dogma, not words—but *awakening itself,* is the answer. Awakening is the end of all suffering, incompleteness, and dissatisfaction. Awakening ends your nightmare forever.

THE ABSOLUTE: TRUTH

When your nightmare ends, what you awaken to is absolutely satisfying: your true nature. Your true nature is your spiritual essence. Complete, peaceful, and free, your true nature is beyond all comprehension and ultimately fulfilling. Because it is beyond all relative values, we can call it *the Absolute.* Awakening to the Absolute is everything you could ever want or need.

One way to look at the Absolute is that it is *absolute truth.* The Absolute is Truth* because it is what is revealed when you remove everything that is false. When you realize that you have been suffering from false ideas for as long as you can remember, it shocks you—and then you can begin to see what is actually there, what is primarily and ultimately true, the fundamental condition that *you already are.*

Truth is what you are.

Awakening is Truth-recognition. It is not an experience, state, or form of anything you can mentally *know.* Awakening involves finding false ideas, or *lies,* and seeing their falseness. When you see their falseness, you see truth. When you see nothing but Truth, you are awakened. This true seeing is *awareness.* Awareness is identical with your true nature.

---

* Capitalization denotes absolute quality of a term. For example, "truth" means truth in a relative or general sense, whereas "Truth" means absolute truth.

To find Truth, you have to be a detective. You have to notice that things don't add up, like a bad alibi. Then you have to find clues and follow them to their source, arriving at Truth no matter what, freeing you from your pain.

FREEDOM

To free yourself from pain, you must remove what keeps you bound to it. The absolute freedom of awakening in the average person is obscured by pain. You have to remove the cause of your pain to be free, just as a prisoner must break the chain of his leg-iron to escape. Eliminate what binds you, and Freedom is revealed. You don't create Freedom; you *are* it, and you fall into it when you get rid of false ideas.

The unawakened condition is like a powerful state of hypnosis that you are convinced is true. For example, if you were hypnotized into thinking that you were a convict and your leg-chain were real and unbreakable, you would not be able to break it—because the chain is an idea in your mind, an impenetrable thought. You have to break the thought—the chain in your mind—by fundamentally recognizing that *there is no leg-chain.* That is what frees you—not the *thought* "there is no leg-chain," but the *actuality* of it, the clear seeing that the leg-chain is just a thought, a hypnotic suggestion.

Because the Absolute cannot be grasped, it is difficult to try to attain it as a positive value. It is far more effective to get rid of what blocks it in your awareness. To do this, notice that you are dissatisfied, trace your dissatisfaction back to its origin, and eliminate its cause—a false belief—revealing the Satisfaction that is already there. Otherwise, you will not likely find it. This approach is not for the faint of heart because you have to face your deepest fears. It may be challenging, but the ultimate satisfaction of awakening is beyond anything you could imagine: better than sex, better than drugs, better than success, incomprehensibly, ultimately, absolutely better than anything.

THE TRUE TEACHING

Spontaneous awakening is rare, and the path that leads to it is long and arduous. This random, self-guided path is the way of most people. Waiting for awakening to occur in this way is like wandering aimlessly on a desert planet, expecting to stumble upon a hidden diamond by accident. It's not likely to happen. For this reason, it is ill-advised to leave your spiritual progress up to random events. It is much easier to embrace the *true Teaching*, the active form of Truth in the world that is reaching out to you, even now.

The true Teaching doesn't just materialize out of ether; it enters the world through awakened human beings. Because the awakened person embodies Truth completely, it is helpful to find an awakened person, a true Teacher, to help you. Awakened people are true Teachers because that is their function. Although there is only one Truth, it has many relative forms. The Teaching is one; its forms are many. The outward form of the Teaching is a body of instruction whose purpose is to awaken all beings.

Most people think that a spiritual teacher is a person *outside* you. This is not necessarily the case. The ultimate Teacher is Truth, or who you are in your essence, so you already have a Teacher *inside* you. Everyone does. You are your own Teacher. But having an external, flesh-and-blood Teacher makes your work *easier*. It is easier to listen to a voice outside of you than it is to listen to a voice inside, especially when you are a beginner on the path. Having a Teacher is a great benefit, as if the internal voice of Truth had been conveniently externalized for you as a person.

A Teacher has been there, has taken the steps that you must take if you are to awaken. He* is the one who can pull you from the quagmire. To a person who wants to awaken without an external Teacher, I would say that although it is possible, it is not advisable. It is extremely difficult to access your own spiritual wisdom consistently

---

* To honor men and women equally, I have distributed gender references to reflect a balance between male and female and to avoid awkward constructions such as "his/her." Half of the chapters refer to the Teacher as male and others as female, and the other half vice-versa.

without help. On a self-directed path, your progress is sporadic and regression is common. Why would you want to prolong your suffering? A deliberate path of study with an external Teacher is far easier.

Remember: you are not alone. The Absolute knows about you, is trying to reach you this very moment. Don't think that it is up to your own limited, conceptual intelligence to figure a way out of the quagmire. Your own, limited, conceptual intelligence *is* the quagmire. That is why it is so challenging to find a way out by your own effort. The harder you struggle, the deeper you sink. You need leverage, a stable platform that doesn't move when you grasp it and pull. You have such leverage, waiting for you to extend your hand so it can pull you out.

The platform is this book. Let it help you.

TIPS FOR GETTING STARTED

If you are serious about awakening, here are a few guidelines.

First, *you cannot know what awakening is with your mind.* Waking up is radical, not to be approached casually, as if it were a trifle. You cannot know what it is. If you assume you know what awakening is, you will miss out. Strive to be the person who admits he knows little or nothing, and you can go far—as long as you realize that even the little bit you *think* you know is next to go out the window.

Second, *true Liberation does not come from anything of this world.* Nothing of this world satisfies. To awaken, you must be profoundly dissatisfied with everything the world has to offer. No possessions will save you, no ideas will save you, and no feeling-states will save you. No matter what you own, no matter what you believe, no matter what you experience, it's all temporary and ultimately unsatisfying. You must abandon looking for salvation in anything of this world. That doesn't mean that you don't own, think, or feel anything; it just means that you have given up looking for salvation in those things. It also means that looking for salvation in those things is painful.

Third, *you are inflicting this pain on yourself.* No one is hurting you but *you.* This is the best news you could ever receive. Since you are the cause of your pain, you are also its solution. Blaming others doesn't work. You are the cause of all of your suffering as well as the only one who can free yourself from it. If you don't free yourself, no one else will.

Fourth, and finally, *you must want awakening badly to have it.* A Zen parable tells of a monk and his Master who are fishing in a small boat on a lake. The monk asks his Master, "How badly must one want awakening to have it?" The Master answers by throwing the monk into the lake and holding his head under water. When the monk is near drowning and desperate, the Master lets him up for air. He then asks the drenched, sputtering monk, "When you were under the water, what was it that you wanted more than anything else?" The monk gasps, "Air!" Then the Master says, "You must want awakening this badly or you will not have it."

You must want awakening this badly or you will not have it.

ABOUT THIS BOOK

This book would be worthless had I not lived it myself. I woke up. How did this happen for me? Good question. The essence of it is as follows:

1. I found a Teacher.
2. I did the work.
3. I gave it everything I had.
4. I kept going until I was done.

Aside from this, my personal story is not that important. The most important thing about my story is that it ended. I am more interested in helping you find Freedom than narrating my personal history. Instead of telling you about my own process, I decided to leave its essence in this book of instructions. This book is a guide to awakening based on my own experience. Although the particulars are missing, you can assume I went through all of it in my own way.

And that's just it: I was in my own way, and now I'm not.

So here we are: you, I, and these words. It is as if my path left behind muddy footprints, and compassion is making them available for you to follow. Truly, compassion wrote this book. I have no ulti-mate need for it—but at the level of compassion, I am both giver and receiver, doctor and patient, author and reader, so I don't mind us being here together, as long as someone needs to get what the writing contains. If we leave all the fiction behind, you will realize that *there's only one of us.*

I can stay if you're interested.

———————————

This book comprises ten chapters. Each chapter describes an approach to awakening involving a path of Truth-recognition. Each chapter can be used as a path in itself or in combination with others. Taken as a whole, the book is a progression of foundational ideas to more advanced concepts, each one adding further depth and complexity. It is designed so that someone new to the path could begin at Chapter One and read each chapter in succession all the way to the end. Those already familiar with it could read it in any order.

If this book seems redundant in places, realize that sometimes it helps to hear the same thing said many times in different ways. If you are dying of thirst in the desert, it helps to hear "The oasis is *this way*" as many times as it takes to find it.

I prefer the term *awakening* because it is most descriptive, like waking up from a nightmare. But because awakening frees you from false ideas, it can also be called *Freedom* or *Liberation.* It can also be called *enlightenment. Enlightenment* is a term that, while useful, is less so because it implies that awakening necessarily involves seeing visions of light, which it doesn't. The "light" of enlightenment actually refers to *consciousness,* which is more like the figurative light bulb of clarity that comes on when you are hit with a sudden insight. These terms— *awakening, Freedom, Liberation,* and *enlightenment*—basically all refer to the same thing, and I use them more or less interchangeably.*

---

* I capitalize the terms "Freedom" and "Liberation" and not the terms "awakening" and "enlightenment" because the former two represent a greater degree of absolute quality than the latter two, although their meaning encompasses that of the latter two. In general, awakening and enlightenment occur in a physically embodied state, whereas Freedom and Liberation both include and transcend the physically embodied state, as in Liberation in the between, covered in Chapter Nine.

Some of the ideas in this book may be considered metaphysical, such as what lies after death or beyond the reach of the ordinary five senses. These ideas are based on my experience. I had to discover them for myself. I suggest you do the same. I am not asking you to *believe* in anything. Some things are called "metaphysical" because they lie beyond the ordinary experience of most people. That does not make them any less real to you when you encounter them for yourself. I would rather you be prepared for what lies beyond the fragile skin of this world than meet it without a prayer.

The authenticity of this book cannot be proven by anything other than your own wisdom, intuition, and experience. You have to find out for yourself. If you are ready for fundamental change, keep reading.

You've been warned.

Remember: The world is a prison, and you are holding the key. You locked yourself into imaginary bondage and only you can free yourself from it. No one else can do it for you. Use this book. Let it guide you.

Make a break for it.

I AM waiting on the other side of the wall for you.

James Wood
June, 2007

CHAPTER ONE

HONESTY

You will know the truth, and the
truth will set you free.
                                    —Jesus Christ

God is Truth.
                                    —Gandhi

LIES

If you are looking for Truth, the world is not going to help you. The reason for this is simple: *The world is made of lies.*

The world is like a mental institution whose occupants—including the doctors, nurses, and administrators—are insane, thinking they are sane. They are insane because they believe the world is ultimately real when it is ultimately unreal.

Most people assume that the world is ultimately real, a kind of bedrock upon which everything else rests. It's not. If you examine it closely, you will find that the world is insubstantial, the play of shadows on a wall, a mere projection of your mind. Everything we know as "the world" is a conglomeration of thoughts, a gauze of hypnotism that falls apart under scrutiny. Like a dream, it is a mental drama playing out on the screen of your awareness, a phantom composed of thoughts.

If you find yourself objecting to this, notice that your objection is a thought.

Think about this for a moment.

The world seems solid because we cling to it, giving it a sense of power that it would otherwise not have. We cling to it because we believe that we depend upon it for our existence. In fact, the reverse is true: *it* depends on *us*. It depends on us because we project it as a dramatic display on the screen of our awareness. We think that it's being done to us when we're the ones doing it.

Everything in the world is *relative* because it exists relative to and dependent upon awareness for its existence. Awareness depends on nothing but itself, and therefore is absolute, identical with Truth. Everything arises within awareness. Even your body arises within awareness. Because awareness is your true nature, the world arises within you and depends on you. Once you recognize this fact, nothing can scare you.

Truth is who you are.

An awakened person acts in the world just like everyone else, only she knows that the world has no independent power. A projectionist is not afraid of her own movie, because she knows it's just a play of light and shadow on a screen.

She also knows that the projector can be turned off.

BASIC HONESTY

To awaken, you have to align yourself with truth in all its forms. You have to break free. You have to get honest. On a relative level, being honest is speaking, writing, or otherwise conveying truth. On an absolute level, being honest is waking up to who you are. Either way, it means being real. It means untangling the web of lies that binds you. First, clear up your relative thought process and communication, then you can approach the Absolute with clarity.

Start by speaking the truth. Truth-telling is the last thing most people want to do, but it is one of the most effective ways to get started on the path of awakening. People want to be free of unhappiness, but most are unwilling to give up their lies, the social glue for their drama. People want to be rid of suffering without getting rid of its cause: dishonesty. You can't just ascend above the insanity of the world. You have to clean up your part of it. Until you clean up your part, how can you be trusted with What lies beyond it?

You have to be bold. You have to get mentally and emotionally healthy. Many students of awakening just want to ascend, to attain some pleasurable state, but trying to ascend without taking care of your own basic psychological dishonesty is like trying to take off in a hot air balloon with too much baggage on board. You'll never make it.

One of the basic misconceptions about the spiritual path is that you can awaken by avoiding or denying the world. You can't. The world is the Absolute in disguise. You have to penetrate the illusion of the world directly and see its falseness. Avoidance of the world is what gives it its sense of substance, like avoiding a monster under your bed. The only way to get rid of the monster is to shine a light under the bed and see that it was an illusion to begin with. Instead of avoiding it, see it for what it is—a false appearance.

You have to find out what's true. Do this by finding what is false and recognizing its falseness. Seeing what is false *as false* is true seeing, like seeing the falseness of the statement, "2 + 2 = 5."

Start with *basic honesty,* or telling the truth about the relative world—the world of day-to-day living—whether speaking, writing, or otherwise communicating. To practice basic honesty, you have to know what constitutes a basic truth. A *basic truth* is a thought that matches your experience. A *basic lie* is a thought that does *not* match your experience. Simple, isn't it? If you see a cup on the table, the statement "The cup is on the table" is a basic truth and the statement "The cup is *not* on the table" is a basic lie. Basic honesty, then, is communicating a basic truth, and basic dishonesty is communicating a basic lie. Basic honesty is a form of *relative* honesty, the honesty of day-to-day living. Relative honesty prepares you for *absolute* honesty, the conscious activity of awakening.

Awakening is rare because most people lie. Few are willing to commit to honesty in their daily living. To awaken, you have to be uncommon. You have to be willing to embarrass yourself if necessary, and most people avoid that. You have to humiliate the arrogant parts of your personality that resist relationship to your true nature. You have to be willing to shock your family, your friends, even your thera-pist. You have to free yourself from the false self-image you have been projecting, the one that keeps you from being free. Most people avoid this level of honesty. If you want to awaken, you must embrace it.

Start looking closely at your life. Find the lies that you tell, both to yourself and to others. This can be challenging, but it must be done if you are to become sane and healthy. You have to be a lover of truth, to want the truth at all costs, beyond even comfort, security, and cer-tainty. Find the ugly facts about yourself that you avoid. Reveal them so completely that they lose the power to contaminate your sense of self. Be brutally honest about how you live, how you treat yourself and others, how you deceive others—everything. Seeing yourself as you are is crucial. Hitler was able to rise to power in Europe because German citizens were unwilling to admit the heinous character of their own government. Your nature is like this. If you let lies go un-checked within your borders, you doom yourself to a perpetual inner holocaust. Be courageous. Rigorous self-honesty is necessary, other-wise you blind yourself to your own illusions.

Get clear about your experience, and don't allow yourself to live a lie, because it will hurt you. Get in touch with your senses. Pay at-tention. Notice the flavor of food, the texture of fabric, the fragrance of plants, the color of the sky, the sound of laughter. The clearer you are in your sensory nature, the more accurately you can match your thoughts with your experience, because you are aware of what is hap-pening. Check and double-check to make sure that you are honest with yourself. Don't assume anything. Investigate. Notice things, ask questions, and find out for yourself. Face facts, or strive to find the facts until you are satisfied that you have found them. Live in accord with what you find, no matter how painful it may be to do so. A pain-ful truth heals if faced openly and honestly, but a painful lie festers like an infected wound and cannot heal until exposed to the clear light of your awareness.

Once you reveal it, you can heal it.

SITUATIONAL HONESTY

If someone asks you what you think or feel, tell him the truth, or don't tell him anything at all. We lie because we believe that it will cause less pain than being honest. It doesn't. We lie to protect a false image of ourselves, and the false image is a constricting suit of armor. We must give up comforting illusions about ourselves to find out who we really are. Even a healthy self-image is a miserable caricature that must eventually be left behind. Who we ultimately are is infinitely more than any image we could have of ourselves.

Lying builds a wall that blocks intimacy. If you lie to people, you cannot connect with them, you cannot establish any real rapport. The false sense of self is a barrier, a social mask that gets in the way. Don't pretend to be something you're not. Lying reduces the possibility of intimacy—"into me you see"—with others. People can't see into you because you're putting up a false front. Even if someone likes you, it's not the real you, but a cardboard cutout, and you have to work to maintain the facade. Give it up and get real.

Allow yourself to confess to someone you can trust. Confide in at least one person, such as a counselor, therapist, or spouse. Be as honest as you can and keep going. Buried lies will reveal themselves.

When confessing, make sure you can trust the person who's listening. To whom you speak is important. It would be inappropriate to reveal your deepest, darkest secrets to a complete stranger. The general rule is this: the more intimate you are with someone, and the more intimate you want to be with someone, the more you reveal. It is appropriate to get to know someone before you reveal intimate facts about yourself. The relationship must be developed first. Otherwise, you could be harmed.

Honesty involves more than just telling the truth, or *what* you tell. It is also *when, where, how, why, if,* and *to whom* you tell it. Some information is appropriate to reveal in a given situation and some is appropriate to withhold. This is called *situational honesty* because it depends on the situation. It does not mean changing truth to fit the situation. It means communicating at the right time, in the right place, in the right way, to the right person, for the right reasons. A statement can be honest in one moment and dishonest in the next because the situation has changed.

Practicing situational honesty requires a clear assessment of what is going on around and within you. You have to pay attention. You must know both what is basically true as well as the appropriateness of revealing information or withholding it—based on the situation. Situational honesty requires clear reasoning, and you must be able to assess the situation appropriately. For example, can you trust the person to whom you are speaking? Are you in a private place where no one can overhear your conversation? Are you communicating to establish or develop intimacy? These are all important considerations.

To practice situational honesty, start paying attention to your surroundings, to what is happening around and within you. Notice your environment, who is there, what is happening, what you are feeling. Make this your practice. This practice brings you into the present moment more fully and makes you more aware of what is appropriate to say (or refrain from saying) in the moment. The more you pay attention to your experience in the moment, the better you get at trusting what you feel is appropriate to say, or not to say. Eventually, you can pay attention to your experience in the moment so fully that you begin to tap into the Absolute directly. This tapping into the Absolute directly is called *absolute honesty.*

ABSOLUTE HONESTY

Absolute honesty is the conscious activity of awakening, the way to approach the Absolute as well as the nature of the Absolute Itself. The key to absolute honesty is this: *You are not a thought.* You are not your mind. Awakening involves seeing the entire domain of mental content and recognizing that it is not who (or what) you are. Whereas relative honesty involves communicating thoughts that match your experience (basic honesty) and under what conditions to do so (situational honesty), absolute honesty involves *how you relate to the thoughts themselves.* An awakened person relates to thoughts consciously; an unawakened person relates to them unconsciously. An awakened person recognizes that thoughts are ultimately false; an unawakened person assumes that thoughts are ultimately true.

To appreciate absolute truth and absolute honesty fully we have to examine their opposites, *absolute lies* and *absolute dishonesty*. For clarity, we will consider all four of these categories in detail: *absolute truth, absolute lies, absolute dishonesty, and absolute honesty*. First, we will look at absolute truth.

ABSOLUTE TRUTH

- Absolute truth is *who you are in your essence.*
- Equivalent terms for absolute truth include *Truth, Being,* and *Reality.*

The Absolute may have many names, but they all boil down to one thing: you. Your true nature is the essence of all that is: pure, complete, one without a second. It is beyond who you *think* you are. Although the Absolute is an unbroken wholeness, names for it abound because language demands that we describe it in relative terms. Although it may seem confusing to call an essentially unnameable unity by various names, it is problematic only if we confuse the names with Reality. Words for the Absolute are like symbols on a map; you can use them to get to your destination as long as you realize the difference between them and the Reality they symbolize. We can use these names to our advantage by looking at different dimensions of how the Absolute presents Itself to our understanding—similar to the way a map shows different routes to the same locale—and gain a deeper appreciation of how to approach it. Once we gain a clearer view of the map, we can begin to walk the Territory and find out who we truly are.

Truth

The term *Truth* refers to the Absolute. This term is useful because it is abstract enough to feel universal, applicable to all situations, yet concrete enough to grasp, like "2 + 2 = 4," a concept even a first-grader can understand. I don't use the term "God" often because it implies an anthropomorphic male deity on a throne somewhere. That is not God. The term "God" is sometimes useful but it is commonly misconstrued. The term "Truth" is more useful because it is harder to objectify, implying an abstract essence or principle, like the principle of mathematics. The principle of mathematics is a kind of ultimate truth, at least in worldly terms. It's everywhere, but you can't see it. It has no visible boundaries, but if you disagree with it, you experience disharmony: you can't balance your checkbook, build a house, or do the laundry unless you can add, subtract, and measure in accord with it. Truth is like this. You can disagree with it, but your life will be painful, like arguing with the law of gravity. You can step off a high ledge, fully convinced that the law of gravity is wrong, but you will lose. It is appropriate to live in accord with it. To awaken, you must strive to live in accord with Truth—as much as you can—until you awaken to the fact that you *are* it.

Being

The term *Being* refers to the same absolute essence as Truth, but with a connotation of Truth *as identity*—or *Truth is what I am.* The good news is that you already *are* Truth, and nothing can keep you from being it, regardless of what happens in your life. You have simply gotten out of touch with it in your awareness. The path of awakening is the process of getting back in touch with it. We all know how to feel into Being; we just don't often make the effort to do so. You could ask a random person on the street to feel into his sense of Being, and he would likely be able to do so just by pausing, taking a breath, and feeling into the inner space of his body. We all instinctively know what Being is and how to cultivate it, but only a few make the effort to cultivate it to a high degree. To feel into your sense of Being is actually quite easy. Just sit down, relax, get quiet within yourself, breathe slowly and steadily, and become aware of the inner space of your body, noticing thoughts, feelings, and sensations with silent attention, staying with it until a ground of deep Stillness begins to reveal Itself to your awareness.

Reality

The term *Reality* points to *what is,* the absolute nature of what we think of as the world. Since Truth is the true nature of the world, it is also called Reality. While the term *Truth* conveys an abstract idea like the principle of mathematics, and *Being* implies a sense of who you are in your essence, *Reality* refers more to the true nature of the *outer* world. *Truth, Being,* and *Reality* are just words that represent ways to view something that is essentially unqualified and inexpressible in language. You could actually use *Being* to refer to the inherent majesty of a mountain or *Reality* to convey the inner nature of an emotion. No absolute boundary exists between inner and outer. The key is to use these terms to find the Freedom toward which they point. Words are representations of the Absolute, not the Absolute Itself. You must *use* the relative to *attain* the Absolute, not as a substitute for it. Reality is not conceptual, but is the Truth that makes concepts possible. Thoughts get in the way of the clear perception of Reality, as it is. Therefore, although thoughts are useful for getting around in the world, they are ultimately false, or *absolute lies.*

ABSOLUTE LIES

- ♦ Absolute lies are *thoughts.*
- ♦ Equivalent terms for absolute lies include *judgments, the mind,* and *the world.*

In the unawakened state, we confuse thoughts with Reality. As we have seen, a basic truth is a thought that matches your experience. Although thoughts can match your experience, they do not ever *exactly* or *ultimately* match your experience. For example, the statement "The earth is spherical" may seem true until you look at it more closely. Careful scientific measurements show that the earth is actually *oblate,* or flattened at the poles and slightly bulging at the equator. The statement "The earth is oblate" may seem true until you consider the earth's topography, which is highly irregular, with mountains, valleys, and canyons. As you examine it even more closely, the earth becomes a molecular soup, and then a mysterious "something" that our current science cannot penetrate, leaving us with *I don't know what it is.* Ultimately, no thought matches the shape of the earth or the essential nature of any *thing.* The statement "The earth is oblate" is a useful generalization, but not an absolute fact. It can be useful if you're navigating an airplane from New York to Beijing—but it's not what it ultimately *is.* Therefore, thoughts can be *relatively* true but cannot be *absolutely* true. If the thought "The earth is oblate" gets me to my destination, does it matter what its ultimate shape is? The whole point of a conceptual map is to use our descriptions in a way that gets us where we want to go—but the map is not the Territory. Thoughts do not capture essence, but they can be useful in navigating the world. They are problematic only when we confuse them with Reality.

What we call *things* are really just *thoughts.* You cannot separate any object from the thought that represents it in your mind. When you perceive an object in space, you are witnessing a projection of your mind. The ultimate nature of things lies not in their form, but in their formless essence, or Reality. We can know things on their surface, but we do not know them ultimately, nor can we. When we look closely enough, we find that it's *all* surface. There's nothing underneath. I cannot prove this to you. You have to find out for yourself. The way to be free of this confusion is to closely investigate the nature of things until you realize that what you call a *thing* is just a *thought.* People miss finding Truth because they are looking for some *thing,* and *Truth is not a thing.* People want something hard, reliable, and solid, like a rock—but all rocks dissolve, even diamonds. As long as you are looking for some *thing,* you will miss the Ultimate.

Judgments

Another name for a thought is a *judgment.* A judgment is basically an opinion, a description, a subjective evaluation. The statements "That dress doesn't look good on you," "The earth is oblate," and "The cup is on the table" are all judgments. Judgments are statements of relative truth, not ultimate truth. Judgments have only relative value because, like the earth, I cannot know what a dress or a table ultimately *is.* I can form an opinion, but I cannot ultimately *know.* Therefore, all that matters is whether a judgment is practically useful. For example, I may ask someone in the room to "Please hand me the cup that is on the table." We both experience the cup as being on the table and both know what the verb "to hand" means. The request refers to a relative truth, and is therefore useful. However, the ultimate nature of what we are describing is boundless and unknowable. We cannot know what it is.

A *description* and a *value judgment* are not the same thing. If I see a cup on the table, the statement "The cup is on the table," is an accurate description of my experience, a basic truth. If I say, "The cup *shouldn't* be on the table. It *should* be in the dishwasher," I am making a *value* judgment, because I am implying that my experience should be other than it is now or would be better if something else were happening. This is also true if I say "The cup is ugly," "You're an idiot for owning such an ugly cup," or "I hate myself for being so careless as to leave a cup out on the table (again)." A value judgment implies that something is *wrong* or *bad* about my experience. In this case, the badness or wrongness—the "shouldn't be-ness"—can be attributed to the cup, to its owner, or to myself. You can judge anything or anyone for any reason. Descriptions are useful because they convey information about the world. Value judgments are confusing because they conflict with Reality. Notice the difference.

The Mind

A term that refers to the collective accumulation of thoughts is *the mind.* The mind is *everything that you can name.* The mind refers to the entire field of phenomena that we experience as the everyday objects of life. Everything is a projection of the mind, including all thoughts, feelings, and sensations. The mind is like a map that can be useful for getting to your destination, but has no independent substance. The mind is different from Reality because it is the stream of thoughts in your awareness, but not awareness itself. The mind is both personal and collective, and the two blend, as a harbor blends with the ocean. The key is to get beneath the surface.

The World

We can also call the mental collective *the world*. The world is the narrative of life, an ongoing description in our heads that we confuse with Truth. The world is an illusion because it is not what it seems to be. Like a mirage, the world is a misperception of the way things really are, a distortion that makes illusions seem real. Like a reflection in a mirror, it seems to exist independently, but its source lies elsewhere. A movie is really just light that is dependent on a projector, a screen, and an observer to give it a sense of reality that it wouldn't otherwise have. If any of these conditions are not present, a movie cannot exist.

The world is a drama with highs and lows, birth and death, and with no independent existence. Like a soap opera, the world is a story that fascinates you and keeps you from discovering Truth. You get preoccupied with how it's all going to end—but it never ends, so you keep tuning in, day after day, week after week, mesmerized by the rising and falling of fortunes. "Happily ever after" never happens, and you remain enthralled by the spectacle.

When we attach to the story as if it were true, we get mired in *absolute dishonesty*.

ABSOLUTE DISHONESTY

- Absolute dishonesty is *unconsciousness*, or seeing thoughts as absolutely true.
- Equivalent terms for absolute dishonesty include *attachment, identification*, and *resistance*.

The unawakened state exists in you because, on some level, you are avoiding the conscious recognition of your ultimate nature. Therefore, we can think of it as a form of fundamental dishonesty. This designation is not pejorative, but useful. Unconsciousness is not bad or wrong—but calling it absolute dishonesty puts the responsibility for awakening on you, where it belongs. This is not about blame, but responsibility. Awakening is your responsibility. No one else can do it for you. Absolute dishonesty is just a way of looking at suffering, bringing you to a place where you can recognize that you are both the problem and its solution. You just have to be honest about it. Anything else is an abnegation of responsibility and will not help you. It all begins and ends with you.

Attachment

Thoughts are not painful unless you attach to them. *Attachment* means attributing absolute value to thoughts, when they have only a relative value. Thoughts are only relatively true, not absolutely true. Degrees of attachment proceed in severity from mere thoughts to *opinions, views, beliefs,* and *knowledge.* A thought is the least severe degree of attachment, as in, "I'm not sure, but I *think* so." An opinion is something you hold somewhat lightly, but is stronger than a thought. A view is more serious and implies that you are taking a stand on something. A belief is a thought that has been hardened by many layers of judgment until it takes on the characteristics of sedimentary rock. Knowledge is the strongest degree of attachment, where you don't even question certain thoughts but accept them as Reality. Knowledge is a locked cell into which Truth cannot penetrate. Sometimes knowledge and belief are confused, as in religious belief, which is knowledge cloaked in absolutist garb. A religious belief is an attachment that you would die for—and usually do. Some people even kill for their religious beliefs. Religious beliefs cause much violence in the world. They nail you to the cross of suffering with a vengeance. It takes great effort to remove them. Views, on the other hand, are easier to remove, like staples.

Identification

Another way to look at how we attach to thoughts is to consider another term, *identification.* Identification is in effect saying, "I *am* my thoughts." Identification is living a lie. If you identify with thoughts, you obtain a false sense of self from them. Since thoughts come and go, you fear losing them because it feels like you are losing yourself. The more you identify with a thought, the more it hurts when you lose it. Notice how identification with thoughts makes you feel nervous and afraid. Once you identify with a thought, you fear losing it, just as you fear your own death. You cannot *know* who you are; you can only *be* who you are. You are not a thought. You must go deeper than thoughts to find who you are. For example, recognize that the statement "I am not a thought" is just another thought.

Identification is sticky, saying, "This is my story, and I'm sticking to it." When you identify with thoughts, you block Truth from entering your awareness. Concepts seem independently real only because you attach to them. Flypaper doesn't bother you if you're not stuck to it, but flies are attracted to it, even though it's sticky—and deadly. Discover what thoughts trap you and begin to free yourself by noticing them without judgment. Realize that ultimately, you're stuck to a false sense of self, a fabricated "me." Notice how you use the words "I," "me," and "mine" and derive a sense of self from them. Notice how, when you identify with things, you experience pain when you lose them. Because Being is the fundamental Reality, loss of something with which you have identified causes suffering. Notice how you project a sense of self onto people, places, and things. Some people become so distraught over losing things that they become suicidal.

Resistance

Another word for attachment is *resistance*. Attachment resists Reality, like the mental patient who, attached to his paranoid fantasy, resists joining society. Resistance is the disease of "This shouldn't be happening," the basic tendency toward stress and unconsciousness in the world, the cause of the unawakened state. When what you think *should* be happening is different from what *is* happening, you experience the fundamental pain of existence. Attaching to thoughts resists the radical Freedom of non-attachment; the mind clings to thoughts to feel safe. Resistance hurts because it shuts you out of Paradise, like a lab monkey that has been caged for so long that it rejects its native habitat when given the opportunity to escape, afraid of the freedom it doesn't know. A person shut in a dark room for years resists the "painful" light of an open doorway. Your mind is conditioned to prefer the suffering of "me." "Me" is like a little cage to which you have become accustomed, even though it hurts. When it's all you know, it can be hard to leave behind. Resistance is negativity, or saying "no" to Freedom. The unawakened condition is defined by negativity, a painful cringing away from Truth. For example, if you complain about things, hate your job, or get irritated, you are resisting Reality. This resistance perpetuates your suffering. Notice when you do this. When you notice it without judgment, you are practicing *absolute honesty.*

ABSOLUTE HONESTY

- Absolute honesty is *consciousness,* or seeing thoughts as absolute lies.
- Equivalent terms for absolute honesty include *recognition, disidentification,* and *radical acceptance.*

Absolute honesty is the conscious activity of awakening, the recognition of thoughts as ultimately false. The more thoughts you recognize as ultimately false, the more conscious you become until you awaken and no longer identify with the mind. Awakening involves a conscious relationship with thoughts. It's about your conscious relationship to the world. That's what awakening is about. It's not about *things.* It's about your conscious *relationship* to things. It's about breaking your identification with form. Awakened Reality is no different from unawakened Reality; it's just fully conscious of Itself.

The hallmark of absolute dishonesty on the feeling level is *pain.* The easiest way to know if you are actively resisting something is to recognize pain in the feeling space of your body. Resistance is always painful on some level. Notice what you are feeling. Acknowledge any pain that you feel and be present for it without judgment. Be present for any thoughts, feelings, and sensations that arise in relationship to the pain. When emotional pain or negativity arises in you, ask yourself, "What thought am I believing in that isn't true?" Let absolute honesty kick in like a thermostat when you feel inner pain, cooling the frictional heat of resistance.

Absolute honesty is the essence of all spiritual practice, which at its heart is *conscious relationship with what is.* Any spiritual practice, to the degree that it is effective, is a recognition of Being. Traditional practices such as meditation, inquiry, and prayer are all forms of absolute honesty.

Recognition

When you pay attention to thoughts without attachment, you can see their ultimate falseness. This is called *recognition*. Recognition is complete because you see not only the ultimate falseness of the thought to which you are attached, but also the pain that is caused by that attachment. When this happens, you immediately drop the attachment. This is not an activity of the mind, but of consciousness. This activity of consciousness leads to detachment, or the ability to be peacefully with thoughts—as well as the things they represent—without judgment, and therefore without negative emotions such as anger.

Maybe you're dissatisfied because the world seems meaningless or empty. If so, you're on to something. It *is* meaningless and empty. It has no more substance than a stage play. The way to find value in the world is to see that it has no *ultimate* value, only a *relative* value. Like a stage play, the characters, plot, and scenery are all make-believe. When you see its falseness, you will no longer confuse it with Reality and try to find ultimate truth in it. If you are an actor and suddenly wake up to the fact that everything around you—characters, plot, and scenery—is fake, including your own role, any anguish you had about the theatrical "world" vanishes. Whatever scary ideas are being whispered by the other actors, you are free of fear because words cannot scare you unless you believe in them.

Confusing drama with Reality is the same as confusing lies with Truth. If you think "The earth is flat" is a true statement, you are deluded, at least by modern standards. Not only that, but you cannot help but be terrified of falling off the edge of the earth into the abyss that lies beyond it. The way to rid yourself of this insanity is to investigate it for yourself. You could study astronomy, circle the globe, or view the planet from a spaceship. Then you would see that the statement "The earth is flat" is a lie. Seeing lies *as lies* is truth. Once you begin to see lies as lies, you begin to see Truth. You begin to awaken.

When someone dies in a movie, no one dies. It's acting. You don't feel bad about a movie death because you know it's not real. You might allow yourself to feel bad if you feel like it; this is called suspension of disbelief. If you suspend disbelief, you do it on purpose, for your own enjoyment—not out of confusion between drama and Reality.

People who mistake movies for Reality are mentally ill. People who mistake the drama of birth and death for Reality are *confused.* The unawakened state is a state of confusion between drama and Reality. Suspending disbelief is what you do to enjoy a movie. If you want to enjoy life—the awakened life—practice seeing thoughts as absolutely false but relatively true. Thoughts are not a problem if you see them as the insubstantial phantoms they are. Then you can be *in* the world but not *of* it.

Disidentification

Disidentification is the antidote for identification. If someone asks you who you are, chances are you'll stop to think about it before you answer. If you have to stop to think about it, you are already lost. You are not a thought. You are the Truth that sees thoughts as lies, the Reality that sees drama as illusion. You cannot know Truth because you *are* Truth. Give up thinking that you know ultimate truth or even *can* know it. Some students grasp at ultimate truth intellectually, thinking they can somehow "get it." You cannot get it. Do not clutch or grasp. Instead, see that your false ideas are false and let go of your struggle to know. The thought of "I" is not who you are. Assuming you are an I-thought is like thinking you are a character in a movie. It may seem real, but it is an illusion. Your character is fictional. Can you verify yourself? Can you prove that "you" independently exist? Your essence cannot be comprehended by thought, belief, or knowledge. Awakening clears away the cobwebs of false ideas, revealing who you really are.

Radical Acceptance

Instead of resisting thoughts, allow them to be what they are. This is *radical acceptance.* Radical acceptance is not the same as mere mental acquiescence or resignation. Radical acceptance is being with what is, as it is, without judgment. Practice being with what is without judgment. Notice that you judge all the time—then, notice if you judge yourself for judging. When you notice it without judgment, you break the cycle of unconsciousness. Practice letting things go. You have to get really quiet within yourself and become conscious of the part of you that is holding on to judgment. You cannot let go of a judgment by judging. The only way to truly let go of a judgment is to be with it as it is. Then *it* lets go without your having to employ your mind.

Let the mind be still.

If you can simply be aware of resistance and be present for it fully without judgment, it loses power and disintegrates. This is not the same as repression. Repression holds things in, stuffs them into the unconscious. Being with what is allows the de-repression, or un-doing, of painful memories. Repressed emotions rise to the surface of your awareness to be melted in the warmth of your unconditional presence like chunks of ice in the sun. Imagine melting an ice cube with a beam of warm sunlight. The cube is your false sense of self, made up of erroneous ideas. The beam of warm sunlight is your atten-tion. Awakening is the melting of the ice.

Practice saying "yes" to the "no" of resistance without grasping and see what happens. Allow it. Eventually, you will find that it lets go all by itself, like a flower opening. The key is to notice the content of your awareness—thoughts, feelings, and sensations—without judg-ment, to allow the field of your awareness to be present for what is, as it is, without trying to modify it. If you judge what is created by judgment, you add to it and strengthen it. If you can simply be with it, the judgment has nowhere to go, collapsing into the infinity of Now. If judgment arises in you, just be with it. Notice that you usually judge yourself for judging.

For example, notice if you get angry. If you judge yourself for getting angry, you are strengthening the false self out of which the anger arises, and the anger continues, even if you repress it (especially if you repress it), because you are just driving it underground where it will gather steam and emerge later. Anger arises out of a strong sense of saying "no!" to something. To get rid of the anger, simply notice it without judgment. Allow it to be. That dissolves it. It may flare up and try to scare you, but just be present for it down to the roots because it doesn't have any power over you. If it persists for a while, stay with it until it dissolves or at least weakens. Do this with any negative emo-tion you feel and notice that you naturally settle into deeper feelings of peace, satisfaction, and joy. Radical acceptance destroys negativity. The "no" has nowhere to go.

Many people think that mere acknowledgment without vocal complaint is radical acceptance. For example, most people can acknowledge that there is terrorism in the world, but extremely few can be present for terrorism without any residue of judgment, without resistance or even a moral sense of self-righteousness. Terrorism isn't ultimately wrong, no matter what we think about it. It has no power but what we give it. Terror is based in fear. Fear is based in judgment. When you judge terrorism, you are strengthening its power base. Radical acceptance may seem passive, but it is actually quite active. If you radically accept the existence of social ills, you will still take action to stop them—but from a place of peace, not resistance. This empowers *you,* not the problem. The mind resists perceived injustice because it wants to make things better. It judges some things as insufficient, so it strains against them in order to improve them. This doesn't work. This just adds to the confusion and misery in your life.

MOMENTARY HONESTY

Eventually, when you tap into Truth directly, you begin to experience a form of communication called *momentary honesty:* the spontaneous arising of words from the domain of Being within you. It is called momentary honesty because it is absolute communication in the moment. Whereas situational honesty arises from the mind and depends on a clear assessment of a given situation, momentary honesty arises from Being and depends upon nothing but Itself. Whereas situational honesty is of the relative, momentary honesty is of the Absolute. Transitioning from situational to momentary honesty is a transition of conscious perspective from thinking to Being, or growth in consciousness. The more conscious you become, the more you tap into the moment and speak from your essence.

It has no reason. It just is.

Basic honesty helps clarify the mind so that your thoughts and speech match your experience, and situational honesty helps you to become aware of what is happening around you and thus more present for your experience. Eventually, along with the practice of absolute honesty, situational honesty takes you deeper into the moment, into Being Itself, making momentary honesty possible. You cannot exactly *practice* momentary honesty because it is spontaneous and unpredictable. You can, however, practice absolute honesty, and your capacity for momentary honesty will increase, making it more likely to occur.

Momentary honesty is the spontaneous communication of the awakened person (and occasionally of the conscious person). Although momentary honesty may relate to circumstances, it does not depend on them. Momentary honesty is communication that arises from momentary truth. Momentary truth is the absolute truth of the moment of Now, and momentary honesty flows out of it.

Momentary honesty is important because it is the communication of an awakened person, a true Teacher. This kind of communication comes from the realm of Being, deep within you, even though it may appear to come from outside you.

This book is an example.

EMPTINESS

Emptiness is the absolute quality of all things. Things have no absolute value in themselves but in a relative sense are useful for awakening to the Absolute. In other words, the Absolute is recognized by seeing the relative as relative, or empty of absolute value. For example, when you recognize a thought as ultimately false, you are recognizing its relative nature, and thus its Emptiness, or lack of ultimate "thingness." Emptiness doesn't mean "nothing"; it more accurately means "formless substantiality," "reality beyond all form," or "formless essence of all that is." It is what is left when Truth is recognized. Emptiness is the ultimate substance of all that is, of the Formless as veiled by the appearance of form. As Gautama Buddha says in the *Heart Sutra,* "Form is emptiness, emptiness is form."

Emptiness is the ultimate quality of Reality. Because the "thingness" of the world gets in the way of your awareness of its Emptiness, you must deepen your practice of absolute honesty until objects are recognized as essentially empty. The primary distortion blocking awareness of Emptiness (and therefore awakening) is the core of the false sense of self, the *ego*.

THE EGO

The ego is the controlling core of the personality, the root of all unconsciousness, and it is your duty to destroy its "thingness" by recognizing its Emptiness. Destruction is the only sensible way to approach it. The ego is not a thing, but a compulsive tendency, like an addiction: a vain grasping for satisfaction that is never fully satisfied. When you unravel the false self down to its core, it disappears as if nothing had ever been there. When it disappears, what is left is your true, formless nature. The ego is that part of the personality that struggles to survive at all costs. It will try to dissuade you from acting consciously (even now). Because consciousness destroys the ego as sunlight destroys darkness, the ego tries to hide under lies to survive the onslaught of your practice. You must find the ego and eliminate it. You must focus and persist until it gives up the ghost. The ego wants to survive, and fear of death is a smokescreen that keeps you from putting it out of your misery. Destruction is the right attitude to have toward it—not as violent action, but as focused attention. Make sure you line it up in your sights.

If it moves, destroy it.

"Destruction" is a dynamic word, a metaphor for how far you must go: all the way to the end. This is not extreme, but sane. Consider the following example. If someone surgically implanted a computer chip in your brain that made you do evil things to people, destroying the chip would make sense. Destroying it would revert you to your original nature. Your actual situation is similar to this. Just as your brain cannot properly function with malicious computer code directing its activities, you cannot function optimally with the ego controlling your life.

A common misunderstanding of awakening is that it involves destruction of the personality. That is not true. The ego is the *root* of the personality, not the personality itself. What is destroyed is *identification* with the personality. The ego is the root of personal identification. Once awakening occurs, the personality functions as a free emanation of consciousness, rooted in Being.

The activity of the ego is like an addiction to thinking—a mind-made "me." Its nature is unconsciousness. When you make it conscious, you destroy it. Start with disidentification from your self-concept, your personality, and work your way down to its root. The sense of self is a tendency, something you are doing all the time— more of a "selfing" than a self—making it seem solid. What you call "me" is a constellation of false ideas whose root is a tendency toward dishonesty. The ego maintains itself by straining against Truth, creating a false sensation of self that is like a cramp. It seeks forms in which to encapsulate itself—ideologies, religions, worlds, physical bodies— and it cannot be satisfied with just one. It multiplies itself endlessly. It cannot stop itself. That is why you must destroy it.

This selfing activity and the cramping sensation it causes can be called the *self-contraction,* similar to a clenched fist. Whereas a fist is closed and basically non-relational, an open hand is functional and able to relate to others. It grasps, touches, manipulates, makes itself known through its usefulness. Try it now. Close your hand tightly into a fist and hold it for ten seconds. A cramped, closed fist creates a painful sensation in the palm that is like a "something that is there," when nothing is there but a tendency toward contraction, producing a painful sensation. When the cramp of self-identification is all you know, you protect it at all costs, even if it's painful. From the perspective of unconsciousness, it's scary to let go into the freedom of openness. As understandable as this is, notice the absurdity of protecting that painful cramp as a "precious something" when it is really *nothing.* Not only is it nothing, but it renders your hand dysfunctional: you cannot use a tool, caress a child, or pick a flower because you are afraid of opening your hand and losing your "treasure." Further, the cramp hurts, even numbs. That is what the self-contraction is like. That is what we are doing to ourselves, all the time.

Another name for the ego is the *controller* because its selfing activity is a vain effort to control Freedom—a contradiction at the core of all unhappiness, a grasping for satisfaction that is never satisfied. When it disappears, it can no longer run your life. The true nature of things is Freedom, and Freedom cannot be controlled. Control is a lie. No one ultimately controls anything. Being simply *is*. Does a river control itself? Of course not; it just flows. It just *is*. Being is like this. It is perfect control because it fully *is,* without obstruction, from its essence. It knows how to flow. It also knows where, when, and how much to flow, perfectly, in the moment. It is so naturally in control that even the *sense* of control is allowed, even though this sense is ultimately an illusion. Your true nature flows perfectly, even now. It is the *illusion of control* that perpetuates your suffering. Surrender your need for it. Give it up. Let Truth take you over.

Although Truth is who you ultimately are, it seems like something outside you. From the unawakened perspective, the ego seems like who you are and Truth seems like something other, when the opposite is actually the case: Truth is who you are, and the ego is something other. When you are new to the path of awakening, the feeling that you are handing the reins over to an outside authority is natural. Don't let it discourage you. Give yourself over to Truth and trust what happens. Take a chance.

When you destroy the ego, you destroy the false sense of self at its root, and the world at its root. The world arises from the mind, and the mind arises from the ego.

No ego, no mind, no world.

THE PATH OF HUMANITY AND THE PATH OF AWAKENING

Like it or not, you are on a path. The only relevant question, then, is whether your path is dedicated to consciousness or unconsciousness. The path of most human beings is dedicated to unconsciousness. If you want to be free, you must dedicate your life to consciousness. When you do this, you transform your unconscious path into a conscious one. You transform the *path of humanity* into the *path of awakening.*

The path of humanity is the path of the relative world, the way of the average human being. The path of awakening is the path of the Absolute, the way of the sincere student of Truth. The path of humanity begins at birth and ends at death, a closed loop that refers to itself as the absolute value. When it refers to consciousness as the absolute value, it is transformed into the path of awakening. It is redeemed by its conscious connection with Truth.

Without the path of awakening, the path of humanity is an endless cycle that has no ultimate value. Birth and death repeat themselves over and over again in a continuous loop called *cyclic existence*. The ego is the cause of cyclic existence because as soon as you lose your physical form at death, the "selfing" tendency seeks another form in which to be born and persists until it gets one. Death does not end it. It compulsively exists in one form or another and is never satisfied. Awakening breaks the cycle and makes death and rebirth unnecessary.

It doesn't matter whether you believe in cyclic existence or not. You may believe that we live once and death is the end, or you may believe that we live once and reap a singular eternal afterlife. Regardless of your beliefs, what saves you is not adherence to a belief, but in finding out what is true.

Everything in nature is cyclical. Forms are created and destroyed continually. The mistake is in identifying with form. If you identify with form, you will seek a form in which to be reborn. It makes sense just to observe that, on every level of existence, things are created, they exist for a while, and they die. Nature is constantly recycling itself. Why would human beings be any different? Why would we be the only exception to everything else in the universe?

The path of humanity is a misperception of the nature of the relative world and its ultimate usefulness as a means of awakening to the Absolute. The path of humanity, rightly seen and used, is a path that leads to Liberation, like a hidden walkway inside a prison that leads to an unlocked gate and beyond. If you fail to recognize that there is a way out, you won't start taking steps toward the exit. Instead, you will just wander around aimlessly, pursuing goals within the walls of your cell block. If you know the path and how to use it, you can escape and be free.

For example, when you earn money, you are doing something conventional, or relative, but your action can lead to awakening if you use the money you earn to empower your practice, as in paying the tuition for a meditation retreat. If you use the relative things in your life—work, time, relationships—for awakening, you transform your relative path into an absolute path. This makes your progress faster and more direct, like a trail that leads straight up a mountain instead of winding slowly around it for eons.

This redeeming usefulness of the relative gives practices such as basic honesty a deeper focus in your life than just being a good person. These practices also serve as vehicles for awakening. Once you realize that using your life for awakening is the way out of relative misery, then the ordinary things in your life are given extraordinary value. You see that your efforts can fuel something truly worthwhile and permanent instead of meaningless and transient. You see that the true nature of the relative is to use it to attain the Absolute. This insight gives your life true purpose and meaning. As soon as you begin working toward awakening, Truth helps you meet daily challenges with more faith, courage, and perseverance.

The path of humanity is like a vast dome with a human-sized opening at the top that few can see, and the path of awakening is a rocket that takes you straight up through the opening and beyond. The apex begins to touch into the transcendent, into the Absolute, but most never climb that high. From the top, you can see that any notions of a path, a dome, or a summit are illusions. But you have to get there to see That.

You can—if you dedicate your life to consciousness.

CHAPTER TWO

STUDY

An indispensable prerequisite for insight is to use the wisdom gained through study and reflection to develop knowledge of reality.
　　　　　　　　　　　　　—Tsongkhapa

The unexamined life is not worth living.
　　　　　　　　　　　　　—Socrates

LEARNING

The unawakened state is characterized by ignorance. Ignorance means lack of knowledge, understanding, or awareness. It does not mean stupidity. Ignorance means, for example, not knowing about the path of awakening, that life is suffering, or even that a solution is necessary. If you don't know that unawakened existence is suffering, you won't become disillusioned with it and seek a way out. Even if you do sense there is a way out, you may not know how to find a true path. The cure for this kind of ignorance is gathering information, or *learning*.

But gathering information is not enough. You must use what you learn. The path of awakening requires that you *do* things—practices—that produce growth in awareness. First, you learn how to practice, then you practice. On the path of awakening, both are necessary.

This is like baking a cake. First, you find a recipe. The recipe tells you what ingredients, tools, and materials you will need and how to use them properly. Then you combine the ingredients, using your tools and materials, and bake it until it's done. If you just read the recipe and don't do anything else, you will never be able eat the cake. You must actually assemble the ingredients and *use* them according to the recipe. Similarly, if you just read about the path of awakening and don't use what you learn, you will not make much progress. To liberate yourself, you must both read the recipe and follow it thoroughly.

That is what you are doing with this book; you are learning how to wake yourself up spiritually. If you want to awaken, you must use it. But there is more. *How* you read it is important. You must read attentively, or *study* it. Because spiritual texts contain an inner level of Power that is hidden from casual eyes, how deeply you focus on this text determines how much you will get from it. Spiritual study is not just a learning process; it is also a practice in itself, a discipline. When you study spiritual literature, you are recognizing the absolute Source of the words, the awakened consciousness of the one who wrote them.

If you studied the above paragraph attentively, you are already practicing.

Because understanding multiple layers of meaning is required to study effectively, it is important to learn how to read for maximum benefit. As you read this chapter, you are both studying and learning how to study at the same time. As you learn the finer points of how to deepen your practice of study, both your understanding and awareness will deepen.

HOW TRUE TEACHERS COMMUNICATE

Communication occurs on relative and absolute levels. It is important to understand that an awakened Teacher communicates on both levels because as a student, you must be able to discriminate clearly between the two levels and use them appropriately to maximize your benefit. You must be able to both understand the words a Teacher communicates and recognize the Truth of his essential nature without conflating the two and losing some of the value of what is being transmitted.

The awakened Teacher is different from most people. Most people communicate through ideas. Awakened Teachers also communicate through ideas, but simultaneously from *beyond* them, from conscious *relationship* to the ideas, the absolute honesty or consciousness that imbues them with the living presence of Truth. This living presence is transmitted through the words beyond the mere concepts that are conveyed on the surface. The concepts are like froth on the surface of the ocean. Truth is the ocean.

On the relative level, a Teacher is a person who conveys information. On the absolute level, he is identical with the Absolute and conveys Truth by virtue of who he is. Truth is who he is as well as what he teaches. The Teacher and Teaching are the same. Any words spoken or written by a true Teacher possess both relative and absolute value. The absolute value is found not in the logical validity of the words, but in the essence of the one who produces them, carried on the words like a fragrance. It is a common error to focus on the relative value of a Teaching to the detriment of its absolute value. It is important to be able to discriminate between these two levels of meaning.

Absolute truth cannot be conveyed in the strict denotative meaning of language. Concepts cannot contain it. It is conveyed by the degree of consciousness of the communicator. The words of an awakened Teacher are living representations of Truth, just as they are, simply because of his degree of consciousness. A true Teacher, firmly established in Truth by definition, simply *is* the Truth and is therefore flawless in absolute communication, irrespective of the quality of the verbal formulation of his teaching. The Source is crucial, not the content. An illogical statement spoken by a true Teacher, while having little relative value, has just as much absolute value as a logical one, simply by virtue of who says it. However, since sloppy formulation is an obstacle to cognitive understanding, the Teacher strives for relative precision when teaching. He strives for basic honesty.

The value of intellectual precision in teaching is the *ease* with which the inner meaning becomes a focus of study. In other words, an effective Teaching grabs your mind and says, "Look at who you ultimately are." Any statement by a Teacher can be meditated upon no matter how senseless or conflated it seems as potently as any other statement he makes—but perhaps not as easily. Even gibberish, if uttered by a true Teacher, will produce results if meditated upon, but not as easily as a clear, coherent statement. Entire schools of enlightenment have been based on illogical verbal formulations called *koans*. Unlike gibberish, koans are carefully formulated. They stop the mind, using thought against itself, and can be quite effective. A good koan fosters meditative insight. Ultimately, gibberish, koans, and clear logical statements are identical.

The absolute value of a statement is directly proportional to the degree of consciousness of the one who utters it. A verbal teaching has absolute value only if the person who utters it speaks from consciousness. A logically accurate statement uttered unconsciously has no absolute value. Consider a purely relative statement pertaining to matters of absolute truth, as in some academic philosophical writing. A relative expression, if divorced from consciousness, as by a scholar with advanced intellectual skill but no actual recognition, has virtually no value, even if it is logically precise, because it isn't good for anything. If the formulation is about a relative matter, such as how to bake a cake, it has relative value, because you can bake a cake with it. A relative statement pertaining to spirituality, if divorced from an origin in awakened consciousness, has neither relative nor absolute value because you cannot do anything with it except perhaps line the bottom of a birdcage. Of course, in scholarship, degrees of consciousness vary, so different texts may display varying degrees of absolute value.

An awakened person is the complete true Teaching and does not need to express himself verbally to convey Truth, except to hold your attention and give the mind something to masticate while his silent transmission makes words unnecessary. For example, this book draws you in and holds your attention (to this point, at least) with descriptions, points of view, and philosophical arguments, but it is the liberated consciousness of the one who writes it that sets you free. A useful statement draws you in, keeps you interested while the Absolute speaks to you in your depths. A strong Teaching gives you food for thought and words to chew on, but in a way that stops your mind and brings you to the gateway of Truth deep within yourself, prior to words.

Absolute communication is from Truth to Itself. The one who communicates and the one who listens are the same. You are listening—now—as Truth, to Itself.

THE WISDOM OF NOT-KNOWING

If you attach to thoughts as absolute truth, the intellect is a barrier to Liberation. It doesn't have to be. Use the mind instead of letting it use you. See thoughts as symbols on a map, and you will avoid getting lost. Intellectual development is important because you need a good map to get to your destination, just as you need a good recipe to bake a cake. Without a clear map, awakening would be impossible, because you must be able to assess relative truth clearly before you can discern absolute truth. You must develop the intellect carefully, see how you identify with it, then work to eradicate the identification. You must use the intellect against itself by whipping it into shape and pinning it down; then it can't escape the force of your insight.

Therefore, do not suppress critical thought. The intellect is a valuable tool if used properly. Instead of suppressing thoughts, destroy the belief that thoughts are ultimately true. As long as you clearly discriminate between the relative and the Absolute in this way, you will be able to use the intellect effectively without being dominated by it.

Use your conceptual maps appropriately by seeing where their usefulness ends, recognizing the difference between information and Truth. Truth is a form of absolute intelligence, or Wisdom. Wisdom is not knowledge *of* things, but *as* things. It's the essence of things, a kind of pure, absolute knowledge beyond thoughts, the supreme Intelligence beyond all thinking. The Absolute comprehends the relative completely because it *is* the essence of the relative. An awakened person looks at something and "knows" its essence, because he *is* that. Being is absolutely intelligent, way beyond what you could imagine. Some assume that Being's simplicity implies dullness or stupidity. It does not. Its order of intelligence is off the scale, and the mind cannot grasp it.

Wisdom recognizes concepts as ultimately empty—albeit relatively useful—phantoms. Wisdom can be called *not-knowing*, because it is neither conceptual knowledge nor the absence of conceptual knowledge, but the Intelligence beyond all thinking. Not-knowing is the radical intuition that concepts are ultimately false, or empty. Not-knowing discriminates clearly between the relative and the Absolute, allowing the Absolute to manifest as the Wisdom that you are. It sees conceptual knowledge as conventional and allows the world to be what it is. Knowing is ignorance; not-knowing is Wisdom. Not-knowing gets thoughts out of the way so you can *be* fully as you move through the mind-field of life.

If you are mercilessly honest with yourself and investigate your hard-won opinions, views, and beliefs, you will find that they have no ultimate substance whatsoever. You cannot know anything with absolute certainty, although you can comprehend the essence of all by *being* the essence of all. Not-knowing is a useful way to dissolve attachment to conceptual knowledge. The recognition of your essential nature or Being means not-knowing. Thoughts may arise for you—but you no longer confuse them with Reality. Your locus of identity shifts from thinking to Being. Use thoughts by holding them lightly, like snowflakes—beautiful, geometric, evanescent, gone. You can't know anything with absolute certainty. Why hold onto anything tightly, as if for dear life? To let go of the known means to trust the Wisdom that lies beyond it.

Recognizing the Truth of something is "knowing" it deeply by seeing "I am That" deeply. Recognition is like light dawning in a room, illuminating its contents. Until you have enough light to see the objects in a room, you keep bumping into them as you move around. Darkness makes them look like monsters. Eventually, when there is enough light, you see there are no walls.

SACRED MEDIA

One of the best ways to learn about the path of awakening is to study educational materials, whether written or otherwise recorded. This practice can be done in private and at your own pace when you are new to the path—important because you may not be ready to meet other students or the Teacher in person yet. You may want to feel things out for yourself before embarking on a public quest. Recorded teachings help provide a conceptual framework so that you can more effectively determine which teachers are true, so study as many of them as you can. Because you are reading this book, you have already begun. As you continue to study, you will both learn about the path and deepen your awareness of Truth.

Study is effective to the extent that you do it *consciously*. This requires effort, intensity, and focus, as well as an awareness of your attitude toward the Teaching. If you read a sacred text with contempt, for example, it will not help you. Reading it with reverence helps you. You must deal appropriately with any negativity, whether subtle or overt, you may harbor toward the Teaching. Reverence is important— not reverence for any *thing*, but for the Absolute Itself. You must listen deeply within yourself and recognize Truth to get the ultimate benefit.

When you grasp the Teaching mentally but do not recognize it as Truth, you lose the absolute value of your study. You must be able to grasp the relative meaning as well as listen into the absolute meaning. Both are necessary, and to conflate the two is a basic error. If you confuse the relative teaching with the absolute Teaching, you will think that a Teacher is only as great as the words he says. He is much more than that. Allow his absolute nature to reveal itself to you. It is identical with your own absolute nature. Because your absolute nature is awareness, you must focus your awareness, or become attentive. It is as if you are allowing awareness to listen into Itself as you read.

The three main forms of recorded material that you can study are written texts, audio recordings, and video recordings. Each of these media requires a somewhat different focus or approach, and we will consider each one separately.

Reading Texts

To get the maximum benefit from your study, read *scripture*. Scripture is awakened literature—the written words of a true Teacher, whether written by the Teacher himself or transcribed by a student. If the words of a true Teacher are faithfully reproduced, the resulting text can rightfully be called scripture. Although the word "scripture" has a religious connotation, it really means "literature possessing absolute value" and is not necessarily religious. It is a powerful source of awakening in the world.

Scripture is fairly common. Most literate people have read scripture and been moved by it on some level, because most people have read at least some sacred texts, such as the ones that serve as the basis for the major religious traditions. In that way, most people have had contact with the awakened Teachers who serve as the source of those traditions. For example, most people in the world have read or heard recitations from either *The New Testament* or *The Dhammapada,* connecting them with either Jesus Christ, the source of Christianity, or Gautama Buddha, the source of Buddhism. All true scriptural writings refer to the absolute Source from which they came.

The validity of scripture must be verified by your own Wisdom. Just because a text is considered scripture doesn't mean that it is authentic, although you can start with popular texts and go from there. When you read a text written by a purportedly awakened Teacher, listen within yourself for the profound recognition that says, "Yes, this is It. This is authentic." True scripture takes you deeper within yourself to a place of preternatural Stillness that is its own validation. Keep studying various texts until you feel certain that you can appreciate the difference between authentic scripture and mere academic writing.

Study scripture meditatively by listening to your own inner Wisdom as you read. You cannot understand the Absolute with your mind, but you can recognize it as your own inner essence. Read with the appreciation that Truth is deeper than anything words can describe on their surface. Ponder and meditate upon the words of the Teacher, taking them into the silent Space of recognition within you.

For example, as you read, you may find that at times you pause, perhaps close your eyes, breathe deeply, and become quietly introspective. This still, inner awareness is the doorstep of Wisdom. You may feel a silent shift within your Being, a peaceful "Yes" deep within you. This is evidence of recognition. When you take the Truth of scripture deep within your Being, the Sacred is revealed to you—but only if you have fully surrendered any sense of personal grasping and given yourself fully. Lay yourself down at the threshold of Truth. Give yourself to Wisdom and listen with great humility into what you cannot know, as if you are listening into a great space of Intelligence beyond the mind. Trust that you are receiving what you need, deeply and silently.

This listening is like inhalation or inspiration deep within you. "Inspire" means both to inhale and to "breathe in" the spirit of Truth. What you take in is already who you are; you're just contacting it consciously. Recognition comes from your essence, which you can feel in the depths of your Being as stillness, peace, clarity. Inhale it deeply. Let it awaken you.

In addition to scripture, you can study academic literature. As long as you use it for intellectual development and clearly discriminate between absolute and relative truth, it is highly useful, because it teaches you to think clearly and logically. The key is to avoid confusing strictly academic or theoretical writing on spiritual matters with writing by an awakened Teacher. You can use academic writing to develop your intellect along certain lines of reasoning. You can also use it to recognize the intellect's limited scope, and use that new awareness to find literature that originates from a more profound level of consciousness. This is an ongoing process: finding the most Truth-filled writing you can and letting go of what doesn't speak to your depths.

You can also learn from fictional literature. Great poetry and fiction is made great by virtue of the author's insight into the human condition. Use it to deepen your understanding of life's beauty, grace, and futility. Great art, whether written or otherwise, hints at something transcendent in the nature of human beings. Great literature develops your mind and builds language skills, and this can be useful when contemplating awakened literature and communicating with others. Great fiction usually conveys something about the bleakness of the human condition while hinting at the potential of consciousness through struggle and suffering. Literature reflects the evolution of our understanding and shows us how to live more authentically. At the same time, realize that fiction can sometimes be an escape into unconsciousness, into the fantasy of drama. Let it wake you up instead of lulling you to sleep. Focus on quality. Use literature just as you would use your own life by asking, "What is authentic? What is valuable? How can I use this fictional experience to grow in consciousness?"

If you are going to study non-scriptural writings, dedicate your efforts to the pursuit of Truth, not just to the accumulation of ideas and theories. Dedicating your study to awakening gives it power, even if you recognize certain texts as limited and eventually discard them. It is just as important to recognize texts that don't serve your growth in consciousness as ones that do. Spend your time wisely. Use all literature, whether academic material or casual reading, for spiritual growth.

For best results, study not only the work of great thinkers, but also of true Teachers. The most sublime philosophy ever put in writing is transmitted by awakened beings. Meditate on scripture instead of just reading it for information. If you read it consciously instead of just scanning it mechanically, you receive a fuller measure of its awakening power. Just to read a few words in this way has power. See if you can take your study to the next level by reading more consciously. Let it speak to you. Let the deeper meaning recognize Itself as the unknowable, mysterious Truth you already are.

Listening to Audio Recordings

An awakened person is the direct transmission of Truth, appearing as profound Silence, even while he is speaking. The direct transmission is always available, no matter what is being said (or not said) verbally.

Truth uses consciousness to reveal Itself to Itself. Therefore, even when a Teacher uses words, he is still communicating from the Absolute to the Absolute. Your true nature is absolute, and when you listen to the words of a true Teacher, you are listening to your own voice, your own essence. The voice may appear to come from outside you, but in a very real sense, it arises from within you, from within the greater space of consciousness that you are. Your job as a student is to listen to what is being communicated on a progressively deeper level until you recognize it as the Truth of your own essence.

A true Teacher works silently. His message works beneath the surface, in the domain of the Real that is not perceptible to the senses but can be intuited by recognition. When you recognize the Teacher, you actually recognize your own true nature. Because a Teacher is a portal into the domain of Reality, you can use his presence to wake up to who you are. Just make sure that you discriminate clearly between the relative and absolute aspects of his nature. When you connect with the Teacher on the level of Being, you connect with yourself on the level of Truth, and this is what awakens you.

When you listen to a recording of his voice, pay attention. Discriminate between the relative and absolute dimensions of what he is saying. He may seem to conflate these dimensions at times while speaking, but this is not what it seems to be. Because he *is* the Absolute in human form, his relative statements are free to shift from one point of view to the other without warning. Watch for this. In other words, the perspective between relative and absolute may shift back and forth, and you have to listen carefully to what he says and not confuse one with the other. If you can't follow what is being said, just become more quiet and listen more deeply. He may say things that seem confusing to you. Just let it go and trust that you are getting what you need from his speech. Pay attention and listen inwardly, letting the words sink into your depths.

Listen to the silence between his words. Listen into his absolute nature as deeply as you can. Listen to the tone of his voice. Listen into the resonant space of your throat, chest, and heart and let the sound of his voice vibrate your body from within as if it were a dynamic Stillness. Let the deeper meaning speak to you in your body as a felt movement. Let the quality of his voice contact the natural peace within you. If the voice is disturbing, let it be what it is. Listen to the silence and not just to the sounds, like listening to the rests in a symphony.

Watching Video Recordings

Watching a video presentation by a true Teacher is the next best thing to actually meeting him in person. You can see what he looks like, notice how he moves, and match his moving image with his voice. A moving image gives you a much clearer idea of what the Teacher is like in person. Meeting a Teacher in person can be daunting at first, especially if you are new to the path, so it is often easier and more convenient to watch a video. As you watch him, feel into who he is as deeply as you can. Watch until you feel that you could recognize him instantly anywhere you might see him. Watch him until you strongly feel that he is your helper, guide, and Mentor.

By viewing a video, you can get a feeling for how the Teacher moves through the world. You can see his mannerisms, facial expression, and so on. Let who he is convey itself to you through the visual medium. Let him impress Truth upon you. Let his visual image, resonant with Grace, burn itself into your heart's memory.

In a video recording, the Teacher does not have to speak. He may sit for a while in silence. You can still derive great benefit from this by simply watching him and listening into the space of conscious relationship with him. Remember that the true Teaching is Silence—even while the Teacher is speaking—and that his true nature is no other than your own.

Protecting the Transmission

If carefully maintained, sacred media can last hundreds or even thousands of years. This ability to preserve the Teaching allows you to discover Truth in the recordings of awakened Teachers who lived in ancient times. If you are drawn to a Teacher who is no longer alive, find his clearest and most powerful recorded teachings, study them, transmit them faithfully, and maintain them with care.

When the Teacher dies and attains final Liberation, all that is left are his recordings, the teachings he has left behind: writings, sayings, images, and insights in the hearts of his students. His students uphold the Teaching and embody his words. If the scriptures are maintained and made available to those who seek them, the Teaching can endure indefinitely.

Maintain a reverent attitude toward these sacred teachings and avoid creating interference in their transmission. Examples of interference include: academic interpretation; harsh commentary;

quibbling over minor doctrinal details; over-intellectualization of the Teaching; hoarding it for only a "select" few; cultic fascination with the "object" of the Teacher; proudly proclaimed misinterpretations by followers; false rehashings of the Teaching by false teachers; false teachings amended to texts as adulterations; belittling the Teacher's awakened status; distorted translations; saying that *these scriptures are the only ones that are fundamentally true;* using true teachings without respect for their source; physically destroying them; or otherwise failing to adequately maintain them.

An ancient Teaching can possess as much power as it does while the Teacher is alive, as long as texts and other recordings are protected and at least a few students are devotionally connected to it in their hearts. The spiritual influence of an awakened being continues well after the death of his physical body.

Make sure to take care of the physical media, such as books. For example, do not place anything but other sacred literature on top of them. Do not soil or damage them. Do not abuse them. Put them in a special place away from other media, preferably on a shelf by themselves. Do not let just anyone borrow them. If you use them, you are responsible for their care. Take care of them with great reverence. This in itself is a practice.

THE PERSON

Like an overlay covering Being, the *person* is the personal structure—the mental, emotional, and physical vehicle—for the functioning of awareness in the world. Although you may feel that the person is who you are, it is not who you are in your essence, but merely your relative mode of expression. The person is best viewed as a vessel through which consciousness operates. It is to be used, just like everything else in life. The mind rightly seen is not a problem, but a tool to be used. This is also true of the body and emotions. For any tool to be used effectively, its structural integrity must be preserved. For the mind to be used for awakening, its structure must be strong, healthy, and balanced. It must be durable enough to withstand the force of awakening without being damaged or destroyed.

For example, psychological wounds must be healed. Most spiritual seekers have been wounded in some way and usually have suffered more than most people, or at least more poignantly. All beings are traumatized, even just from the birth process—but while minor trauma is relatively easy to repress and ignore, major trauma generates tremendous suffering that drives a search for relief and healing. Pain relief provided by distractions such as sex, drugs, and entertainment are not enough to heal the profound ache, so the seeker keeps seeking, perhaps trying conventional religion, philosophy, or other mind-based practices. Eventually, perhaps after many lifetimes, awakening is intuited as the only solution, and the wounded aspirant finds a true Teaching that can heal the cause of her profound suffering.

If an early childhood trauma is severe enough, a person may need psychotherapy or other forms of mental, emotional, or physical therapy before safely engaging in advanced spiritual practice. In most cases, a student is wounded enough to drive the search to heal, but not enough to render the person unusable for awakening. An unusable person is a body-mind that is disturbed beyond safe limits, beyond the help of spiritual practice or psychotherapy, such as in severe mental illness or trauma. Minor disability is not an absolute barrier to awakening, although certain conditions, such as schizophrenia, make it extremely difficult to relate to the Teaching coherently. Physical disabilities present challenges, but not ultimate barriers, because awakening is possible as long as the mind is healthy.

It may seem strange to consider that your body, mind, and emotions are not fundamentally who you are, but as a student, it is essential that you at least begin to appreciate what that means. We are so accustomed to identifying with our minds, emotions, and bodies that we confuse the person with our true nature. On the path of awakening, the person is neither to be affirmed as important in itself nor denied as useless. It is to be used for living in the world, both before and after awakening. After awakening, the person is required to speak, write, play, love, and be physically present for others—all components of the work of a Teacher.

The person must be developed to prepare for awakening. In those cases where awakening is more or less spontaneous, some kind of preparation has taken place. Awakening occurs only in those who meet certain standards of personal integrity. Do not force awakening, but let it come to you naturally, at a pace you can safely handle. A structured Teaching will help you do this.

The person is like a block of ice that is carved into a more functional form by dedicated practice. Awakening melts the inner core, leaving a functional outer interface with the world—a thin, weblike, evanescent shell—that is further refined into progressively more useful forms. The person is constantly developed, both before and after awakening, manifesting continually greater levels of refinement.

In awakening, there are no hierarchies of attainment. There is one goal, and that is Liberation. Once Liberation occurs for that person, it's over. Some schools teach that there are degrees of enlightenment. There are no such degrees. There are, however, levels of depth of expression that are gradually refined and eventually transcended completely. This gradual refinement occurs on the relative level of the person, not on the absolute level of Truth. These are not levels of attainment; they are degrees of refinement and occur naturally, like the falling away of leaves.

THE AWAKENER

The *Awakener* is another name for your true nature, specifically the functional capacity to awaken others. The Awakener is both the *inner* potential we all have to become an awakened person as well as the *outer* manifestation of the actual awakened person—both the inner and outer Teacher. Although they appear to be different, the Awakener within you and the Awakener outside you are the same.

Since the person you think you are is "other" from the point of view of consciousness, first you awaken yourself, the primary "other," then everyone else, or secondary "others." The Awakener is pure consciousness, the interface between relative and absolute, the sense of being *in* the world but not *of* it. The Awakener appears in many forms as worldly Teachings and Teachers, or expressions of the one Truth. Awakeners are the Absolute as it consciously manifests in the world.

The Absolute Itself is so sublime that there is no easy way to approach it. The Awakener puts a human-looking face on the ineffable, appearing as an awakened person, a fleshy frame around Emptiness, so to speak. From the relative state of awareness, the Awakener appears as a person. If you were having a dream and I tried to wake you up by speaking to you, you might hear my words and convert them into an image of a person in your mind. The image is not important in itself, but its origin is. Since the awakened person is the functional aspect of his origin, listening to him awakens you from the dream.

You are having that dream now.

Just as an open doorway into space is identical with space itself, the Awakener is identical with the Absolute, although the Absolute is, in a sense, greater. From the absolute perspective, there is only Emptiness, and the doorway is also Emptiness. As Jesus said, "I and my Father are one ... [yet] my Father is greater than I." Which is greater, the space outside your house, or the space framed by its doorways? From a practical perspective, the space outside is far greater— but since space has no size or shape, they are essentially identical. Do this: make a circle with your thumb and forefinger. Notice the space you are framing with your digits. Regardless of content, is there any fundamental difference between it and interstellar space?

What does it mean when Emptiness is framed by an illusion?

The Awakener is pure awareness, or consciousness, and can be seen both as an *essence* and an *activity*. Consciousness is both the essence of Truth and the conscious activity that brings you to full awareness of Truth. Who you are in your essence is both consciousness as well as the activity of conscious relationship. This is like looking at yourself in a lake. When you look at yourself in a lake, you are simultaneously *being* yourself and consciously being *in relationship* with yourself. Narcissus is the one who forgets who he is and falls in love with his own image. He is who he is, but he does not *recognize* his image, so his *conscious relationship* with himself is lost, and he becomes fixated on the image as an independent "thing." If he would but recognize the dependent nature of his own image, he would, in a sense, "wake up" to himself. This is similar to what you must do, only your reflection is everywhere.

Awareness is like a clear space that allows things to fully be what they are. Reality is pure, unobstructed awareness. Consider an open doorway; nothing obstructs it. Awareness is the interface between the relative and the Absolute, as well as the essence of the Absolute, just as an open doorway is both an opening into space and identical with the essence of all space. The door's frame creates an appearance of an interface, saying *Enter Here (no obstruction).* An awakened person is identical with the Absolute as well as a doorway into the Absolute for others to use. Without the frame, we might miss the doorway, and thus miss an opportunity to enter.

LEVELS OF INVOLVEMENT

When becoming more involved as a student, it is helpful to consider entering the path by degrees, at a pace you can safely handle. You may not want to dive into the Depths right away, and it is helpful to recognize the levels of involvement in a Teaching so you can proceed at a deliberate pace. It can be a relief to know that you can modulate your progress to serve your particular needs.

A true Teaching has four *levels of involvement.* Each level of involvement has two dimensions: outer and inner. For convenience, each outer dimension can be called a *level;* each inner dimension can be called a *stage.* The level represents the outer form of your participation—literally *what you are doing* with respect to the Teaching. The stage represents the inner form of your participation—*who you consciously are* with respect to the Teaching, based on your level of involvement. The levels are numbered one through four; the stages are named, respectively: *interested, involved, committed,* and *awakened.* Each stage implies that you have reached a certain degree of spiritual maturity and depends upon how involved you are. Realize that they are merely conventions. Don't take them too seriously.

If you are practicing at any of these levels, you are a student, except for level four, at which you are no longer a student, but a Teacher. No level is "better" than any other. Each simply reflects how involved you are. Each stage reflects that it is what you *do* in relationship to the Teaching that determines who you consciously *are* with respect to the Teaching. If you want to grow inwardly, you must act outwardly. As you progress through the levels of involvement, your practice will naturally deepen. As your practice deepens, you grow in consciousness, and with growth in consciousness comes responsibility.

Level one means that you are *interested.* You have read some texts, listened to audio tapes, or watched videos of the Teaching, but you have not yet made physical contact with the Teacher or any students who are at level two or above, although you may have met or talked to other level one students. For example, you are already at least at level one because you are reading this book. Notice that the word "interested" implies more of a mental process, a participation on the level of thought—reading books, listening to tapes, watching videos, as if you were browsing in a bookstore. At this stage, you are considering whether you want to become more deeply involved. Even though you are "just looking," so to speak, there is a definite movement within you toward Freedom and away from mind-identification.

Level two means that you are *involved.* You have met at least one student at level two or above (with the Teaching as a context)—or the Teacher himself. This brings you into closer contact with the Teaching because you are in contact with an actual person, not just a book or video. The more you get to know other students and become involved at this level, the more you are transformed by that contact.

Level three means that you are *committed.* You have made a commitment to awakening in the presence of the Teacher—either outwardly or inwardly (this is covered in Chapter Five). This vow may be made silently or audibly, but it must be made consciously and definitively to the inner Teacher, the Awakener within you. Being at level three also means you are a *disciple* of the Teaching. At this point, your responsibility to practice deepens considerably.

Level four means that you are *awakened.* At this level, you are no longer a student, but you remain involved in the Teaching because you *are* the Teaching. The form of your participation will suit your particular personal expression and may vary from that of your original Teacher. At this level, you develop your own outward form of the Teaching.

The further along on the path you are, the more your sense of identity shifts away from thinking and toward Being, or away from your relative identity and toward your absolute identity.

The levels of involvement are similar to the process of courtship leading to marriage. When you meet someone you like, at first you are *interested*. You talk to her, flirt, get her phone number, and think about how involved you want to be with her. You may have a sense of knowing that "This is the one," or you may want to go on a few more dates to get to know her, or you may want to date other people.

If you are interested enough to date her regularly, you get *involved*. You make an agreement that the two of you you are dating, that you are in a relationship. At this point, you're "together," but not engaged or married.

If you date her for a while and decide to get married, you get engaged. You tell your other romantic partners that you are getting married and you are committing to this one person. Then you are *committed*.

When you get married, you join with her, symbolically becoming a single one. This is analogous to being *awakened*. Jesus said that "When you make the two into one … and when you make male and female into a single one … then you will enter [the kingdom]." When form and Formless are united as one, you awaken to your true nature.

Again, do not take the levels of involvement too seriously, but use them to gauge your progress on the path. As with any intimate relationship, it makes sense to proceed with careful abandon.

SOLITUDE, SILENCE, AND SPACE AS DOORWAYS TO BEING

Since we are considering a typically early level of involvement (study can be and often is a strictly level one practice, not having met other students yet), it is appropriate to look at things that you can do on your own to deepen your practice and make the most use of the first level. When you are ready, you will know when to take that step up to the second level by meeting level two students or the Teacher himself. For the time being, if you are engaged in solitary practice, you can focus on three main areas—*solitude, silence,* and *space*—to deepen your awareness.

Solitude

Solitude is a condition that most of us experience every day, but few people use it consciously. Most of us either use solitude as an avoidance of relationship or just randomly let it happen. In other words, most of us approach solitude unconsciously. Solitude can be consciously used as a form of spiritual practice. It can be cultivated, maximized, and maintained. It can magnify your awareness of unconscious mental patterns that ordinarily cause you pain but go unnoticed because of the distractions of daily life. Make sure you spend plenty of time alone, unless you already do. In that case, make sure that you balance your solitude with relationships. Both are important. Often, people avoid solitude, thinking it is "bad." It is not. As with anything else, solitude is redeemed by its usefulness, so use it appropriately.

Take some time to be by yourself. Experiment with different lengths of time, perhaps a day or two at first. Even an hour of solitude, if practiced consciously, can be highly useful. Notice what you feel. Notice any resistance to being alone or a craving for the presence of others. Notice how it can deepen your appreciation of the presence of others. If you must be alone for extended periods of time, use it as an opportunity to be present with what you are feeling. Instead of distracting yourself (e.g., with television or telephone), pay attention to the thoughts, feelings, and sensations that you experience, whether positive or negative, pleasant or unpleasant. Notice them without judgment. Just be with them, allowing them to be what they are.

Silence

Silence is a retreat from the noise and chaos of life. Sometimes it is helpful to go into silence by not talking for a day or two. If you have never done this, you may find it unsettling at first. You may become aware of an unconscious need to talk or make noise—something that is difficult to notice in the busy habits of daily life. It helps when you practice silence to do it either alone or with someone who is practicing with you, especially someone who has done it before or an experienced guide who can help structure your environment. It also helps to take time off from worldly concerns—work, family, entertainment, socializing—and just be in a quiet, relaxed environment, preferably in a retreat setting. Rest, sit in quiet meditation, go for walks in nature, and luxuriate in the magnificence of silence. Listen into your depths for quietness, stillness, and peace. Take your time with it. After a whole weekend, you may find yourself deeply rested and rejuvenated because you have tapped into your innermost Being, the source of vital energy and peace in your body. Once you learn to take time off like this, make it a regular practice and you will develop the ability to become deeply relaxed and present in your daily life, listening into the silence of your surroundings.

Space

Space is another useful element of solitary practice. We talk about space, but what is it? Nothing. How can we talk about something that is not something? We refer to it obliquely, by conceiving of it as some *thing* that is left when there are no objects. When we talk about it, we act as if we knew what it is, and we don't. We only know the concept, not the actuality. Use the concept of space to take you into the actuality of Spaciousness and Freedom. Use the concept of space as a meditation on Emptiness. The answer to the question "What is space?" is not a verbal answer. A verbal answer might sound something like "a place where nothing can be found," "an area void of contents," or something along those lines—but these are still *things,* concepts that do not really describe what space *is.* The only way to truly know what space is is to be with it, meditate on it, breathe it in. Look up at the stars and ponder the void in which they blaze. Go to the Grand Canyon and witness its massive stillness. Sit with it and be open to what you experience. You may find a spaciousness inside of you that you never noticed before.

You may lose something or someone in your life that will show you what space is. Instead of rushing to fill the void in your life with things—possessions, concepts, stories, people—allow yourself to sit still with the space and just be with it. Breathe into it. Allow your awareness to deepen, without judgment, into the feeling of absence. Your mind will try to convince you that it is nothing, but if you sit with it consciously, you will notice a stillness, a domain of peace and wakefulness that is also a quiet joy and gentle brilliance within your awareness. Recognize it as the glimmerings of your true nature. If you experience pain, be with it without judgment. When you lose something or someone, meditate on the space created by the loss. When disaster comes, let it be your best friend. Invite it in for tea.

Ultimately, you don't need anything but what you have in the moment. Learn to live with less. Be with the feelings of loss and notice how within grief and mourning is a stark sense of beauty that bleeds through your inner awareness. Notice how alive you feel when you can be present for loss without judgment. Notice that it shows you how to treasure what you have—and especially how to treasure Emptiness, the value at the heart of all mourning. See if you can feel the Emptiness in loss, death, and poverty.

Create space in your life by getting rid of old junk that you don't need. Go through your life and sell, recycle, donate, or throw away anything that is old, useless, and unnecessary. Get rid of old ideas, furniture, clothing, inappropriate relationships—anything that no longer serves you. Get rid of more than you think you can comfortably tolerate losing. Once you have purged, feel that space. Sit with it. Let it speak to you.

In the Zen aesthetic tradition, space is considered as important as the objects that occupy it, even more important in some cases. Study Zen calligraphy, gardening, architecture, and ink painting. Notice how anything unnecessary is excluded, providing a sense of openness, stillness, and serenity. You don't have to live in an extremely spare, minimalist fashion, but you can at least begin to create more space in your life by getting rid of what you don't need.

EXISTENTIAL ANXIETY

When you consciously cultivate solitude, silence, and space, you may stir up feelings that are extremely difficult to handle. You may become more introspective and notice a feeling of hollowness, nothingness, or vacuity at the center of your being that causes you to feel ill at ease or upset. This feeling is called *existential anxiety*. Emptiness is your true nature. When you feel this "voidness" inside yourself, you are feeling

Emptiness on the surface of what it seems to be—a hollow nothing, non-being, or nonexistence. This can be a shock to you when you first encounter it.

The void of Being appears to be a meaningless "nothing" at first and may cause profound feelings of boredom, anxiety, or pain in your emotional body, often of a severe nature. This painful sensation is hard to describe—something like a ragged, hollow fear tinged with sadness, meaninglessness, and despair that can become extremely intense, even to the point of suicidal ideation. While suicide is never a solution to severe existential pain (or a solution to any problem, for that matter), consciousness is, so cling to the Teaching. Instead of letting the ego do you in, let existential anxiety abrade your attachments.

In the presence of Truth, your sense of Being deepens and becomes more serene if you can allow yourself to feel into it. If you resist, the feeling may become more intense for a while, but it always feels deeper and more integrated once you make conscious contact through practice. The only way to get through existential anxiety is to surrender to what you are feeling: raw, naked fear. What else can you do but be with it as it is? Often deeper feelings will arise—sadness, grief, despair. Extended crying jags are common. Sometimes existential suffering lasts for weeks, months, or even years. The key is to be with it, allow it, let it move more deeply into you until it dissolves. Don't judge it or avoid it. If you do, witness what you are doing and be with that as consciously as you can. Be with what you feel.

Remember that hopelessness, nothingness, and despair are one step away from surrender. Existential anxiety is an emotional reaction to the intuition of the Emptiness at your core. Existential anxiety is not true Emptiness but a feeling of resistance to it, like clinging desperately to the wall of a bottomless canyon. It hurts. Emptiness itself is not painful. The key to being at peace with Emptiness is to be with what you feel without judgment. Keep practicing until peace is revealed to you.

Recognition of Emptiness may bleed over into your awareness of the world as you go through your day, changing the way you perceive it. The world may begin to seem strange, absurd, or meaningless. You may feel a sense of nothingness within yourself. Allow this feeling. Within it is a vibrant touch into Being, so don't assume that it is something wrong, bad, or unhealthy. Stay with it until your fear dissipates. What remains will astound you.

THE PARADOX OF GENEROSITY

A paradox is an apparent contradiction: It seems like a contradiction when you say it or think it, but its true meaning lies beyond what you say or think about it. Its true meaning transcends its apparent logical inconsistency. For example, consider the statement, "The only way to know something is if you know nothing." This statement means that the only way you can truly know something—know it absolutely—is if you know nothing, or recognize its Emptiness. In this case, "knowing" has a dual meaning. On the surface, the statement appears to contradict itself, but it indicates a way of knowing that is beyond the mind's capacity to grasp. The paradoxical structure of the statement tends to challenge the listener's notions about what it means to know something.

Other examples include the following:

> *The only way to have something is to let it go.*
>
> *The only way to get rid of what you don't want is to accept it completely.*
>
> *The only way to limit something is to give it space to be.*
>
> *The only way to get everything is to give everything away.*

Paradoxical statements convey how we do everything backwards. We see the world as independently real when it is only dependently real. We see thoughts as absolutely true when they are only conventionally true. We see ourselves as finite when we are infinite. Paradox breaks the straitjacket of unconscious language that restricts happiness. The mind cannot capture Truth. Paradox stops the mind and makes it reconsider itself in the Light of what it cannot control.

You get by giving. Make this paradoxical truth real to you by giving to others in need. In our absolute nature, we are all one. Giving to others affirms this oneness and begins breaking the back of egoic self-grasping. Greed blocks Freedom, and generosity gets it moving. Therefore, be generous. Keep what you need, but give away what you can spare. When you give, you receive recognition of the oneness of all beings. This strengthens you and sustains your path.

Generosity is an excellent practice for those new to the path, because it is a simple, physical action. When you give, you affirm the body of humanity as your own body, seeing others as yourself, and this is what gets you there. When you give away what you don't need, you create more space in your life, reduce clutter, and as a consequence feel lighter and freer. Keep doing this until you are living only with what truly serves your conscious growth toward awakening.

CHAPTER THREE

INSTRUCTION

They said to him, "Tell us who you are so that we may believe in you." He said to them, "You examine the face of heaven and earth, but you have not come to know the one who is in your presence, and you do not know how to examine this moment."
                                    —Jesus Christ

What is the best thing a spiritual aspirant can do? Carry out his Teacher's instructions.
                                    —Shankara

THE TRUE TEACHER

Now that we have looked at relationship with the Teacher through awakened literature, let us look at that relationship through personal contact. This in-your-face, lived relationship is quite different from relationship with an unconscious individual. An awakened Teacher challenges you to grow in consciousness at every turn, by every means necessary, all the way to awakening itself. This relationship requires that you approach it in a certain way if you are to use it to your full advantage. It is in your best interests to do so. If you use it inappropriately, you will miss an opportunity to deepen your awareness of Truth in tremendous ways, and you may miss the only feasible opportunity for awakening you will get in this lifetime.

As we have seen, you must have a relationship with the Teacher for awakening to occur, even if that relationship is experienced through the inner Teacher or through a text or other recorded medium. Meeting the Teacher in person takes it to the next level. The Awakener appearing as a human being to help you is the most powerful aid to awakening there is. Although study can help you, it is far more powerful to meet a true Teacher in person and receive his transmission directly.

Although the Awakener is ultimately who you are, many people perceive Teachers as external authorities and would rather pursue their own path. Many resent being "told what to do." On some level, you have to decide whether to serve consciousness or unconsciousness. If you serve consciousness, you can't have things on your own terms. No matter what you do, the Teacher is going to seem somewhat of an outside authority over your life. He is not. This is just a misperception. Are your lungs telling you what to do right now by breathing? Is air an outside authority? Would you fight your own breathing because "something else" is doing it "to" you? The awakened life is a surrender to what is already true, giving up the fight with Reality. Because working with a true Teacher intensifies this process, it can feel as if he is trying to dominate you. He is not. When you go to a true Teacher and ask for help, you get help—just not on terms that your ego will find palatable.

The awakened person teaches from who he is. He is spontaneous. He is always listening into the moment, always moving authentically, just being Truth. Regardless of any plans he may have made, Truth is the only determinant of his actions. While an unconscious person's movements are dominated by a false sense of self that fights Reality, causing suffering and conflict, there is no conflict in the actions of a Teacher. The hand moves, picks up a glass of water, drinks from it, puts it down. Like the wind, his movement may change suddenly, without warning. It is not uncommon for the spontaneous actions of the awakened Teacher to seem unusual to those who witness them. The Teacher's movement is Wisdom and responds to Itself in the moment. It has no authority but Itself. It arises naturally from the radiant intelligence of Stillness. There is a profound sense of *this is It* in it. There is no ultimate "me" in it. In the awakened person, movement is stillness for the Absolute to see Itself.

The awakened person exhibits a dual instrumentality, consisting of the relative and absolute elements of his nature. Fundamentally, the Absolute is who he is, and the relative is his expression. He is like a jewel with many facets. Once the mud is cleared away, the jewel of awakened radiance is clear to be as it is, infinitely complex, yet startling in its clarity and simplicity—a perfect, brilliant, vibrant human being. However, just because a Teacher is authentic doesn't mean that he is without apparent flaws on the level of his person. It is incorrect to assume that because a Teacher is awake he is somehow outwardly "perfect." On the absolute level, he *is* perfect, but on the relative level, he may seem to have imperfections. It is not even necessary to *like* the true Teacher on the level of his person. He may apologize for apparent lapses of behavior. If a Teacher seems to wrong you, it is a powerful opportunity for you to forgive.

In the case of the true Teacher, know that his nature cannot be fathomed by the mind, because he is Truth in human form. All beings are Truth in human form, but the awakened person is fully conscious of this and lives from that awareness. His relative aspect gives him a human appearance, but do not confuse that with who he is. He is the same as you in your absolute nature, only openly and without obstruction. If you find him, you find your own true essence. Let him guide you. Do not listen to his words as mere thoughts; listen to the Space underneath. If you find who it is that speaks, you find who It is that listens. Do not surrender to his person or relative form, surrender to who he is in his essence, the same as your own Being.

A Teacher's awareness deepens into the Absolute when necessary and shifts to accommodate demands placed upon it while maintaining the appearance of a person. He allows the person as a kind of dramatic role, but he never confuses it with who he is. Sometimes he may seem more grounded and ordinary and sometimes more transparent and extraordinary. He is occupied with eliminating the negativity caused by unconsciousness from your field. The Teacher takes on massive amounts of negativity every day, a truly unimaginable amount. He literally meditates the planet into surrender by taking on others' suffering, even that of people he has never met.

Can you appreciate this?

Because a true Teacher is free of negativity, everything he does serves awakening, regardless of what it may look like. Since a free person generates no negativity, he is free to do as he pleases. Everything a liberated being does benefits humanity, regardless of the outward form of his behavior.

A true Teacher will always be essentially inscrutable as experienced in relationship, as if you are meeting Emptiness Itself. The Master lives in the world but is not of it. He is the Awakener appearing as a person. It is important to realize that the true Teacher's actions serve at the highest level, regardless of their form. Get to know him. The inner, true relationship to the Teacher is not subject to the limitations of time and space, so you can do it, even now.

RELATING TO THE TRUE TEACHER

The proper attitude toward the true Teacher is respect, kindness, and generosity. It is proper because it is useful. Surrender to his absolute nature is a kind of subtle prostration or bowing, a constant listening-into-the-heart attitude that connects you with his essence, the same as your essence. You would not be able to adopt this attitude toward an unawakened person because there is no space for it. The true Teacher makes space for that relationship by recognizing who you are. You will either welcome this invitation or reject it. Learning how to listen into this space is at the heart of all authentic spiritual practice.

To relate appropriately to a true Teacher, your conscious attention is required. If you are not truly present, Truth cannot come to you. If you do not listen inwardly, into the space of recognition, if you listen with your mind and filter what you hear through a meshwork of concepts, all you will get is static. You must want it. You must listen inwardly. You must enjoy the flavor of the Teaching. If you do not enjoy the flavor of the Teaching, you will not be able to receive it because you will not be able to recognize it. It is a taste that can be acquired by anyone sincere and dedicated enough to develop it.

Listen deeply into what you hear. Tune into the stillness out of which the words arise. Do not rely on your Teacher's words as mere intellectual objects, but as resonant signifiers that can take you into the realm of Being. Otherwise, they become dead and rattle around in your head like cadavers. You must go beyond the graveyard of your mind to unlock their significance.

Look at him. Something happens when you look at a true Teacher, especially if your eyes meet. It's not necessary for your eyes to meet if you have faith that he is who he is. Recognition of his absolute nature means that, in that moment, you recognize Truth. A degree of ignorance is removed from you. This can be full awakening in one glance; more likely it is a small fraction, depending on your receptivity to who he is. It helps if you can recognize who he is beyond his personal appearance. That empowers you tremendously.

Of course, he is usually set aside from others, perhaps even sitting on a dais. Regardless of what this may look like, it is not egotism. He is not "above" you or "better" than you. He is placed higher because he is that to which you aspire, and when you respect him you are respecting yourself in the most profound way possible by honoring your true nature. When you place him higher, you are honoring yourself. That is why people often bow or prostrate themselves before the Teacher; they are honoring Truth by lowering the person, placing it in service to consciousness. In the *Tao Te Ching*, Lao Tzu notes that "The supreme good is like water, which nourishes all things without trying to. It is content with the low places that people disdain." When you make yourself lower in this way, you allow the supreme good of Truth to flow into you, filling you with blessedness. The ego is diminished; Being is exalted.

When you are with him, allow yourself to feel what you feel. Your bond with a true Teacher is not emotional, although emotions may arise. Your bond with him is Freedom Itself. Just remember that the true Teacher is your best friend in the most profound sense possible. Your relationship with him may seem like other relationships, and it is—but only on the relative level. On the absolute level, his true nature calls to you, drawing you toward Freedom, toward the world-shattering peace of Liberation, and is the greatest gift you can be offered.

Do not become attached to your Teacher or you will treat him as an object. Just *be* with him, finding a way to let yourself feel the presence of Freedom between you without attachment. This is a sacred relationship that is essentially wordless and of the purest unconditional love possible. Do not fixate on him as an object, idol, or image. Instead, feel into his essence. This relationship can induct you into conscious oneness with your fundamental nature. This induction is the most powerful way for you to move forward on the spiritual path. Induction is the awakening of Being in you by the presence of the Teacher. A true Teacher can induct you with a look, from a photograph, from a video, or from a voice recording. You must be able to feel into who he is, not just fixate on an idea of who he is.

To be close to an awakened being is difficult. It means that you stand face to face with your true nature, like staring into a deep well. The closer you get, the deeper It gets. Ultimately, you and It are the same.

You don't have to quit your job, leave your family, or sell your possessions to get deeply involved in a Teaching. The main thing is that you practice, work with other students, and spend some time in the Teacher's company. Your primary involvement is on an inner level, not an outer one, so you don't have to become a monk or live in an ashram. Just do the work and listen. Don't stop until you're finished. When you're finished, you'll know. As far as believing in what your Teacher says, don't. Don't attach to the words as if they were ultimately true; take them in and meditate on them. Be with them. Digest them. Assimilate them deeply.

If you are fortunate enough to have a personal, one-on-one relationship with a Teacher, it is important to use it properly. You probably would not have a personal relationship with him unless you were using it properly to a significant degree already, but learn how to deepen that relationship so you can deal creatively and effectively with its unique challenges. If you misperceive the nature of the relationship and react negatively to it, you could lose it. Sometimes the Teacher's behavior may seem shocking, abrasive, or even rude. It's not. He just seems that way to your ego, because the ego likes to think highly of itself. An insult to your ego is actually a blessing; the challenge is in recognizing that *you are not your ego*. Because the unconscious state is ego-identified, it feels and looks as if your true friend—the Teacher—is attacking you or acting rudely. Regardless of the situation, it is not possible. If you have a tendency to defend your ego and reject recognition of who your Teacher is, strive to overcome it. Strive to be respectful and forgiving under all circumstances. An insult to the ego is a gift. Use it.

On an absolute level, a Teacher will provide you with conscious relationship; on the relative level, he will help you develop the person—your mental, emotional, and physical vehicle—to handle the forces involved in the awakening process. Although study prepares your mind to receive the force of Truth, the Teacher will provide further instruction for strengthening your mind, body, and emotions. If you are not prepared to withstand the force of awakening, it will not likely happen. If you force a premature opening through unbalanced practices, you can become mentally, emotionally, or physically unstable. A true Teacher can help you take appropriate steps on the path so that you don't force your development. When you are ready, awakening happens naturally, and you can safely tolerate it. The more suitable the person is, the more likely it is that awakening will occur. Basic training in moral discipline, physical integrity, and mental resiliency is important. The person must have weight, just as a sculptor must have something solid to carve.

To some, the Teacher-student relationship may seem childish, as a child clinging to a parent. The truth is that everyone who is not liberated from the mind is childish to some degree. The ego is molded by early childhood experience of a mother and father, forming the basis for the sense of self. When a student projects a parental image onto a true Teacher—which she can hardly help but do—the Teacher may be perceived as a punishing parent. A Teacher doesn't punish you; that's a projection of parental authority. A Teacher confronts you with your own unconscious patterns, and his authority is of Truth, transcending the parent-child dynamic. The punishment, if there is one, is the pain caused by your own unconsciousness. Let it wake you up. The Teacher gives you an opportunity to see what you are doing to yourself. Eventually, the negative patterns transferred in early childhood are undermined, and the person is transformed into a useful vessel.

Massive amounts of negativity—truly, incomprehensibly massive amounts of it—can be cleared in an instant in the presence of a true Teacher. With the proper attitude of respect, service, and love, you are on your way to the end of suffering. Take his words to heart and see if you can find the Truth in them. Take them into your awareness, deep within your Being. At least be open to who he is and what he has to say. Do not say, "Oh, I know what this is" and close your mind. Take some time to get to know him.

While many spiritual seekers are really seeking ego-gratification, you will not get that from a true Teacher. The Awakener cannot be bargained with, cannot be won over with flattery, cannot be a source of ego fulfillment. To the ego, the presence of a true Teacher is like sunlight to a vampire and the ego cannot stand it. It's like looking into the sun, only infinitely brighter. You don't look into it; you *are* it. You look into it with your Being. The ego cannot tolerate the brilliance of your true nature. You are not the ego. You are absolute, magnificent, brighter than a billion suns. Stop looking with the you that you know; start looking with the you that you can't see because you are identical with it and don't know who you are yet. The one that you are is looking into the one that It is, and you are That, looking into Itself.

SKILLFUL MEANS

Sometimes, as a form of practice, a Teacher will guide you to do something that makes no apparent rational sense. If a true Teacher asks you to do something, do it, even if it seems unreasonable. Anything you do as guided by a true Teacher will generate awakening power, even if it's something as simple as washing the dishes or stacking rocks. Directives from a true Teacher are always for your benefit, even if they seem not to be. Because they are for your highest benefit, they are also for the highest benefit of all beings. This is not unlike a wise parent or guardian who tells a child what to do when the child does not know what is in her best interests. Sometimes a Teacher's guidance seems absurd, impractical, or contradictory. It is always in your best interests to listen to him, no matter what. The Teacher is your refuge.

Of course, use your best judgment.

The true Teacher uses any means necessary to reach people and help them move toward Freedom. This is called *skillful means,* like using candy to lure children out of a burning building. Freedom is so valuable that anything the Master does to help others attain it is worth it, no matter what. The relative level of truth is so radically different from the absolute level of Truth that the Master acts one way out-wardly while simultaneously, the true work is being done on a hidden level, like a spiritual sleight of hand that puts diamonds in your pocket when you're looking the other way.

A true Teacher may speak or act abrasively toward certain stu-dents. The Teacher doesn't attack you; he attacks your false sense of self. It just *feels* like he's attacking you. A true Teacher will not do this without being asked, either explicitly or implicitly, for help. If he is asked or told to stop vehemently enough, often enough and with sufficient force, he will continue but in a different way. Once you've asked, it's too late; you're on your way.

Some Teachers exhibit outward behavior that defies rational understanding and appears strange or contradictory. A true Teacher can be unpredictable. See if you can stay with it, even when your ego rebels.

AVOID PROJECTING NEGATIVITY

Not all teachers are true. If you feel that a teacher's style is not to your liking, you can move on to another teacher. You can even describe your experience to others. But if you project anger, spite, or judgment toward a true Teacher, it could harm you greatly. It is wisest to simply describe your experience and be done with it. Castigation is not help-ful. Thinking that you know a false teaching when you see one is a mistake. You can't know. You can only discern its quality as best you can and decide whether to get involved or not, doing so with respect for the teacher's humanity.

Criticizing a true Teacher is harmful to you because you are judging what is essentially blameless. If people ask you about your experience of a teacher, share your views and let them know that you ultimately know nothing about the matter and urge them to investigate it for themselves. Share your experience, feelings, and observations. If you do so respectfully, honestly, and with humility, it will help you and may even save you.

If you project negativity at, around, or about a true Teacher, you can harm yourself greatly. A true Teacher is a spiritual amplifier whose effects can be experienced either positively or negatively. Just as reverent attention can liberate you from negativity, disrespect or angry attacks can incur extreme repercussions. No one can hurt a free person. Anyone who attacks an awakened person is really only harming herself—far more so than by attacking an unawakened person. It's like a boomerang that comes back to you a thousandfold. Since it is difficult to discern who is awakened and who isn't, it is best to treat all teachers with respect and kindness, just as you would any other human being. The person who bumps into you at the grocery store may be an awakened being. Always assume the person you are dealing with is worthy of your respect unless his behavior proves otherwise. If someone tries to harm you, leave. Forgive him and move on. If you say or do something to harm another person, make amends. That's all it takes.

When sharing your experience of a teacher with others—even if he seems to be blatantly false—it is pointless to criticize him beyond sharing your experience honestly. A false teacher is his own worst punishment, and a true Teacher is his own highest reward. Why attack either one? When sharing, speak from your experience. For example, you could say: "I don't really know, but this is my experience. I saw this, I witnessed that, and I experienced such and such. This is what I felt, thought, and sensed." Your only important decision, then, is whether to study with him or not. Either way, you have done so based on your own well-considered views. Why gossip, attack, or criticize? He may be true. You cannot know with absolute certainty.

If you have insulted, disparaged, or otherwise projected negativity at a Teacher, you can always contact him and tell him what you have said or done and ask for his forgiveness. Be honest and willing to do whatever it takes to make up for it. If you are sincere, it is likely that you can correct your mistake in a relatively short period of time. But contact him directly, or your actions won't have the power to eliminate the negativity that you have accumulated.

FINDING A TRUE TEACHER

To participate fully in a Teaching, you have to be there. Showing up is half the battle. Make the effort to see a true Teacher in person. If you don't go, you may not get another chance. The more true Teachers you see in person, the better. Talk with them if you can. One meeting with a Teacher can liberate you or at least benefit you massively, as long as you have the right attitude.

In this modern time, you are fortunate enough to have a range of Teachers from which to select. Some are popular and more difficult to get close to than others. Do what you can to see them. Most actively working Teachers hold talks, workshops, seminars, and retreats around the world, or at least in the local community where they live. If you don't have the time to do this, make the time, because it's worth it.

When you attend a talk by a teacher, listen to him speak. Is his meaning clear and consistent? Does he seem to be speaking from a higher or deeper place of wisdom than the mere educated, intellectual mind? Most importantly, are you moved by his presence, voice, and manner? If so, you may want to get more involved. Ask him questions if you can. Does he take the time to talk to you? Do you feel a connection when you talk to him? Ultimately, you must decide how you feel about working with him further.

If you feel genuinely moved and intrigued by your interaction with him, find out how to get more involved. You may want to wait a while after the talk to integrate your experience and meditate on the teaching some more. Typically, if he is true and his style is appropriate for you, you will know almost immediately.

Sometimes, if you cannot meet a true Teacher in person, you can seek out his students and practice with them, or just talk to them.

Meeting other students can be helpful because they usually have access to resources and information that can aid you in deciding if you want to become more deeply involved. Talking to a student who has met the Teacher in person can help you get more insight into his character, methods, and presentation. Because of their deeper involvement, students can give you information and guidance about taking the next step of involvement, what kind of effort that requires, how much it costs, how long it takes, and so on. You can usually get the same information from an official representative of the organization, if there is one, but a student will give you the lowdown, if you will, on what participation in the Teaching at a deeper level is like. This is similar to investigating a school that you are considering attending. If you ask school officials about what student life is like, you will usually get good information, but it will have a more official tone, whereas actual students will give you a much more personal, off the record, and intimate view of the institution. Both are useful.

Evaluate a teacher first on an absolute, then a relative level. In other words, is he truly awakened? Then, does his teaching style work for you? To determine if a teacher is truly awakened, use your powers of discrimination. Listen within yourself as you listen to his words. Get a feel for what he is like. You may have a silent recognition within yourself that says "This is It."

How do you determine if a teacher is true? There is no way to be absolutely sure about it. If your discriminating wisdom is strong enough, you will automatically be drawn to a true Teacher, and you will recognize him. Eventually, everyone develops enough discrimination to recognize a teacher's awakened status to some degree. To develop discriminating wisdom, study and practice until you recognize Truth when you encounter it. Then, when you meet a teacher in person, you will have a basis for making a distinction. Just attending one event or reading one book by a true Teacher will develop your inner wisdom, allowing you to at least begin to detect Truth. Your ability to recognize Truth in others is directly proportional to your ability to recognize it within yourself. Keep practicing. Develop a deep commitment to Truth instead of a tepid desire for comforting ideas.

Keep researching available teachers until you are certain that you have found the right one for you. True Teachers are still quite rare, but there is always one for you if you are sincere in your search. Don't be satisfied with the cheap glitter of fool's gold. Hold out for the real Gold, the awakened Teacher. If you're not sure about a teacher's quality, do not commit to him until you are.

You don't have to dive in right away. You can just sit silently and listen to what he says. It is ideal to get close enough to a true Teacher so he can get to know you, observe you, and hear what you have to say, because then he can speak directly to you, and you can listen. This kind of personalized instruction is invaluable because it is a direct communication of the Absolute to Itself through you, and it's tailored to your specific, personal needs. For example, you can receive guidance on what you need to do to live most in accord with the Teaching and develop spiritually in the most rapid, yet healthy and balanced way. If you are listening to a public talk with many people present and cannot be addressed individually, you will not get personal guidance as you would in a smaller meeting, but you may get specific guidance from a message given to the general audience.

Whereas an unconscious person is like a mud-covered window, a true Teacher is like an open window. A mud-covered window lets in no light, and the room is dark. You cannot see the way out. A dirty window lets in a little light, but still it is hard to move around without bumping into the furniture and hurting yourself. An open window lets in all the light of the sun, and you can see your way around and the way out, easily. Even if the window's frame is flawed somehow, it doesn't matter to the functionality of the open space it surrounds. Regardless of the state of a frame, the open space still lets in light. The key is to discriminate between the space of the window and the frame around it. Then you can use it properly and not be troubled over the frame. In the same way, do not confuse who the true Teacher is in his essence with who he is in his manifested form. He is identical with Freedom, in the same way that an open window is identical with space that allows light. If his personal style is not to your liking, keep looking. Eventually, you will find him.

PRIMARY AND SECONDARY TEACHERS

You can work with a variety of Teachers, but it is best to find one with whom you are most in accord and make him your primary Teacher. Get as close as you can, listen carefully to what he says, and follow his instructions. What could be easier than that? If you trust your Teacher, you will do the practices that he recommends, even if you resist doing them sometimes. If you are fortunate enough to find a true Teacher, learn from him. Learn from as many true Teachers as you can find. Cling to true Teachers as if they were life preservers and you were a drowning person. Trust them with your life.

Ideally, find a Teacher with whom you can work closely. One primary Teacher and a handful of secondary Teachers is excellent. One is good, but more is better. The more true Teachers you are in relationship with, the stronger your affinity to Freedom. But you cannot have more than one primary Teacher. If you try to serve more than one Master, your practices and loyalties will be divided, causing conflict between them. Your primary Teacher is the one from whom you take direct instruction, and that instruction must take precedence over all others. You would not take direct instruction from secondary Teachers, because their guidance might conflict with that of your primary Teacher. Stay with one primary Teacher until your course of study has ended, if it has an end. If it does not have a scheduled end, let your Teacher guide you.

Try to receive personalized instruction from him, if you can. Some Teachers are not available for personal contact. In such a case, that Teacher might be best suited as a secondary Teacher for you. It is ideal for you to have a primary Teacher from whom you can receive individual attention tailored to your specific pattern of unconsciousness, supported by more generalized instructions from others. Even having a brief conversation with a Teacher can be beneficial. The greatest benefit is derived when you work closely with the Teacher and receive feedback and guidance on your path.

If you can't get personalized instruction, it is still highly beneficial to sit in the presence of a secondary Teacher, especially when in the company of a number of dedicated students, because the effect of the presence of Truth is amplified greatly by collective listening. Make use of whatever instruction is available. If you are serious about awakening, you will find a way to meet at least one Teacher in person and perhaps even exchange a few words or ask a question. Depending on the format, it is often possible to ask a question even in a large gathering. Do so if you can.

Once you have found your Teacher, stay in relationship with him. It is up to you to find a way to be with him. The lessons you need will then come to you as you live your life. People and situations will force you into a deeper relationship with yourself, because your contact with Truth is changing you from the inside out, and your lived, day-to-day experience will reflect that. The acceleration of your personal evolution will give you enough material to keep you busy. Just make sure that you continue to practice, focusing on issues that have arisen from contact with the Teaching.

THE EMPOWERED TEACHER

An *empowered teacher* is a disciple of the Teaching, a student at the third level of involvement who serves as an associate in the teaching of new students. A disciple who respectfully represents the Teaching is a powerful teacher in her own right, but because she is not yet liberated, she must teach with great humility and discipline to hold her ego in check. Sometimes, it may be difficult to see or work closely with an awakened Teacher because of the sheer volume of his students, and it is common for advanced students to help with the large workload.

Being an empowered teacher can be helpful to both the Master and students if done properly. If she teaches in homage to or with respect for the true Teaching without any credit or claims for herself, this actually serves awakening tremendously—both hers and others'. The empowered teacher's surrender to the true Teaching serves to awaken others, even though she is not yet awakened. When teaching, the compassionate humility in her heart says, in effect, "These words are not *for* me or *about* me and the Teaching does not *originate* with me, but I lay myself down at the feet of Truth in complete and utterly grateful surrender." This kind of teaching is extremely powerful.

If you are a student at the first or second levels of involvement and are studying primarily with an empowered teacher, you need to consider some important issues. First of all, does your empowered teacher have a primary Teacher who is alive and currently teaching? If so, is she in contact with him? Are they on friendly terms? Has your teacher received a dispensation to act in an empowered status? If not, it is best to find an empowered teacher who is an active disciple of a true Teaching and authorized to teach. Even if your teacher is truly empowered and teaching at a high level, why would you not at some point consider working with her Teacher directly? The awakened Teacher is the source of the Teaching, and there is no reason why you cannot work with him directly, unless he is too busy. Go straight to the source, if you can.

FALSE TEACHERS

The vast majority of those who are currently calling themselves spiritual teachers are false. Using a false teacher for spiritual help is like using an anvil to escape drowning. Those who claim to be enlightened, awake, free, liberated, or somehow a source of Truth beyond that of a scholar, pundit, or student—when they are not—are false teachers. Basically, they say: "I am awake, free, liberated, enlightened. If you sit with me, you will realize the Truth. I can teach you. I can get you there." This is like standing on a public platform and shouting, "I have the keys to the Kingdom" and passing out pull-pins to live hand grenades. This is fundamentally dishonest, not to mention destructive. This is so even if they say, "I have nothing to teach, there is no such thing as enlightenment, no one has ever been enlightened, and I have nothing to give you"—because these statements imply the ability to evaluate (recognize) Truth and communicate from That position, something they cannot do—even if they communicate that they have nothing to communicate.

Devious. Watch out for it.

False teachers muddy the waters and make it hard for sincere students to see clearly who is true and who is false. This factor adds a challenge to your quest. Do not let it dissuade you or draw you into an unconscious path. You must listen more deeply than your intellect to determine if a teacher is true. Although the abundance of false teachings creates a bewildering racket, you must persevere until you succeed. It is your responsibility to find a true Teacher and avoid following a false one. If you become a student of a false teacher, on some level you prefer darkness to Light. Many false teachings sound authentic and seduce you into an egoic fantasy of absolute understanding on an intellectual level. There is no such thing. You cannot comprehend the Absolute intellectually. You must be sincere in your quest for awakening and keep searching until you find a true Teaching.

One way the mind keeps us enthralled is by speaking through false teachers, mimicking words of Truth, but with subtle differences that render them false. If absolutely true words are spoken by an awakened Teacher, the exact same words spoken by a false teacher have no power to awaken you. Fruit plucked from the tree is no longer fresh once it is devoured and excreted. What is left over is not fit for human consumption. If the words are spoken with reverence for Truth, with great love and respect for the original Teaching, those words have the same power to awaken as they ever did. This is also true of the written word. Since false teachers have no reverence for Truth, their fruit has no power to nourish, only to sicken, putrefy, and poison.

Do not underestimate this factor.

With a false teacher as a guide, even technically correct practices such as meditation are worthless. Fine wine looks like grape juice. To find out which is which, you have to get close and smell it, taste it, drink it to know the difference. A true Teaching is like fine wine. False teachings are like imitation grape juice laced with arsenic.

Know the difference.

How can you tell a true Teacher from a false one? Watch him and see what happens when confronted with conflict or chaos. Whereas a false teacher will become nervous, angry, or afraid, a true Teacher will become calmer and more deeply present. Above all, trust your valid reasoning and deepest intuitive feelings to tell you if a teacher is true. Investigate carefully to discern the authentic from the counterfeit. Don't allow false teachers to lead you astray.

ABSOLUTISM

False teachers embody *absolutism,* or the erroneous attribution of absolute truth to relative statements. Because false teachers' statements often sound philosophically valid, many people mistake their relative meaning for absolute truth and get mired more deeply in unconsciousness. Absolutism is evidence of a lack of true awakening because it fails to clearly discriminate between the Absolute and the relative.

Most potential students do not know the difference between a relative philosophical statement with absolute implications and a statement having absolute value. For example, the statement "The world is an illusion" has absolute implications, but it has absolute value only if made by an awakened person. It takes practice to develop that level of discernment.

The world may be an illusion, but you have to recognize this Fact before it has absolute value *for you.* The Absolute must be accessed through relative means. It is something you must *do.* You must use the mind properly to discern its ultimate nature. The awakened person has done this work. The unawakened person has not done this work, at least not yet. An unawakened person saying that the world is an illusion is like a death row inmate saying that prison walls don't exist. The statement is true on an absolute level but false on a relative level. It's not true for you unless you are awakened. This is not a value judgment, but a fact. It is one thing to say "The world is an illusion"; it is quite another to consciously *be* That which transcends the world and speak from that perspective.

Absolutist claims mimic statements of ultimate Truth but are false by virtue of their relative origin. Typical statements include the following:

> "There is no such thing as enlightenment."
>
> "You're already free, so you don't need a teacher or a teaching."
>
> "There's nothing to do."
>
> "All is one."
>
> "Just be."

Offering intellectual statements such as these in lieu of Truth is like offering poisoned cookies to starving children when real food is available. It is a profound mistake to think that the shallow intellectual understanding of absolutism is the same as the absolute authority of awakening. Anyone who falsely claims awakened status or authority—either explicitly or implicitly—and spews absolutist dogma as a viable facsimile of Truth is doing egregious harm to herself and others.

Absolutism is often falsely referred to as *Advaita* (Sanskrit for "nondual"), a term borrowed from the valid philosophy of *Advaita Vedanta*. Actually, it is fairly easy for a person who has read *Advaita Vedanta* texts to fabricate a "teaching" that has no awakening power. *Advaita Vedanta* in its original form is a valid Teaching; it takes great humility and reverence to transmit it properly. A true Teaching has Power because of its origin. *Advaita Vedanta* has Power because of Shankara, its originator (plus others who have transmitted it reverently). If an unawakened person such as a scholar writes a book about *Advaita Vedanta* and dedicates it wholeheartedly to Shankara (or any other true lineage-holders) and makes no absolute claims for herself with a supreme intent to transmit the essence of the Teaching, it actually empowers her (and anyone who reads it to some extent) because she has surrendered humbly to Truth in a mode of devoted service to its transmission. If the author makes erroneous claims for herself—in other words, if she is not free but claims to be and writes from that perspective, especially if she does so with disdain for the Teaching—it harms her greatly.

HOW TO AVOID BEING A FALSE TEACHER

It is wise to avoid falling into the trap of becoming a false teacher. But as a student, it may be helpful at times to share your insights with others. The key to responsible sharing is to speak from your *experience*. This protects you from communicating abstractions that sound true, but aren't. For example, how has the Teaching touched you, affected you, helped you? Stick with what you feel or sense is true based on *what you have lived*. Speak from that place of basic honesty, where your thoughts match your experience, and no further. This protects you from teaching falsely.

Protect the "green shoots" of new insight or understanding sprouting up in your awareness. Do not trumpet them to the four winds before they have had a chance to take root. If they take root in the laboratory of your experience, they can grow into great trees. But this takes time. Keep them to yourself until you have lived their effects on the relative scene long enough for them to root deeply in you. If they have not yet rooted deeply, remain silent until they do. As Lao Tzu notes, "What is rooted is easy to nourish." It is not that you must hoard the Wisdom-treasures for yourself like a miser, but rather that you respect the Teaching enough to remain silent until it is appropriate to share what you have learned. It is more important for you to reflect the Teaching through the quality of your consciousness than through the sophistication of your words. If you live the Teaching in a responsible fashion, others will eventually ask you to share your wisdom. Until then, it is best to remain silent and let your consciousness do the talking.

Before you share your wisdom with someone, make sure that she is asking for it, either explicitly or implicitly. Listen into her space for a need to receive what you are considering saying and into yourself for an honest and humble willingness to give it. If that space is not present, do not share. Listen into your heart, and compassion will help you determine whether to communicate it or not. Watch out for a feeling of self-will or pride in telling your story, a sign that the ego is co-opting your willingness. This in-the-moment determination is an example of situational (or even momentary) honesty. Because of this, make sure that you are paying attention to the dimension of *intimacy with Truth*. You are both creating intimacy with Truth by listening into the space of relationship and honoring it by either sharing or not. Let Truth determine your action. Make sure you speak from the deepest truth you can, adhering closely to your experience, and you will be less likely to move into your head, set up shop, and spout mental fabrications.

Remember that you cannot help others see Truth before you have helped yourself do the same. Living your insights successfully in the relative field of experience gives your words the weight of basic honesty, and others will hear it. When you live the Teaching in this way, you embody consciousness to a degree. To that degree—and no further—you know what you are talking about. Wisdom comes from deep within you, from beyond your intellect. Sometimes the most honest thing to say is *I don't know*. Maintain your humility and remember that you cannot know anything with absolute certainty, having reverence for That which cannot be known by the mind. The more conscious you become, the less likely it is that you will be deceived by your ego.

If all else fails, remember that *if you maintain humility, not-knowing, and reverence for the Teaching, you cannot go wrong*.

NEUTRAL TEACHINGS

As we have seen, the source of a true Teaching is an awakened person, a true Teacher. The source of a false teaching is a false teacher—an unawakened person who claims to be awakened, either explicitly or implicitly. It is important to realize that, between true and false teachings, a middle ground of *neutral* teachings exists—teachings that are neither true nor false, strictly speaking. These teachings are basically harmless because they are not represented by a person who claims to be an awakened Teacher, but by a set of ideas, a sort of colorful playground for the mind. Although neutral teachings are many and varied, a useful modern example is the *New Age* movement.

The New Age movement is an amalgam of old ideas traditionally considered occult, metaphysical, or mystical, now packaged for modern audiences. "Occult" means "hidden" or "covered up." In ancient times, groups who studied witchcraft, astrology, alchemy, divination, and other occult disciplines had to hide what they were doing from the church or they could have been burned at the stake or worse. So-called "mystery schools" practiced arcane rituals in secret and summoned mysterious deities for the purpose of obtaining spiritual power, but typically only mesmerized themselves with exotic belief systems. The New Age movement is a modern, sanitized version of this kind of study, typically for those who have rejected mainstream religion and are reaching out for something to replace it. There is really nothing new about the New Age except that now it is out in the open, whereas before it was hidden.

The spirit of the New Age is finding ultimate truth within one-self, on one's own terms. Although noble in intent, the problem with this approach is that its unstructured "do it yourself" mentality provides ample hiding places for the ego. Often, New Age practices are geared toward the empowerment of the individual without involving any true spiritual practice, or surrender. For example, a New Age enthusiast might try to meditate, but without the structured and often demanding environment of an authentic Teaching, such a practice usually leads to a trance state instead of true meditation.

The New Age implies that you can be in control of Reality, and you can't. Reality is what it is, regardless of what you do. To grow in consciousness, you must surrender control of your life to Truth, not sugarcoat the controller with esoteric philosophies. While dabbling in subjects such as astrology, tarot, and witchcraft can be fascinating, it's not ultimately liberating.

Below is a description of three common New Age ideas—*visualization and affirmation, channeling,* and *evolution of consciousness*—and their ability (or lack thereof) to aid you on your path.

Visualization and Affirmation

The New Age Movement claims that you create your own Reality and can therefore *control* Reality through techniques such as *visualization* (imagining vividly what you want) and *affirmation* (mentally affirming what you want). While it is true that you create your own Reality, it is true only on an absolute level, because on an absolute level you literally *are* Reality, and phenomena are an appearance of your form. Striving to control Reality implies that things should be other than they are—the basic misconception of unconsciousness—and this tends to strengthen the ego.

While these techniques sometimes get results, it is only by Grace that it happens. If you use these techniques and are conscious enough to interpret your experience symbolically, as if you were having a dream, you might get a message that in effect says: "Stop it. You are only hurting yourself." You then might be led to recognize the Truth that underlies the sometimes magical confluence of events and begin to surrender to it, weakening the ego's hold on you rather than succumbing to its demands that Reality conform to your desires.

Your spiritual development does not depend on the ability to control your experience. It depends on finding the Power that makes such an occurrence possible. Eventually, what you want and what you have are the same thing: Reality. It already is. Investigate your tendency to argue with it until there is no more tendency. Otherwise, confusion is the result, regardless of what you affirm or deny.

Channeling

Channeling is a popular New Age phenomenon in which a disembodied being supposedly speaks through a person as a form of teaching, but few channeled teachings are honest. Disembodied beings sometimes speak through a trance channel, but only rarely. Most channeled teachings are not channeled at all, but are produced by personalities split off from the "channeler," similar to a person with multiple personality disorder. These personalities are unconscious aspects of the individual's psychology that are not claimed by the integrating consciousness. If a disembodied being does speak through a channel, it is almost always (and perhaps subtly) malevolent because it is accorded independent power by the channeler. But Truth is the only Power. And Truth is who you ultimately are, not something external to or separate from you. It must be embodied to be transmitted effectively—not split off from you and "channeled." Because of this inherent split, channeled teachings do not possess awakening power. They are mostly ineffectual, unless you see them as mind-based and move on to a more embodied teaching, having learned from your experience. If you are interested in any channeled teachings, investigate them, keeping in mind that they are likely a comfort to your ego and not much else.

Sometimes "Ascended Masters" are said to speak through channels, but this is a false notion. Disembodied Teachers do not speak through people, and the true Teacher is not a channel for anything. He is *here,* not in a distant realm. As long as you rely on a source of information that is coming from another realm, you are still functioning within the realm of the mind. All beings seek Liberation, even ones in other planes and dimensions. To be awakened means that beings in all realms, planes, and dimensions long to be your friend—whether they know it or not. Compared to awakening, even to be a god is to suffer. You are a human being. Isn't that mysterious and fascinating enough? Find a true Teaching and get involved.

Evolution of Consciousness

Another popular New Age idea is the *evolution of consciousness,* a theory that the universe is some kind of school in which we are evolving to a higher plane of functioning.

First of all, the universe is not a school in any conventional sense. It's more like a prison.

Second, consciousness does not evolve. The world evolves, but this is an effect of consciousness, not a cause. In other words, the relative evolves, but the Absolute does not; the Absolute is revealed through a conscious process that appears as relative change.

Third, and finally, it is a mistake to look to future events to save you, because your salvation is available now. True Teachers are available today, so waiting for another day is an avoidance of your present opportunity. If a teaching emphasizes future events as your salvation, it is masking its current lack of substance and trying to get you to avoid the Freedom that is available to you as you read these words. Eventually, we will all be liberated, but not through an evolutionary process. Although the bulk of humanity is becoming more conscious, it is a mistake to wait passively for collective awakening to occur. If you wait for the bulk of humanity to be liberated, you will be waiting a *long* time. Freeing yourself now contributes to the evolution of humanity, and you don't have to wait.

GRATITUDE

Once you find a Teacher with whom you feel comfortable working, allow yourself to be grateful. Practice *gratitude* for all you have, especially for what serves your growth in consciousness. Take moments throughout the day to reflect on the blessings you have received in life that have led to this point. The practice of gratitude tends to instill humility, a condition that is favorable for awakening. It also leads to joy and faith. If you are grateful for what you have, regardless of how little it may seem, more will be given to you, and you will also be more likely to use what you have for noble purposes.

CHAPTER FOUR

ACTION

Read as few words as you like
And speak fewer.
But act upon the law.

—Gautama Buddha

Practice not-doing, and everything
will fall into place.

—Lao Tzu

SPIRITUAL PRACTICE

Spiritual practice is action that leads to growth in awareness. Those who practice assiduously and with great devotion align themselves with the Power that seeks to awaken within them. Getting there is the whole point. Once you are there, you can decide what to say about it. Until then, practice. You must *do the work* to get there. If you practice consistently and sincerely, you'll get there and realize that there's no getting there. All is revealed *there.*

Your next breath is not guaranteed. Although we habitually ignore the fact of our mortality, death can occur suddenly. Cerebral aneurysm, heart attack, stroke, auto accident, natural disaster, and routine surgery can be instantly fatal. Don't leave your spiritual health up to fate. Take charge of it and take the necessary steps toward solidifying your practice. If you neglect your practice and die unexpectedly, you may lose this precious opportunity to awaken. Practice like there is no tomorrow, because you never know if tomorrow will be there to meet you.

Very few phrases are as important as *do the work.* This means *take action and do the spiritual practices that your Teacher has given you to do.* Make practice a habit, like brushing your teeth, and you will be less likely to skip a day. This activity does not have to be compulsive to be consistent. It does not necessarily involve stress or strain. It becomes integrated into a conscious regular movement in your life. Informal mindfulness practice, for example, can be done anytime, anywhere. All you have to do is listen, breathe, and pay attention to what arises in the field of your awareness without judgment.

When disaster strikes, do the work. Disaster is your opportunity to grow spiritually. Measure your spiritual progress by how you react when things go awry, when accidents happen, when you are faced with catastrophe. If you react negatively, blame factors outside of you, or don't practice, you are wasting a precious opportunity to become more conscious. When things go wrong, say "Yes" to them—not because they are necessarily right or good—but because they *are.*

If you get stuck in lethargy, stress, or indecision, just *do* something. Anything. It doesn't matter. You will discover what is best for you more quickly by taking an action than by mulling over an issue in your mind. To maintain your serenity when confronted with a problem, you must either change the situation or radically accept it. There is no other stress-free option. You must act, even if that is to sit still and breathe.

Ultimately, there is no such thing as a problem. The mind generates the appearance of problems to maintain a sense of self. Practically speaking, a problem is a *painful situation.* The only way out of a painful situation is to take appropriate action. This does not require value judgment and stress. Conscious action dissolves judgment and relieves stress. The term "problem" implies that there is something wrong, hidden, out of place, or not as it should be. Everything is as it should be because it *is.*

The world is an illusion, like a mirage. If you are afraid of a mirage, you must take steps toward it—toward the "lake"—until you get close enough to see that it is just a perceptual distortion. Some people are more willing to go the distance to find out this truth than others. We can talk about it, although conversation doesn't help much. Action is more important. If you must talk, do so consciously and constructively. Sometimes humor helps.

Use the mind against itself. Use the mind to attain no-mind. Use doing to attain not-doing. Using the mind against itself is like stopping a train so you can step off onto the platform. It's the stopping that lets the stepping happen. The mind cannot stop itself, but you can *use* the mind to stop itself. You must take action. If you leave the mind to its own devices, it creates hell then complains about the heat.

NOT-DOING

On the absolute level, doing is an illusion. On the relative level, doing is everything. You cannot help but take action, regardless of what you are doing or not doing. The key is to take action that leads to growth in awareness. For example, sitting still is a form of action: a decision you make, an action you take to sit down and be still. If you sit still in meditation with a Teacher, your action becomes a form of spiritual practice. You are always locked into the relative cause and effect of an action unless you use it to produce growth in consciousness. If you fundamentally recognize the Emptiness of the moment of action and are unattached to its outcome, it is *not-doing*, or conscious action. Conscious action arises from beyond the mind.

Action is relative in nature because it consists in a person—someone—performing an action—some*thing*. Absolutists often mistakenly claim that because action is an illusion from the absolute perspective, it is a mistake to do anything in the way of spiritual practice. Rather, they say, you should just recognize who you already are. The problem is that the instruction to "recognize who you already are" is a directive to take action. It is dishonest, not to mention confusing, to say, in essence: "Doing is an illusion. Don't do anything. Now do something."

It requires great effort to become conscious. This effort is non-effort. It looks like effort, but, from an absolute point of view, nothing is happening. If I pick up a glass of water, my person, the action, and the water are illusions—and yet, I can drink it. If I don't drink some form of water, I will die of dehydration. The key is to *use the relative to attain the Absolute.* Drinking water is useful for quenching your thirst. Similarly, embracing a conscious path of action is useful for awakening to Reality. There is a path, and you must walk it, although ultimately there is no path and no one to walk it. Saying "there's no path" is true on the absolute level, but false on the relative level. You must walk the path until you discover its Emptiness for yourself. Because true spiritual practice is given to you by awakened beings, it reveals your true nature. It is like a beacon from the Beyond.

The not-doing of the awakened person is not mere inaction, but conscious action. As a student, you must practice in order to recognize this Truth. You must do *something,* even if only to take your attention into the awareness of this fact. Not-doing doesn't mean that you just sit there, doing nothing, although you may do that sometimes. Becoming conscious is recognizing that action is ultimately insubstantial, although relatively important. "Doing" is a concept that is redeemed by its usefulness. Spiritual practice is action that is redeemed by its being performed in service to awakening—not to concepts *about* awakening, but to awakening *itself.*

Absolutists don't understand this. They say "don't do anything," but then they give you directions on what to do—or not do, which is still a form of doing. "Just become aware" is a directive to do something: become aware. The contradiction here is trenchant and foul. If anyone tells you to "Just let go and don't do anything," he is telling you to do nothing and let things take their course. Only a mind-dominated person would tell you this, because it is the very thing the mind wants you to do: nothing. True not-doing is neither doing something nor doing nothing. Not-doing is beyond concepts. It is so radical that if you were able to speak it, the earth would catch fire and everyone you know would run screaming in the other direction.

From an absolute perspective, there is only Freedom and no doer or doing—but saying "do nothing" to a student implies that spiritual practices are worthless and nothing needs to be done because "Freedom already is." This is a deadly combination of ignorance and dishonesty that often leads students astray. If someone says "There's nothing to do," meaning that you don't have to do anything to become conscious, that person is conflating the absolute and relative levels of truth. On the absolute level, it's true that there's nothing to do. On the relative level, there is much work in the form of authentic spiritual practice to be done. On the relative level, something is being done by a person who is doing something. On the absolute level, nothing is being done and no one is doing anything. It is important to understand the difference.

Some teachings insist that you must stop seeking, that to seek is the problem. But being a seeker is not necessarily a problem. Seeking is a problem only when you *identify* with seeking. Keep seeking until you find. When you find, you are no longer a seeker. Eventually, the search ends, and no more questions arise.

KARMA

Karma (Sanskrit for "action") is the accumulation of mental tendencies produced by unconscious past action. Conscious action destroys karma. Unconscious action perpetuates karma as a cause that comes back to you as an effect through time. Karma is the stored negativity from your past that must run its course in order to fulfill itself, like an arrow shot into the sky. Eventually, it must fall to earth—unless you pull the earth out from under it. That is what awakening is like.

If you are moved by your mind, you generate karma. If you are moved by Truth, you dissolve karma. A liberated being dissolves karma because she is moved by Truth.

Karma and rebirth coexist. A major misconception is that when you die, you're free of embodied existence. This is not true. Bondage continues beyond death unless you are liberated. Death is not the end of everything. Death is more of the same. Your karma keeps you bound to the wheel of suffering, and awakening is the only way to liberate yourself from it. What is commonly referred to as death is merely the sloughing off of the physical body. What continues beyond death is an accumulation of mental tendencies, a bundle of lies saying "I know who I am" that is irresistibly drawn into the sexual relations of a pair of beings, human or otherwise, then fused with the embryo or fetus at some point in the beginning of a new life cycle. What is born and dies is not who you are. You do not die and get reborn; the mind does. Because you identify with the mind, you adhere to it and go through lifetime after lifetime thinking that the mind is who you are.

Your creditors cannot follow you beyond the transition we call death. Your karma does—until you dissolve it with awakening. It is a mistake to think that you can get away with unethical behavior, even if you manage to evade worldly authorities. It is a mistake to think that murderers who escape courtroom justice do not face the awful consequences of their actions in some way, either in this life or the next. Karmic obligations keep you bound to the wheel of birth and death, so a facile interpretation of karma will not suffice. Karma reaps its harvest with your death, and it is not something to be referred to lightly, as it often is in our culture. Karma and pain are inseparable. Karma is created by unconscious living and destroyed by conscious action.

Karma drives the various realms of suffering. If you have a heavy burden of karma, it must play itself out through many lifetimes until you enter the true path and work toward Liberation. You are not totally free of generating new karma until you are awakened. Once you are awakened, the body persists for a while, then ceases, but you do not generate any new karma. A liberated person is not attached to the consequences of her actions. This does not mean that she isn't aware of her actions or their consequences. It simply means that she is free of attachment to them. The only karma acting on an awakened person is what was set in motion before awakening. Like a wheel, it spins for a while, even when no one is actively spinning it any longer.

Then it stops.

SOUL MEMORIES

From the perspective of the Absolute, there is no past or future. It's all now. Since from the perspective of awakened consciousness everything is happening now, "past lives" are more accurately called *soul memories*. The past exists entirely in the mind as memories. Memories are traces in the mind that are recalled now, if at all. Lifetimes are connected by karma and are part of the illusion that you call *yourself*. If you are one person in one lifetime and another person in another lifetime, who are you, really? The entity that reincarnates is not who you are. You are Consciousness, Spirit, Soul. The thread that connects your lifetimes is attachment to being a person with a story. You are no such thing. You are Freedom Itself.

You do not need to remember other lifetimes until you do. It is wisest first to find out who you are, then see if you are interested in other lifetimes. If you awaken, you may or may not consciously recall soul memories. Awakening means that what is *is,* and you are one with That. Because the ego needs an identity, people often try to discover themselves in the past by trying to find out who they were in a past life. Although this can be useful, it cannot be forced. Soul memories are usually spontaneously revealed and will find their way to your conscious awareness regardless of what you do. If you have a selfish interest in finding out about a past life, you will likely just create a fantasy about it and believe it's true. Instead, find out who you truly are, now. Who you truly are is beyond the wildest fantasy you could possibly concoct.

Soul memories almost always involve profound trauma from another lifetime, usually an excruciatingly painful death. We have all experienced them. These afflictions stamp themselves on your mind like a hot iron and rankle into your current experience, causing distortions in your subconscious mind. They do not have to be resolved for awakening to occur and usually resolve spontaneously as a result of the awakening process. Their outer effects can be managed with consistent practice. If you sincerely devote yourself to the path of awakening, any soul memories that need to surface will surface. If any do, consulting with a true Teacher is helpful. Otherwise, focus on *this* life and not on any other, because that is what is most valuable in terms of awakening.

SERVICE

Service means doing something for someone else. The Latin root, *servus,* means "slave" or "servant." On the path of awakening, you serve Truth. You place yourself below it, in subservience to it, acknowledging it as your Master. For most people, this is extremely hard to do. The false self wants to know *What's in it for me? How can I bend the world to serve my needs? How can I get what I want?* Service means that we turn this relationship around, that we live in service to Truth without attachment to the outcome, bending *ourselves* to serve *its* needs. Paradoxically, being a slave to Truth is what sets you free. It straightens you out and liberates you.

The most powerful way to use service as a liberating practice is to serve a Teacher in some way. This means that you can help move furniture, cook food, raise funds—basically, do something that helps the Teaching. The key is to do this spontaneously and without any attachment either to doing it or reaping any benefits from doing it. If you have an attachment to doing the service, you might get upset over not being allowed to do it or fight with others over the privilege. This does not work. If you are attached to reaping benefits for yourself from doing a service, you will not get any benefit. You cannot curry favor with Truth; you can only serve it and lay down your selfish preferences. *You must value Truth as the ultimate value.* If you value anything over Truth, you are opposing your own Freedom, and it cannot reach you.

Service is *surrendered action.* Resistance is surrendered so that the highest action arises spontaneously by itself. In that sense, you are serving Truth. The easy way to serve Truth is to listen to your Teacher and do what she guides you to do. She is not controlling you, because you are free to leave or do as you please. See if you can listen to her and find the Wisdom in what she says. If you can, trust her guidance and instruction. This is crucial. If you get a direct instruction from a true Teacher, do what she says. A true Teacher will not harm you.

Of course, use your best judgment.

You can serve one of two masters: Truth, or the world. Most people live like slaves because they serve the world and its values. They see the world as intrinsically valuable and act accordingly. For example, if you see money as intrinsically valuable, you will serve money. Money has a relative value only. Seeing money as an absolute value gives it power over you. Money becomes your master, and you serve it by slaving away at a job you hate, cheating others, even committing robbery or murder to get more of it. When you do these things, money is your master. Jesus said that "No one can serve two masters. Either he will hate the one and love the other, or he will be devoted to the one and despise the other. You cannot serve both God and Money." You can *serve* God and *use* money, but you cannot serve both. Some people try to serve money and use God. This does not work.

You cannot use or obtain God as an object. If you are with a Teacher just to get something from her, even something "spiritual," you will not get it. You must surrender to your Teacher as Truth or it is like trying to get something from her. You must be willing for Truth to be the highest value to which you attain. If you value Truth above all else, you cannot be bought, nor can you cheat anyone else. You do things for your Teacher because it is natural for you to do so, because you love her, because you value her as an awakened human being, not as a means to an end. Awakening is not a commodity that you can get, and the Teaching is not a metaphysical convenience store.

You must serve the Teaching by laying down your selfish motives, even to gain Freedom as some *thing* you can own. If you really knew what Freedom was, you would have it. Since you don't have it yet, it follows that you don't know what it is. Why, then, would you try to get it from your Teacher? Trying to get something assumes that you know what it is you are looking for. If you broke into a house to steal Freedom, would you know where it was or what it looked like? To serve the Teaching, you must have only one motive—to serve Truth at all costs. Since the Teacher knows what it is (by consciously *being* what it is) and you don't (at least not yet), you must give up all hope of having it on your own terms. If your motivation to serve your Teacher is a calculated attempt to get something, you will not get what you are after and you will harm yourself in the process, because the calculating mind only serves itself, strengthening its delusion and taking you along for the ride. True service is done without any expectation of reward, such as praise or approval. This is the true essence of service.

Serve the Absolute as you find it in other people. People are intrinsically valuable by virtue of their humanity. If you try to get something from someone, it means that you value the thing you want to get more than who the person is. If you try to con a person out of his money, you value money more than the person. If you view money as an end in itself and people as a means to an end, you have it backwards. If you view people as ends in themselves and money as a means to an end, you turn selfishness around and act in alignment with what saves you. Human beings are the bearers of Truth, the ultimate end in themselves by virtue of who they are. Suffering begins and ends with human beings. If you treat human beings as objects, you are missing an opportunity to serve them and become liberated.

To serve all beings is the standard of service for the sincere student. This service may take on an overt or subtle form. How you serve depends on your particular mode of expression. It may occur through your career, family, volunteer work, or with people you meet as you move through life. The highest service you can render is walking the true path and sharing who you are with all beings, including children, plants, and animals. As you progress on the path of awakening, you become a blessing to all beings, regardless of what you do. All beings are blessed by your growth in consciousness and the inspired service at its heart. The quality of your conscious presence determines the degree of blessing you bring to the world. This blessing has less to do with *what* you do and more to do with *who you are as you do it.* Your conscious recognition of Truth informs your actions. Make awakening your standard of service and you cannot fail because you will not stop until you are free.

Awakening is the greatest service you can render.

LISTENING

Listening does not simply mean hearing. It means *acting* on what you hear. Listening to the inner Teacher and listening to the outer Teacher are fundamentally the same—but make sure that you listen to your outer Teacher as a primary source of guidance, because her voice is clear and unambiguous, unlike the inner voice, which can be masked by mental voices. This takes practice.

Listening is action. If you act on what you hear in the way of Truth, you are listening. Acting on what you hear sends a resounding thunderclap of blissfulness throughout your rotten false zombie self and shakes it ruthlessly. Take action. If you don't, you may lose the opportunity. Spend time with Teachers in person and do the work in whatever form suits you.

Listening is tuning in to the inner Teacher, your inner Guide, and acting on what you hear. Even if you just sit there, seemingly doing nothing, you are listening as long as you are consciously tuning in to Reality and letting it hold your sitting. Be willing for this tuning in to move your body or keep it still. If you remain still when movement is suggested, you are not listening. If you move when stillness is suggested, you are not listening. In those cases, you are letting the mind move you. When you act on inner guidance, your hearing becomes listening, and only then. Acting on what you hear in the way of Truth is power. If you move with Reality, you are saying "Yes" to it. Let it be what it is through the vessel of your person. To the degree that you allow this, you consciously *are* it.

Listen to your Teacher and be guided into perfect mastery, no matter what you hear. This requires trusting who she is, the essence of faith. Trust your Teacher. Make sure you have found a truly awakened Teacher and trust her. The main way that trust is proved in you is by listening to the guidance she gives you. If you don't act on what you hear, you aren't listening, and you don't trust your Teacher, which means that you don't have faith.

If you have a Teacher and you trust her deeply, it is likely that you will listen to her guidance. You will do what she says—not because she dominates your mind, but because you trust her. She doesn't tell you what you want to hear; she tells you what you *need* to hear to break the ego's grip on you. Therefore, let her get to know you and listen to what she says. This is the best advice you could possibly get. If she is a true Teacher, she is your highest advocate. Trust the Teaching and watch what happens. Trust implies consent; otherwise, it's just blind submission.

Asking *how* is more important than asking *why*. Asking *how* represents a mature willingness to act that presumes a *why*. For example, asking "How can I serve?" implies that you already know *why* or you wouldn't already be asking *how*. The answer to *how* involves something you *do*.

Listening doesn't have to make rational sense. It often doesn't. True love is *love in action*; it has nothing to do with reason. If you make an acronym out of "love in action"—LIA—you see that putting the R of "reason" on the end of it makes you a LIAR. True love in action is free of attachment to the mind; that is what makes it genuine. That is what saves the planet. Ultimately, love makes no sense to the mind.

What is love? Keeping it simple, love is being with what is, as it is, without judgment. Love is unconditional relationship. Love is not a feeling, although it causes powerful feelings. Love is the recognition that we're all one (without the schmaltz). Love is helping a child learn to read. Love saves people. Love is the connection that makes us one. Love makes the mind-made self look foolish.

If you love Truth, you must *act* in relationship with the Teacher and risk looking foolish. Take action to talk to her, be with her, take walks with her, whatever. Listen to her, too. Act on what she says. She may not tell you twice. If she does tell you twice, it is not an accident. If she tells you three times, you may not hear it again for a long time, because you are not listening yet and may need some time to stew in your mental juices.

How many times have you heard it already?

Are you listening?

HUMILITY

Service leads to humility, which prepares you for a deeper commitment on the path. Eventually, the deepening of your commitment leads to devotion. Humility, honesty, and a strong commitment to spiritual practice will help you move toward awakening. You will learn humility sooner or later. Cultivating it is a good idea, because then you have less of a need to be humiliated by events beyond your control.

Humility involves giving yourself to Truth without any judgments, qualifications, arguments, saying "yes, but …", asking "why?", or holding back. Your ego is in part a wounded child who wants mommy or daddy on its own terms. That is not going to happen. God is not who you think He is. God is not a he, a she, an it, or an anything your mind can grasp.

You must be humble enough to admit that your life is an ultimate failure on its own terms, that you don't know anything, that it's all a sham. True humility is saying, "I don't know" and meaning it, giving up even the idea that you know you don't know. False humility is just the ego trying to make itself look small and insignificant, which actually strengthens its negative feelings about itself and prevents awakening. The ego feeds on thoughts of worthlessness but starves on humility. See clearly the difference between true and false humility, because one saves you and the other condemns you. The ego hates humility. You love it.

AWAKENED ACTION

Being, as it is manifested on the relative scene, is highly active, even if apparently not doing anything outwardly. The awakened state is dynamically active in the world. The Taoist sense of not-doing, or *wu wei,* captures this active non-action clearly. "Just be" may sound static or passive, but it is anything but that. What if you said to a tidal wave, "Just be"? What if you said it to a mountain lion? What if you said it to a star, a volcano, or a hurricane? Wouldn't this "Just be" be dynamic, active, even explosive? If you say "Just be" to an earthquake, it will level your house. To an awakened person, "Just be" is active beyond comprehension. The activity of Truth is to end your nightmare. In the end, it goes quietly.

Free actions do not arise from the mind, but from Wisdom. The free person achieves results without knowing how they are achieved. The beauty of this is that you don't need to know anything to act as an awakened person. Free actions arise spontaneously in a state of absolute trust, a complete letting go into what is. The mind wants to know the "why," the reason behind Truth's movement. There is no reason. There is only Being perfectly realizing Itself through movement, just as rain realizes itself by falling. It meets obstacles with perfect alignment between what *should* be happening and what *is* happening. The two are one.

Wisdom is not only Being manifesting as knowledge (not-knowing), but also Being manifesting as action (not-doing). Being manifests as a movement that can be called Wisdom, whether that movement arises in the form of thoughts, speech, or physical action. In this sense, knowledge and action are the same thing—relative manifestations of Truth. You do not ultimately know anything, any more than you ultimately do anything. Both are illusions.

Truth knows what to do. It knows when to do it. It knows, way beyond what we need to know—because it *is*. This is not conventional knowledge, but Wisdom. What we need to know is right in front of us and is revealed as *what is happening now*. If I need to know a phone number, it appears. If it doesn't appear, I don't need to know it. If I need to recall a name, I do. If I can't recall the name, I don't need it. What this means is that thoughts appear and disappear like clouds in the sky, quite independently from any sense of a controller. Thoughts rise and fall like everything else that is happening.

What's more relaxing than letting things take their course naturally? Like rafting on a lazy river, no one needs to make anything happen. What happens happens. This is a relief to the struggler, who stops struggling. You put down your baggage and rest. It's so much sweeter that way. I don't know about you, but resting and relaxing is a fine way to live, even in the midst of chaos and turmoil.

Let go.

Spontaneity is the nature of Freedom: now, now, now. This is consciousness, what makes us feel alive, like being on stage or being on the spot improvisationally, having to act without thought; this brings fresh energy and aliveness.

Awakened action involves surrendering to Truth in the moment. Surrender and submission are not the same thing. Surrender means that you give up and stop fighting Reality. Submission implies duality, like there's a separation of power, as between a servant and a master. Submission can lead to surrender, if you do it with gratitude and humility. For example, if you submit to guidance from your Teacher—not that you should, of course, unless you do—in an attitude of willingness and trust, then surrender follows. Surrender is an internal process, a listening to the inner Teacher that occurs once you submit to the outer Teacher. The two are related. Submission may seem like weakness, but submission to your Teacher is strength, because you are listening inwardly into the Power that makes the stars churn and roil in your abdomen.

TRUE MORALITY

True morality is Being in action, Truth as it is lived in the world. True morality arises from beyond the mind. Ultimately, doing the right thing is a matter of listening inwardly into Truth, not adhering to a mind-made moral code. However, mind-made moral codes serve as useful guides to those who are less conscious and need rules to keep them in line. Without such codes, society would collapse.

"Leading with your mind" means that the mind thinks and everything else follows its lead. Stop leading with your mind by noticing what is true. What ultimately leads an awakened person's actions is Truth, which is incomprehensible to the mind. It is possible to have a clear awareness of laws and moral codes and still act in accord with Truth at all times. Truth trumps all worldly rules, but it is almost always of maximum value to obey worldly rules because doing so tends to lead to a stronger Teaching, one that people see as responsible and trustworthy on a basic level. It is usually in everyone's best interests to obey laws and moral codes—but not always. Sometimes laws and moral codes take a back seat to true morality, as in cases of civil disobedience.

A key insight of Liberation is that true morality has nothing to do with ideas about goodness. True goodness arises naturally from the conscious state and is the only true goodness in the world. This is not goodness as opposed to evil, but the indissoluble integrity of Truth that manifests as the perfection of moral values in the awakened human being. True morality knows what to do and when to do it because it literally *is* the Truth. Grass knows exactly how and when to grow, according to conditions. Wind knows exactly when to blow, how hard, and how often. An awakened being simply *is,* and from her being harmonious behavior arises naturally, without effort. Because an awakened person is fully conscious, her doing is not-doing, or pure, unobstructed Being. It only looks like action. Therefore, she cannot act immorally. Everything she does is a blessing, because she has transcended duality. She is aware of relative distinctions and is capable of making descriptive judgments, but she sees that value judgments are pain disguised as morality. She is absolutely conscious, thus absolutely moral.

For example, murder is not ultimately wrong. Saying murder is ultimately wrong is in effect saying that murder should not be happening when it *is* happening. In an absolute sense, murder is neither right nor wrong. Murder is, however, wrong in a relative sense—extremely wrong. It is an action based in profound unconsciousness and therefore evil. Murder is not conducive to consciousness. Murder generates massive negative karma for the murderer. Murder leads one to slip more deeply into unconsciousness, pain, and bloody nightmares.

Unconsciousness causes suffering, the great evil in this world. The degree of consciousness of an action determines its moral value because conscious actions relieve suffering. *Consciousness is the true moral standard.* Evil behavior is immoral only because it is unconscious, not because it shouldn't be happening. No matter how *wrong* an action may seem, it either causes or eliminates suffering, regardless of what we say about it.

And what we say about it matters. If we attribute absolute value to unconscious behavior by using the term "wrong," for example, we lapse into further unconsciousness—and that is a trap, because using the term "wrong" unconsciously is immoral. We may use the terms "good," "bad," "right," "wrong," or "evil"—but if we use them unconsciously, we cause suffering. A conscious person recognizes that these are conventional terms and does not take them too seriously, but sees them as relative distinctions that can be useful.

You cannot get rid of evil by judging it. When you make value judgments about behavior—yours or another's—you perpetuate the very darkness you are trying to dispel. You are saying that people *shouldn't* be doing what they *are* doing. This is insanity. To break the cycle, you must become conscious. You must awaken to the absolute value of Truth. You must practice basic and absolute honesty. You must break the hypnotism of the world, starting with yourself. This is highly personal. It does not matter what others do, only what *you* do. *You* are the one. If you don't do it, who will? You cannot control what others do. If you attach to what others should or should not do, you lock your own cell from the inside. The key is consciousness. The more conscious you become, the more moral your actions become. You must keep doing the work to become more conscious. Forget about judging others and do the work.

From an absolute perspective, good and evil do not exist. From a relative standpoint, good and evil exist and cause suffering. Humanity is mired in the relative and all the suffering that goes with it. The only way out, the only way to establish a moral society, is for individuals to become conscious on the path of awakening. As Vernon Howard notes, "Whatever helps us to awaken is right; whatever keeps us hypnotized is wrong."

To become conscious, you must use the relative to attain the Absolute. Of course, you can use the relative for purely relative purposes. You can use relative honesty to get clear about what is useful for doing relative things, based on your experience. For example, you see that detergent A gets your clothes cleaner than detergent B, so you use detergent A; community C is safer than community D, so you live in community C; employer E pays more than employer F, so you work for employer E. These are basic decisions guided by the usefulness of what is relatively true in your experience, or what works. Of course, perhaps detergent A pollutes the environment, neighborhood C practices racial discrimination, and employer E violates child labor laws. You must be aware of how your actions affect others and try to cause as little harm as possible. That brings your actions into the absolute arena, because you are considering the benefit of others, and thus acting compassionately.

Ultimately, the relative is to be used for awakening. Perhaps you go about it this way: You use detergent A to get your clothes clean so you can wear them to a spiritual gathering; you live in safer community C so you can survive long enough to practice effectively; you work for employer E so you can have enough money to buy books on spirituality and attend seminars by awakened Teachers. You do what serves awakening.

Words don't mean much if you don't back them up with consistent action. Make sure that your actions are in alignment with your values and speech. Don't take an action without carefully considering the consequences. If you're unsure whether to take an action, stop. Relax; take a breath. After getting calm, ask silently within yourself if it is more appropriate to take that action or do something else. If you get a feeling of unease in your body when contemplating an action, it may be inappropriate to take it. Trust yourself—not your mind, but your deeper Wisdom. If your practice is consistent, you will develop more clarity to make appropriate decisions and stand by them.

You can easily take care of a situation by making a realistic assessment of it and taking appropriate action. This is not a painful process. If you can't take action, just stay present for what is, enjoying the scenery. You either take action or you don't. This is not a problem. The action does not arise from a sense of "This shouldn't be happening," but from a sense of *yes*—regardless of what is happening. If a disaster is occurring around you, you either take action or remain still. Fear, stress, pain, and panic are caused by attaching to thoughts about a situation, not by the situation itself.

Learn how to say "yes" to Truth, even when you have to say "no" to a person. Learning to say "no" as a "yes" to Truth is important. For example, saying "no" to someone who offers you a cyanide cocktail is in effect saying "yes" to life, health, and well-being, which serves consciousness. Saying "no" to a person who manipulates you and drains your energy is a "yes" to your path because it supports your ongoing positive functioning. When you say "yes" to Truth, trust the movement that arises out of that conscious space, even if it is a verbal "no" to something that is not in your best interests.

You must be honest and direct with others, even if it ruffles their feathers to do so. Using sound reason, clear awareness, and intuitive listening, you can avoid danger. Just be willing to say "no" and stick with your decision. You must be willing to be confrontational with others if you have to. Some people have a hard time saying "no" or being confrontational with others. Work on it. The key to Liberation is saying "yes" to what is. If you get a strong "no" about taking a certain action but you are afraid of letting others down or hurting their feelings by saying it—say "no" anyway. Your "no" is then really a powerful "yes" to Reality *and all beings are benefited by your action, even those people who appear let down or angry about it.* You must be willing to follow your inner Wisdom at all costs.

It's fun to watch people drive themselves crazy trying to push your buttons when you won't let them. Pull up a chair. Relax. This may take a while.

Another factor to consider when contemplating the appropriateness of an action is *timing.* If you curse a closed window of opportunity simply because it either hasn't opened yet or is no longer available, you block the natural flow of life. If it isn't there, it isn't there. Trust the moment, and what you need is already what you have, opening a door for more to come to you. Friendliness with the moment makes things happen. If you force things, you may get some results, but at the expense of consciousness. To know what to do, just do what comes naturally and makes sense to do in that moment. If you're not sure, listen inwardly until you connect with a "yes" to what is, a sense of communion with Truth. Then it moves, and you are That. You can trust it. The path of awakening involves learning to trust it completely.

PATTERNS

Unconscious tendencies manifest as habits or *patterns* of thought, feeling, and behavior, typically ingrained in the early psyche like virulent software programs. Early traumas to the developing psyche attract similar experiences that reinforce the energy of the original trauma, in varying degrees of severity, over the course of childhood and early adulthood. A person tends to act out these patterns of behavior, causing pain to himself and others, until the pain is severe enough to motivate the search for the cause. Digging through these layers of past pain can be challenging, but it must be done if you are to grow in consciousness. Like a trail of breadcrumbs, you must trace the painful experiences of your life back to their source. You must uncover the childhood traumas that make you think, feel, and act in ways that inhibit your Freedom. You must be present for them without judgment.

Patterns resist change and tend to assert themselves over and over. In some people, patterns can dominate the psyche, manifesting in obsessions, compulsions, and addictions. Patterns block the free flow of Truth in your experience. In most people, though, patterns manifest as habits that, while deadening to the spontaneous aliveness of Being, are accepted by society as normal. Patterns contribute to the false sense of self and its associated compulsive behaviors, often obstructing the growth of consciousness. Spiritual practice and conscious action help to break patterns and create a healthier mode of living that serves the path of awakening, because awakened consciousness breaks patterns. The essence of who you are cannot be a pattern.

HARM

The primary guiding moral factor is "Do no harm." To *harm* means to damage or cause injury to another. If you harm others, you only harm yourself. First, since all beings are one, what you do to others you really do to yourself. Second, by harming others, you reap karma that you must pay. Third, the indivisible oneness of Reality cannot be real to you if you harm others because harmful actions arise from and deepen unconsciousness.

In Truth, you cannot harm anyone, nor can anyone harm you. You are projecting a dream world of suffering that has no independent existence. However, on the relative level, harming another implies a *self* and an *other*—the basic duality of unconscious living. Until you are awakened, you are trapped in this dualistic world and suffer from the consequences of your harmful actions. When you harm another, you violate your true nature by strongly affirming a separateness that is ultimately false. This strengthens the ego and deepens your misery as well as the misery of others.

Harm occurs through the channels of thought, feeling, speech, and behavior. Thoughts harm others only to the degree that you act on them from the point of view of false self-identification. By themselves, thoughts are harmless; they harm others only when we give them power through attachment. Witnessing a negative thought is not harmful if you do not identify with it. We give thoughts power by creating an identity out of them, in believing that they are absolutely true. We give them greater power to harm others when we let them produce negative feelings, when we communicate them to others, or when we make them the basis for actions.

Thinking a harmful thought about another person is not as harmful as speaking it where others can hear (or writing it where others can read), and communicating the thought is not as harmful as physically acting on it, such as by denying the person some kindness because of your judgment about him. Thoughts lead to feelings, words, and actions. Each level in that hierarchy of movement—thoughts, feelings, words, and actions—is more powerful than the one before it in producing a karmic effect. In other words, what you *do* has a more powerful effect than what you *say*. What you *say* has a more powerful effect than what you *feel,* and what you *feel* has a more powerful effect than what you *think.* To the degree that you make thoughts conscious as they arise, karma is negated. A highly conscious person produces less of a karmic effect than a highly unconscious person, and an awakened person produces no karma at all.

VIOLENCE

Violence is an exertion of force that causes injury or harm, typically thought of as physical in nature, but having a mental cause. Only the mind creates violence, even what appears in nature to be violent, as in animal predation, tidal waves, and earthquakes. The egoic selfing activity, operating through the agency of the mind, projects the world and its pernicious savagery. The world is a waiting room for death that keeps looping back around to itself endlessly. The only intelligent thing to do is to end it.

Recognition of Truth ends violence because there is no conflict in it. Violence and war are at their root caused by resistance to Reality. The world exists as a conflict between Reality and what the mind thinks Reality should be. If you can see that you are actively fighting Reality, you can stop doing it. That is the beginning of world peace. Begin by noticing how your anger is caused by resistance to what is, creating an unpleasant feeling ranging from mild irritation to full-blown fury.

Violence begins in you as turbulent emotions such as annoyance, irritation, frustration, and anger that are severe forms of resistance. Annoyance, irritation, and frustration are low-grade forms of anger, and rage is violent, explosive anger. These feelings often lead to some kind of destructive action, such as physical violence against a person or angry speech. All violent actions, even words or harsh movements, are harmful to others. Notice that any form of discordant feeling in you is a form of violence. Notice if your movements become angular and sudden. If so, violence is brewing in you. Observe that, when you get angry, you are contributing to violent energy on the planet. If you really want to contribute to world peace, find the cause of your own anger and eliminate it. Then you can be a cause of peace.

EVIL

Evil is a description of thought, feeling, or behavior that causes harm. Ultimately, no one is evil because the true essence of all is Being—but relatively speaking, unconsciousness makes people resist Reality and fight against it, producing evil. Since virtually everyone fights Reality, evil lives in virtually everyone. This war with Truth manifests as negative thoughts which can then harm others through the production of violent actions. The most useful thing we can do is describe a person's behavior as either causing harm to others or not while keeping in mind his true nature beneath all the violence. The ego is inherently evil in that it causes harm by its very existence. The essential nature of a person is inherently good in that, when it is fully recognized by that person, it is impossible for him to harm anyone.

People often say that certain actions are evil, and sometimes it can be hard to tell evil actions from good ones. The valid criterion is that *evil causes harm*. If it causes no harm, it cannot be evil. Just because you don't like what someone is doing or a person's action violates your ideas of morality, it does not necessarily follow that the action is evil.

God and the Devil are inside you.

Evil is a nice name for "how are you today?", lurking in our most innocuous transactions. People who generate evil are afraid of themselves, afraid of being destroyed. Evil is egoic survivalism taken to an extreme. It is based on a competitive view of life mumbling to itself in a constant inner dialogue:

> *I must assert myself and control everything and everyone around me. I must hurt and abuse others to make them think that I have power over them. I must make the world conform to my beliefs so that I can feel comfortable, loved, and at peace (and look nice doing it).*

This is just the opposite of the way things are. If you really want comfort, love, and peace, you must allow what *is* to be, not force it to conform to your ideas. When the mind is transcended, there is no conflict, no discrepancy between what is and what you think it should be.

The world will never bend to your desires. It may seem to at times, but then it throws you a curve ball to show you how out of control you are. For every action, there is an equal and opposite reaction. If you strive to dominate the world, sooner or later it will dominate you. This is inevitable. Every tyrant reaps his fate.

SOCIAL ACTIVISM

The world may be mad, but it's solving your own madness that cures the world. There is no need to get in anyone else's business. No one else needs to change for your world to be sane. If you wait for the rest of the world to be at peace before you are at peace, you will be waiting a *long* time. It's really not worth it.

Awakening is the greatest gift you can give to the world, the greatest contribution you can make, more than any kind of social service or "feed the world" form of generosity. Fifty billion lifetimes of social service cannot even come close to the benefit to humanity of your own awakening. The enemy is inside you, and defeating that enemy with consciousness is the greatest gift you can offer to world peace. The more conscious beings we have on the planet, the less likely it is that we will destroy ourselves.

Help yourself first, then others. Avoid codependency, or focusing on the perceived needs of others to the detriment of your own progress. Each person who conquers his own limitations, stories, projections, lies, prejudices, and fears helps to dissolve the web of global deception that contributes to universal suffering. Ignorance projected onto others is killing the planet. Liberation is first personal, then global. The collective is best served by liberated individuals. Help others, but not at the expense of consciousness. False compassion, "help-ism," or trying constantly to help people who either refuse help or cannot be helped in an effort to avoid one's own helplessness serves ego, not Truth. You must take care of your basic needs first. In a case of rapid depressurization on an airplane, you are instructed first to don your own oxygen mask, then put one on your child—otherwise both of you are more likely to die. In a similar way, you must awaken yourself first, then others. Trying to change others without changing yourself first is futile.

Social activism is a form of love in action. If you base your activism in a value judgment—e.g., that the world is "messed up"—you will only create more pain in the world. Lao Tzu notes that "The world is sacred. It can't be improved. If you tamper with it, you'll ruin it. If you treat it like an object, you'll lose it." The world cannot be improved, but it can be radically accepted. What is left is literally not of this world. It is already who you are and what the world truly is, now.

Find it.

As far as social activism is concerned, just liberate yourself and trust what happens. Human rights arise from the true heart of all morality, the conscious human being. The more awake you are in the world, the more just, righteous, and fair your actions are. Anger does not produce positive social change. Liberation does. Anger just makes you harder, meaner, and more afraid. Negativity in any form is not necessary for vigorous action that, in its own way, subverts an unjust social order. Freedom is first realized individually, then society feels the effects. A free person votes, takes appropriate social action, all without anger or resistance. A free person breathing is more radical than a million bombs.

Anger will not solve the world's problems, but love can. True love happens when there is not you and someone else, but only one. When you see others as yourself, you naturally become compassionate and helpful to others. Attachment to an ideal is not love, but insanity. Stand up for what you believe is true; just don't make a self out of it. Awakening *is* social change. It creates human beings who are deeply compassionate and can't help but help liberate others. Awakening is established in Truth, and Truth is the only foundation upon which a just world can be built.

You may feel anger about social inequalities. It is this very attitude that throws the world off balance to begin with. People try to improve the world based on disagreement with the way it is. But the world *is* what it is. If you can be at one with it and not resist it, but give it unconditional regard, you can take action based on Truth, not on your mind's idea of how it wants things to be. Resistance is the cause of misery in the world. Before you can eliminate misery in the world, you must accept it as it is—otherwise, you will only create more pain for yourself and others.

But, you say, some things are just *wrong*. Some things *shouldn't be happening*. How can this be? Things *are* happening, aren't they? They're happening, so of course they *should* be happening. You are confusing thoughts with Reality. You cannot change social conditions or eliminate what is destructive to life by proceeding from a sense of *this shouldn't be happening*, because adverse social conditions and behavior are caused by human beings who are acting from negativity based on a sense of—you guessed it—*this shouldn't be happening*, and ultimately, if you act from this premise, you will only add to the misery in the world and keep it going. If you proceed from a sense of this *should* be happening—because it *is* happening—you are acting in accord with the way things are and are thus truly helpful. It is always more useful, peaceful, and liberating to work with a situation than against it.

When you act in accord with the way things are, you change conditions at their cause, regardless of outer circumstances. True change is inner, not outer. Changing social conditions on the outer level without changing them inwardly is like rearranging deck chairs on the *Titanic*. No matter what you do, the ship is going down. To save the people, first you have to find the lifeboat that can rescue them.

You're it.

The only true salvation is spiritual Liberation, so the most effective, most helpful thing you can do for the planet is to liberate yourself. Awakening is unselfish because you are making yourself useful to others in the most powerful way possible. Awakening is the most selfless thing you can do. Awakening is a call to altruistic service, to share with others. Without that, there would be no reason for an awakened being to live. An awakened person's passion is the release of others from the prison of the mind, and this is what moves her, what makes her life meaningful and worthwhile. The world is your greater body, waiting for you to bring your lamp of Truth to light the way. Get involved in a true Teaching and dedicate your awakening to the benefit of all beings. This is what you must do if human life is to survive on this planet.

PEACE

Peace is an absence of noise, conflict, and disturbance. Since the world consists of varying degrees of violence, "world peace" is an oxymoron. The world as seen through a relative lens is violent. Without the relative lens, the world is absolute, and therefore absolutely peaceful—but then it is no longer a world. Without the relative lens, it is impossible to say what it is.

The only way to attain world peace is to establish peace within individuals. If there is no peace in individuals, there cannot be peace in society or between governments and cultures. You cannot have peace between nations or people unless the people of those nations awaken to their true identity beyond the appearance of egoism. As long as you define individuals or groups as entities in themselves with defense tendencies, you have conflict. In such a case, you have already started with the definition of people and places as independent *things*. The mind cannot know or create peace because all it knows are *things*, and *things* cannot help but bump up against, scrape, gnash, and claw at each other when their existence is threatened. When entities are recognized as dependently arising phantoms—no longer independent *things*—peace is automatically established.

To begin to establish peace in your life, first begin to examine your thoughts. Notice the judgments you have about people and the world around you. Realize that thoughts are statements about Reality that aren't ultimately true. Conflict is created in you when your mind-created version of things argues with Reality. For example, you might entertain the thought "Life is unfair," attach to it, and experience sadness, fear, and anger as a result. If you examine the thought closely, you will see life *is* fair because it is what it is, according to your karma. You deserve what you get simply because it is. Then you can work to change your situation, but from a place of peace instead of conflict. If you are poor, you *should* be poor—not because being poor is good or bad, but simply because you *are* poor, relatively speaking. If you are poor, being poor is what is. From that sacred place of allowing Reality to be what it is—in this case, poverty—you can work to get out of it, if that is what you want. Acceptance of your situation gives you hope, optimism, and indefatigability.

Peace is native to you, buried beneath all your thoughts about Reality that aren't true. Beneath mental noise is the Stillness that is like a tranquil lake, like golden sunlight streaming in through a clear window into space. Your thoughts about Reality form a web of deception that ensnares you, and you're in the middle of it. In fact, you're the one spinning it. Since you are creating it, you can stop. Even in the midst of noise, there is stillness, peace, and silence. When you find this stillness, you find peace. Ask yourself, "Who would I be without my story?" Peace is what is left after your story ends. The only reason anyone creates war is to defend a story about "me, mine, and ours." If you investigate your story, you will find that it is a fiction spun from pure nothingness and it's not worth defending. You can defend it, but it hurts when you do.

World peace begins with you. That's the only way it happens. Once you have ended conflict for yourself, you have ended it permanently, and spreading it to others is effortless. The awakened state is inherently peaceful, and recognizing Freedom is all you have to do to establish peace in yourself. If everyone else wants to wage wars and destroy the planet, that's their nightmare. Awaken and end yours. If they want to end theirs, all they have to do is ask for help. It's so easy, really. Everyone is looking for an example of peace, and you're it. Inner peace is the cause of outer peace. If you don't have peace inside you, you won't have it outside you. If you fight Reality, you contribute to war, violence, and death. If you accept Reality, you contribute to peace, joy, and faith. The decision is up to you.

THE SACREDNESS OF NATURE

Nature—what we sometimes call *the environment*—does not include anything natural because human beings have altered it and continue to alter it rapidly. Because we are mind-dominated, we strive to control everything to an unnatural degree, seeking dominance over nature instead of viewing it as our greater body. The mind is not natural, but is antithetical to nature. Nature is the environment before the mind alters it.

Anger about the state of the environment only makes it worse, regardless of how hard you work to save it. You may motivate people with anger, but you will not inspire them. Inspiration is stronger, more patient, more enduring than anger. Mind-domination is destroying life on the planet, and anger is a result of your own mind-domination. If you want to work for the benefit of the environment, do so without judgment; then you are truly helping it. The collective mind is destroying the planet and would destroy all life on it if it weren't for conscious people working to help liberate others from mind-dominance. Because this destruction is becoming more and more obvious, more people are seeking Liberation.

The mind likes destruction, poison, illness, and making the planet a toxic cesspool. It wants you to fight conditions with great anger, because that gives it power. The mind loves opposition, especially violent opposition. Radically accepting what *is* without judgment and acting from that basis is true non-violent action. It makes sense to live so that you have less of an impact on the environment, but it's not as important as entering into and staying on the path of awakening. If you do stay on the path of awakening, you will automatically respect, protect, and help clean up the environment. When you see trash on the ground, pick it up and throw it away, if you can. Notice if you feel angry, self-righteous, or otherwise judgmental about it. Do it because it is helpful and appropriate for you to do so, not to feel special or better than others for having done it. Remember to practice humility.

The environment is not likely to be an overwhelming issue until we are so strongly afflicted by its toxicity and imbalance that we have to do something about it. It's not a big enough issue yet. More pain will likely change that. The earth is a living being, and she may not put up with much more of our abuse. Even if we colonize space, we will likely trash that, too, unless we change.

The natural environment is sacred, and spending time in nature can help you reconnect with Being. Earth may seem beautiful, but beauty arises from beyond the mind. What you are seeing as the beauty of nature is really just more mind forms—except for the essence of Being that emanates from the silent appreciation of natural things. A sunset is not a sunset; it is a phenomenon whose true nature is beyond the mind. Some people recognize the beauty of nature, but most people just desecrate it. Few recognize the radiant quality of Stillness that is the true nature of plants, animals, and geology. That quality is not of this world, but emanates from Being. It is your true nature and the true nature of earth. Try to recognize this beauty in yourself, in nature, in everything you see.

The beauty in nature is sublime, and enjoying it is an aid on the path, because it connects you with Truth. It is important to spend some time in the most pristine nature you can find because you can easily return to the benign simplicity of Being when you are one with it. Nature only appears as a collection of independent objects because of our state of mind-domination. Within the appearance of nature lies Reality, Being. We did not create it. We *are* it.

Is the universe a mistake? Saying that the universe is a mistake implies that someone or something made it and somehow messed things up. This is a complete mental fabrication. Have you ever seen an imperfect cloud, a wrong sunset, or a bad mountain? Nature is perfectly what it is, and thus is sacred.

SACRED SITES

So-called sacred sites have become popular with New Age tourists, but most of these sites are far from sacred. Places are sacred because of the absence of unconscious human beings or the presence of conscious human beings, and not for any other reason.

Some say that "energy vortexes" and "sacred sites" exist in areas populated by humans. This is not the case, except for the areas that support the work of enlightened human beings. If a city or a country supports a true Teacher, that country becomes a blessing, spiritually speaking, for its citizens. The earth does not have energy vortexes or sacred sites aside from unspoiled natural areas, few of which are left. In most cases, so-called sacred sites are worthless as consciousness-raising destinations and prey on people's ignorance of such matters—unless your tour guide is an awakened Master.

If you are a disciple of a true Teaching, your practice area is a sacred site—and the more you do the work on that spot with true devotion, the more powerful is the presence that manifests there and remains even after you have gone. What makes a site profane is the depth of mind-domination of its human inhabitants. Hatred, violence, racism, crime, and other forms of deep unconsciousness create a hell-like field of woe in a place and can be felt by people who visit there. If you are deeply conscious, you can purify it when you visit by taking on the negativity and liberating it through your practice.

Churches, temples, mosques, synagogues, and other places of worship are sacred only by virtue of the degree of consciousness of their clergy and practitioners. The degree of sacredness in these places varies. As you become more spiritually aware, you will be able to identify and visit them if you need a "recharge zone." Nature can be a recharge zone if you know how to use it for that purpose. Just sit in it quietly and breathe, letting thoughts rise and fall without attachment.

The least sacred sites on the planet are easy to find. Ghettos, industrial areas, gangland territories, and prisons are common areas of intense psychological pain and deep unconsciousness. Violence, hatred, anger, addiction, and crime are rampant in such places. Worse are torture chambers, death houses, concentration camps, genocide zones, and areas that we don't know about because they are hidden from public view. Murder, especially mass murder, is usually a factor in the extremely dark, negative atmosphere of these places. It is not advisable for anyone to visit them. It is best to do the work and cleanse the planet collectively, thus reducing its darkness significantly. Areas of past atrocities such as Auschwitz are still some of the most negative areas on the planet and are not ideal places to visit. You don't have to visit dark areas to help the collective. You can do it from your home since your local practice is felt globally.

The most sacred site is *you*—but you have to recognize this for yourself to make it real in your conscious awareness. Every time you actively and sincerely participate in true spiritual practice, you are tapping into your own Being, the source of all authentic spiritual presence.

CHAPTER FIVE

COMMITMENT

For all those ailing in the world,
Until their every sickness has been
healed,
May I myself become for them
The doctor, nurse, the medicine itself.
　　　　　　　　　　　—Shantideva

If you want to be given everything,
give everything up.
　　　　　　　　　　—Lao Tzu

THE COMMITMENT TO AWAKENING

Becoming a student of the Teaching requires a commitment to consciousness, a dedication to spiritual growth in service to awakening. This commitment gets you involved, practicing, and moving forward on the path. Eventually, however, if you want to awaken, you must commit to *awakening itself*—the *end* of the path—as the sole value to which you attain. This is not unlike a mountain climber who, sensing that the summit is near, focuses on attaining it to the exclusion of everything else. When you make the commitment to awakening, you open a channel to the Absolute that powers you the rest of the way up the mountain, like hitching yourself to a locomotive that cannot be stopped.

The commitment to awakening is a deeper consecration than what has come before. Early on the path, you commit to growing spiritually, and you know that something called awakening can occur—and might even occur *for you.* The commitment to awakening occurs when you are so close to Freedom that you can taste it. You recognize that it is there, and that you are within range of attaining it. That is when you commit to the attainment of awakening as if it were the only thing that mattered, putting all other paths aside as trivial. A disciple's life is dedicated to the attainment of awakening—and consequently to the discipline that is required to do the work of discipleship—regardless of the cost, how long it takes, or what anyone else thinks about it.

Some people enter the spiritual path with relative goals in mind, such as happiness, success, or power. Ultimately, you must forgo these relative goals and commit to awakening itself, because that is the only way you will find Satisfaction.

If you become involved with a true Teaching enough to work diligently at the second stage of the path, you prepare yourself for the third stage, *committed.* The second stage involves developing the integrity of the person so that it can withstand the force of awakening and be used for awakening others. Until the person is ready to handle the commitment to awakening, it is not appropriate to make that commitment. Once the person *is* ready to handle the commitment to awakening, it is inappropriate *not* to make it. A Teacher will not ask for a formal commitment to awakening until you are ready for the forces it invokes.

A commitment to spiritual growth serves awakening; but to be a disciple, you must commit to awakening itself. To awaken, you have to want it with everything in your Being. Anything else is a hindrance to your progress. If your goal is not complete Liberation, it's not going to happen for you. If you go for spiritual "relief" and not total awakening, you will not obtain the ultimate prize.

Everyone has something that her life is *about,* something that she devotes the most time, money, and energy to achieving. Even a drug addict has her drug. Everyone has something. If awakening is not your "thing," you won't have it. The only way to make sure is to commit to it.

DECISION

On the path of awakening, your initial commitment is to growth in consciousness through honesty, study, instruction, and action, leading up to a *decision:* do you want awakening, or just growth in consciousness up to a point of relative freedom, safety, and comfort? If you want awakening, you must commit to it. This commitment is a decision. Until you make this decision, awakening will elude you.

You must decide.

The word "decision" derives from the Latin root *decidere,* which means "to cut off." When you make the commitment to awakening, you cut off all but the one path that leads to Freedom. This is something radical, something that cleaves through the mind like a sword and leaves no doubt as to your Truthward direction. It is a bold move.

Decide. Is Freedom *really* what you want? Is your path about getting something, having something, or being somebody? If so, the path of awakening is not for you. You get Freedom by giving everything away. Once you have given everything, a miracle is revealed: You are already That which you have been seeking. You can do it. Just make sure that radical destruction of your illusions is what you really want. If not, you will just chase after shadows, not having the real commitment it takes to get to the end.

Make it your top priority to awaken before you get lost amid the chaos of life and forget about it, until your next opportunity. How long will it take for another opportunity to come around? The next time you find yourself waiting in line at the post office, bank, or grocery store, think about not just one lifetime of waiting, but an endless procession of such lives. You must wait no longer. You must slay the ego-demon with great directness, splitting it to the black heart of its existence. That is what the Awakener does; it does not hesitate. You, in your Being, are the Awakener. The dream of self-existence has no ultimate value. You must make the decision between Freedom and bondage. You must wake up, destroy the lie, and conquer the enemy through surrender to Truth. The decision is yours to make. No one else can do it for you.

You must be fully committed to awakening, or fear may cause you to slip back into the abyss of unconsciousness from which you emerged. Your newly expanding awareness (and newly exposed fears) may shock you. You must not flinch when your blade of decision approaches the seamy egobelly. You must act decisively. You are needed to break free, wake up the planet, and take humanity to the other shore. We are counting on you.

Decision is your sword. Use it.

THE CRUX: AWARENESS OF SUFFERING

Most people "middle along" in life, neither extremely satisfied nor dissatisfied. This kind of life is a vapid state of hypnotism, a murky perpetuity that is sometimes painful, sometimes pleasurable, but mostly somnambulistic. The societal norm is not healthy ordinariness, but typical, average, deadly unconsciousness.

What is your threshold of tolerance for this kind of life? A committed student of the path is someone who cannot tolerate this kind of suffering any longer and develops a profound desire to be free of it at all costs. "I can't live like this anymore" is a typical sentiment. The acute awareness of "normal" dissatisfaction and the desire to be free of it is the basis for awakening. You must realize the enormity of suffering before you decide to end it. Suffering has to pierce you to the core, removing all doubt as to its nature.

Mental sleep causes the entire spectrum of suffering, from garden variety ennui to excruciating torture—but even the most ordinary of suffering is intolerable if your awareness of it is keen enough. If you're okay with life as it is, why wake up? If the dream seems pleasant, why end it? Strong awareness of suffering is practically necessary. It motivates you. If the awareness of suffering becomes intense enough, even a deeply unconscious person can develop a strong awakening potential.

Is extreme suffering necessary to awaken? No, but extreme *awareness* of suffering is. Life is suffering, but people's awareness of it varies. Your awareness of it must be intense enough to make you want to commit to awakening. If your awareness of it is more or less tolerable, you will not be motivated to seek complete Freedom from it. Eventually, one way or another, your awareness of suffering will become acute enough to make you commit to ending it totally. What leads you to this acute awareness is the *crux* of your path.

The word "crux" is related to the words "crucial," "cross," "excruciating," and "crucifixion." A crux is something *crucial,* something extremely significant, important, or decisive. It is also a cross or cross-shaped object. On the path of awakening, the crux is something that leads you to an awareness of suffering that is intense enough to make you want to commit to awakening. What's crucial is what saves you. In ancient times, a *crux* was considered crucial because it refers to a cross-shaped signpost, such as one you might find at a fork in the road. Because it shows you the way to go, it is extremely important in arriving at your destination. It also forces you to leave other paths behind—"cut them off," as it were—hence it is *decisive.* A crux can also be *excruciating,* or extremely painful, because the cross was traditionally used as an instrument of torture and execution, as in *crucifixion.* On the path of life, the crux appears either as *the Teaching*—a signpost that shows you the way—or as *extreme suffering*—a cross upon which you are crucified. The way of the signpost is easy; the way of the cross is hard. One is a decision that you actively make, and the other is a decision that is forced upon you by circumstances.

Not a difficult decision, really, when you look at it.

For example, the unawakened state is similar to an addiction such as alcoholism. For an alcoholic to get well, she can either hit bottom—the worst suffering tolerable—or have an intense awareness of the nature of her current state of suffering established in her through a process in which she actively participates. In *Twelve Steps and Twelve Traditions,* a well-known manual for overcoming alcoholism, it is written that "It was obviously necessary to raise the bottom the rest of us had hit to the point where it would hit them." In other words, instead of waiting for suffering to become dangerously severe, you can increase your *awareness* of your current level of suffering and derive the same effect. It is much easier that way. As Jesus said, "My yoke is easy and My burden is light."

If you take up the true Teaching and follow it to the end with a Teacher to help you, less suffering is necessary to force you to become acutely aware of its nature. If you try to walk the path alone, acute suffering is likely, because unconsciousness tends to perpetuate itself in the absence of Mastery. You do not have to suffer to such extremes. The way of the cross is unnecessary if you can discern the way of the signpost that is being shown to you now. Do the work and commit to awakening. Otherwise, the sleepy middle is a sea of choices as numerous as molecules in all the oceans of the world. There is no end to the soporific delusion that clogs the awareness of most people. You are the one to end it. If not you, who? Because you are reading this book, you are learning how to end the nightmare of existence that is torturing and killing children across the land. All that matters now is how far you will go with it.

No temporary relief will satisfy a dedicated student. The disciple does not stop until she is done.

DECISION VERSUS CHOICE

A decision is not the same thing as a choice. Ultimately, you have no choice, and the viewpoint of having choices is not helpful, regardless of what popular philosophies say. You do, however, have decisions to make. Although they are relative in their execution, they are like calls into the Other Side, awakening through the veil of sleep.

Choices and decisions are vastly different. Whereas "decision" means "to cut off," the word "choice" comes from the Latin *gustare,* meaning "to taste," implying a superficial, "I'll pick this one, or maybe that one," as if from a dessert tray, where you are in control and can just sample what you want. Whereas decision implies commitment, choice implies fickleness.

In New Age circles, choice is seen as a point of power. It's not. Choices imply that you are in control, and control is an illusion. No choice is ever made on a true spiritual path. Decisions, however, though somewhat rare, are made *for* you by your true nature, based on a commitment that is so profound as to "cut off" any possibility of escape. That is why, for example, the commitment to awakening is so powerful. It brings you to the point where you so utterly give yourself away to Truth that it says, in effect, "Okay, hold on to the horse's mane tightly, because you're about to be taken for a wild ride toward Freedom."

The false self cannot decide because it does not have the power to cut itself off. It cannot end its own reign of terror. The false self likes to think that it can choose its way to Freedom—an egregious mistake that, instead of cutting off what is false, cuts the universe in two, perpetuating the myth of duality and creating further suffering. Awakening cuts off the false appearance so that only Truth remains. Since the ego cannot cut itself off, you have to do it. You have to act decisively. Awakening is the ultimate decision—the cutting off of all falsehood. Start with small, conscious decisions about your life and work your way up to other, more crucial ones. As a student, every decision you make either brings you closer to awakening or removes you further from it. The commitment to awakening is one of the most important decisions you can make. The more fully you give yourself to your commitment, the more powerful is your movement on the path.

Choices are many; decisions are few. The Master makes decisions all the time, because his actions originate from Being. A sleepwalker just slogs through the motions. Choices originate from the collective mind, or "herd mentality." The Master is original in the true sense. Actions arise from the original Source of all that is and may go against the grain of consensus thinking, often ruffling the feathers of the sleepy middle, evoking angry reactions that range from mild annoyance to outright hostility.

SAMSARA

In case you are not sure about your commitment to awakening, consider the alternative to Freedom: further ensnarement in *samsara*.

Samsara (Sanskrit for "passing through") is the indefinitely repeated cycle of birth and death caused by karma. Samsara is like a sticky web. You create karma and you get ensnared in it, only to generate more in an endless cycle. You must cut through all of it, not partway. Cleave it off completely, cleanly, as with a sword. Samsara is like a wheel that crushes you over and over. Consider what will happen if you do not make the commitment to awakening. Within the domain of its own logic, samsara is endless suffering. Break the chain, end the cycle, and free yourself from the wheel. I have heard people say jokingly, "Stop the world and let me off." If you have ever felt this way, this is your chance.

Identification with form is what drags you through samsara over and over again. Most of us have come extremely close to Freedom and stopped short and lost the precious opportunity to be free, only to backslide into darkness. Samsara is like a hall of mirrors that reflects the basic illusion of self over and over again, endlessly. When you break the illusion of self, you are liberated. Find a true Teacher and commit to awakening. If you can work with other true Teachers in an accessory capacity, do it. Get all the help you can. But do not stop until you are free, because it is horrific to realize that you had a chance to awaken and squandered it.

Like a bucket that ascends and descends in a well, as you wander in samsara you ascend and descend a vast spectrum of suffering, endlessly. You experience lifetimes of extreme pain that can trap you for what seems like eternities. Eventually, you accumulate enough merit ("good" karma) to earn a relatively pleasurable lifetime—but even these are a form of suffering because they are temporary and lead to more excruciating incarnations. In other words, regardless of any pleasure you may experience in samsara, your karma inevitably carries you into countless episodes of prolonged suffering, many of which are far greater in severity than what you currently experience, and to end the cycle you must awaken from it.

This is your chance to end the nightmare of the mind. How long have you been wandering up and down the spectrum of suffering? It's time for you to deep-six this whole false identity project. Birth is painful. Life is painful. Death is painful. The realm of samsara is pain, and even pleasure is a form of pain, because it doesn't fully satisfy you, only teasing you and leaving you wanting more, and it doesn't last. To escape samsara, you have to realize that *to exist is to suffer.* Notice how unsatisfying everything is, how nothing you do ever really resolves the empty feeling you have inside. Meditate on the pain of it all until the desire for Liberation is like a blazing fire in your Soul.

AVOWAL

The commitment to awakening connects you with a deep Wisdom, a presence within that can help guide your decision-making process. Without the support of commitment, it is extremely difficult to hear through the layers of mental confusion to the Silence beneath. The commitment to awakening is a vow that must be made either in the presence of a true Teacher or within yourself when you are ready. Either one will suffice, but the former is much easier, because it is hard to know when you are ready without the agency of a true Teacher. The form of the commitment is *a compassionate vow to attain awakening for the benefit of all beings.* The form of the vow can vary. It may sound something like "I vow to awaken in this lifetime for the benefit of all beings," or "I vow to awaken in this lifetime so that I may awaken others." Any sincere statement along these lines is sufficient. The vow can be made once or repeatedly, on an ongoing basis, aloud or silently. The one I made, given to me by my Teacher, sounded like this:

> Never will I seek nor receive private, individual salvation. Never will I enter into final peace alone. But forever and everywhere will I strive for the redemption of all creatures, throughout the world.

The exact form of the vow is not as important as the fact that a Teacher must provide the space within your awareness for the profound connection with the Absolute to be given. If you do not have sufficient personal access to your Teacher to check on your readiness to make this vow, or if your Teacher does not recognize the necessity of such a vow, a guideline is to be practicing sincerely at level two for at least two years before making it. In that way, you will have more likely than not received adequate preparation through your studies. If you have not received adequate preparation, do not worry. The vow works only when you are ready, so try again a year or so later, perhaps renewing it formally each season. These are merely guidelines. Eventually, your vow will have a valid effect. Just continue to practice as sincerely as you can.

Avowal is more than mere lip service; it is an ongoing commitment to a way of life that is *about* awakening. It is something you consciously cultivate and maintain as long as you live. Avowal is both a clear demarcation point for this moment of profound life-reorientation as well as the deepening spirit of that reorientation.

Avowal takes you deeper.

Spiritual practice without a commitment to awakening is like getting halfway up the mountain. Why settle for anything less than the very summit? Why waste your time with lesser vistas that just leave you wanting more? Why not give yourself fully to Truth until nothing else truly matters but awakening? That is what gets you there.

If you do not commit to awakening when you have the opportunity, you may get so caught up in worldly events that you never really work toward Liberation. If you do not work toward Liberation, you could backslide into a truly dark and dreary future. Once you are an avowed disciple, your committed practice burns off karma that would otherwise send you into painful experiences. Thousands of lifetimes can be burned away in an instant.

COMPASSION

The commitment to awakening has two components. The first is avowal; the second is *compassion*. Compassion empowers your commitment to awaken others.

Compassion is an awareness of others' suffering coupled with a willingness to help ease their suffering. Compassion is powerful because it takes you out of your selfish tendencies and recognizes other beings as essentially the same as you. Compassion destroys the tendency to view others as objects. Cruelty persists in the world through seeing others as objects instead of connecting through a shared humanity, and compassion is the solvent that destroys this objectifying tendency. The universe is not an object, but is your own living, breathing body. It is a web of relationship, an interdependent nexus of the sacred whose hidden nature is not fully revealed until all beings are liberated. The essence of the universe is the same as your essence. Melt the illusion of cold, hard separateness with compassion, and your true nature will be revealed to you as the essence of all that is. Start with commitment, then practice consistently.

Ponder those trapped in suffering and let yourself feel concern and care for them, as if they were your children trapped in a burning building. Just as a fireman's training is dedicated to rescuing beings and putting out fires, your training as a student of Truth is dedicated to relieving the suffering of all beings. The training may be difficult, but it is worth it. Is there anything you wouldn't do to save your own children from a fiery death? Let compassion move you.

Freedom is something you get only when you give yourself away completely. Giving the ego away to Truth is the very antithesis of self-ishness. When you dedicate your path to the Liberation of others, you are bringing yourself into alignment with the essence of conscious relationship. This compassionate dedication doesn't stop with you, but keeps going until all beings are liberated. Use it to power your way along the path and help you cultivate virtues that are conducive to Freedom, such as patience, kindness, and generosity.

Of course, you *can* seek awakening for yourself without the commitment to awaken others, but it doesn't really work. True avowal summons the Awakener, whose sole purpose is to awaken others. If you dedicate your efforts to awakening others, you are invoking the most potent awakening power for yourself. Further, how can you hope to attain the Goal without compassion? Where is your heart? Do you really think you can hoard Freedom for yourself like a miser? Although there is nothing inherently wrong about striving to realize enlightenment for yourself, doing it for the sake of others fuels your practice. Compassion is the heart of awakened activity, and cultivating compassion aligns you with the awakening power of selflessness. Paradoxically, it is this precise selflessness that gives your own spiritual progress a potent boost. The commitment to awakening thrusts you toward the attainment of Freedom because compassion ignites the Awakener within you.

But do not take selflessness too far. You must free yourself first, then you can help others. Trying to awaken others without awakening yourself first is like a blind person trying to teach other blind people to see. Get it for yourself first, then you can help others get it. Eventually, we all go into final Freedom together. This is the way it works.

It does not work to be selfless to the point that you let others pull you down into darkness, like trying to save a drowning person without having a life preserver for yourself. It is not intelligent or compassionate to try to save a drowning person if the result is both of you being drowned or you being sacrificed without really helping the other swim to shore. The Awakener is firmly established in Freedom and its liberating activity is like saving a drowning person while standing on a stable platform that is deeply anchored in bedrock so that there is no movement, no chance of loss or slippage. The Awakener can then reach out to the drowning person, extending a sure hand, which can either be accepted, refused, or a mixture of both. Usually, the hand is refused because it is difficult for most people to believe that they are actually being born, suffering, and dying over and over again. They have become so accustomed to the "me-sense" that is born and dies that, unless they have developed at least a distaste for cyclic existence and the reaching out for something more, it is not likely that they will even realize that a hand is being offered. They might even confuse it for an enemy and attack it.

Such is the way of the world.

The activity of the Awakener is like that of a rescuer on a lifeboat trying to save people on a sinking ship, only the people are oblivious to the fact that the ship is sinking. The ship is a grand party vessel, and the passengers are busy living life, drinking, carousing, laughing, fighting, socializing, blowing off steam. Unaware that the ship is sinking, they are vaguely aware that something is "off," but they nervously go about their business, ignoring the sneaking suspicion that something is amiss. The rescuer, knowing the certain doom that lies ahead, stays near, one foot on the lifeboat and one foot on the ship, talking to people who pass by. He says: "Excuse me; do you realize that the ship is sinking? If you don't come with me, you're going to die." But these people, firmly believing that everything is fine, ignore him and keep walking. Some people laugh at him, saying: "Oh, dear. You're so deluded. Everything is fine." Only a few courageous souls ever climb aboard the lifeboat, and the rest of the people drown, realizing their doom too late to listen. After the people drown and the ship sinks, the whole tableau is resurrected and reenacted endlessly. Sometimes you're in first class, sometimes in steerage. The Rescuer helps those who can recognize the help being offered.

Compassion is highly instrumental in finding peace in your life because a compassionate person truly cares about the world and its inhabitants. Compassion makes you want to find out why you hurt yourself and others, why you drive yourself crazy, why you stress yourself out every day. Compassion makes you care enough to become a student of Truth, to find the solution to world peace within yourself. You have to really care about beings who suffer in the world to do this work and take it all the way to the end of your inner war. You have to be willing to surrender, to stop fighting Reality, to give up your act.

Compassion takes you to the other side of the river of life. If you remove the last three letters of the word "compassion," you have "compass"—something that leads you in a certain direction. Think of compassion as your best friend that takes you in the direction of Freedom. Think of it as a guide that takes you across the river of the world and beyond. Being compassionate is not the same as being weak and letting people harm you. It is actually the opposite. Compassion, while serving others, protects you from harm.

Compassion is as if you were putting yourself last and everyone else first. As Jesus said, "So the last will be first, and the first will be last." This is a great paradox. Compassion is more than gentleness or friendliness or kindness; it is the Awakener Itself. True caring for beings who suffer is a profound quality of the heart and is its own reward. The nature of the Awakener is one of unfathomable compassion for all beings. When you cultivate compassion, you allow the liberating activity of the Awakener to deepen within you. Because compassion is boundless and varying degrees of it can awaken within you, it is beneficial to develop the most profound depth of compassion you can.

The greater the compassion you manifest within yourself, the greater your potential for awakening.

You must be willing to give yourself fully, all the way down to the core. This giving of yourself arises from humility and is strengthened by it. Compassion lights the fire, and discipline stokes it, keeps it going. All of these lead to devotion, the end of the path, the destruction of ignorance and leaping into Emptiness, final surrender—Grace beyond belief, and Peace beyond all imagining.

To cultivate compassion, put yourself in another's place in your imagination. Imagine what she has been through. Realize that she has suffered. If she is possessed by darkness, consider how she got that way. Think of how others may have hurt her. Think of difficult soul memories she might have. Realize that she is on the same path as you; she just may not have realized its true nature yet.

Tonglen is a Tibetan Buddhist practice of taking on others' negativity willingly and purifying it for them for the benefit of all beings. The basic practice consists of becoming mindfully relaxed, visualizing another's negativity as black smoke (or some other dark material), breathing it into your own Being (visualized as brilliant golden-white light in and around your body), purifying it, then breathing it back out as pure brightness and blessing for that person. This helps the world more than you could imagine, and it helps you awaken more powerfully than just about anything else. This visualization is compassion in action. Do it first with your loved ones and friends, then with your enemies, if you have any. If you have no enemies, do it with public figures (such as politicians) who anger you. Do it with those you hate or perceive as ignorant or evil. Breathing in others' negativity in this way *cannot harm you,* but can only help you and others. Because of the sacred tradition of Tonglen practice, by doing it you cannot take on more negativity than you can safely handle. Fifteen minutes of this practice daily is enough to give you full benefit.

DEEPENING YOUR PRACTICE

Being a disciple requires discipline. You have to do the work consistently. As a disciple, you have to practice more assiduously because your commitment requires that you keep pace with your spiritual growth. The commitment to awakening accelerates the spiritual process, manifested as personal transformation. If you practice rarely or sporadically, your suffering will increase because more dark material is stirred up faster. You must stay active and on top of your process— or *it* will end up on top of *you*. Consistent practice is easier.

Discipline, vigilance, determination, effort, consistency, drive, will, intensity, and desire are burned in the fire of compassion to fuel your movement toward awakening. Once you have made the vow to become liberated for the sake of all beings, you must do the work. If you do not do the work consistently, you are just cheating yourself and everyone else. Holding back and not giving your full effort and feeling to practice is a hindrance to your development. Remember your commitment—your vow to awaken in this lifetime so you can awaken others—in your depths. Your commitment motivates you to work. Avoid indolence. Nothing can stop you but you.

Your consistent practice fuels your avowal and compassion, and your consistent avowal and compassion fuel your practice. They feed off of each other. Waiting listlessly achieves nothing. On the path, you may slow down or rest at times, but stopping and not doing the work is ill-advised. Once you make the commitment to awaken, why not proceed with vigor and consistency? Life is over quickly. Practice while you can. Once you have made the commitment to awaken by igniting the dual flame of avowal and compassion, you can make rapid progress if you practice daily, or at least several times a week. If days go by and you haven't practiced, you will not get the best results, and you may sink into despair. Keep the flame burning. Keep going until you are done. If you lose this opportunity after making the commitment to awakening, you have gotten close only to lose it—something that I wouldn't wish on my worst enemy (if I had any enemies).

Monitor the progress you are making. You are making progress if you function more consciously with respect to people, things, and situations. If you can be in conscious relationship with strong negative emotions for extended periods of time—originating within either yourself or others—you are making considerable progress. For example, if you are an addict, are you staying sober and working a program of recovery? Are you meeting the angry outbursts of others with patience and stability instead of exploding? Are you gentler and kinder with yourself? In general, you can measure progress by noticing that the things that used to bother you don't bother you anymore, or at least not as much as they used to. Stabilize your life situation dynamically by maintaining a steady growth in consciousness through regular practice. This is not the easiest thing to attain, but it serves as fuel for the locomotive that powers you up the mountain of awakening.

If you are unearthing new, deeper emotions—which means that they are older, from early childhood, for example—those "new" emotions are signs of progress, because change is occurring. Generally speaking, change is good. If you are wrestling with bigger demons than before and your practice is strong and you are still on the path, it is usually a sign of progress, because you are closer to the root of your dissatisfaction. Just keep working. If you do, progress is virtually guaranteed. Just make sure that you are honest with yourself and are not skipping over any steps, such as getting psychotherapy when you need it.

Awakening is a gentle process, but you must bring intensity to your practice to keep it going. The intensity that you bring to your practice is like a crucible that burns attachment to your false self until the ego is reduced to ashes. Don't get too serious about your path—you need to relax and be frivolous sometimes—but do the work consistently. Seriousness is appropriate sometimes, and so is frivolity. If you have already made awakening your top priority, maintain your focus and increase your effort if necessary. If your effort is small, maintain what you have and build on it.

Just keep going. Trying to get off the path before you're done means that you think you're satisfied with the limited vista only partway up the mountain. As a disciple, you must forswear this absurdity and keep doing the work until you're done. How do you know if you're done? If you have to ask, you're not done. No one can tell you that you're done. If it's not obvious to you, you have more work to do. Don't stop. Take your time if you must, but don't stop. When you're done, you'll know. Until then, deepen your practice.

TEACHING WITH EMPOWERED STATUS

One way to deepen your practice besides increasing its frequency and regularity is to teach others through your empowered status. Becoming a disciple also means that you are an empowered teacher. They are the same thing. Empowered teaching helps others because it brings them Truth. It also helps you because it is a powerful form of spiritual practice and service. Make sure you know how to do it properly. To teach another with empowered status, you must know whom you are addressing and what the needs of the other person are. You must also have a clear discriminatory understanding of relative and absolute truth and how not to conflate the two. Most importantly, you must not represent yourself as a spiritual teacher unless it is merely as an authorized representative of the Teaching.

Truly empowered teachers are rare, so do not assume that this is something that you can easily do under your own aegis. It is not advisable to try it on your own. Seek your Teacher's guidance to help determine if you are ready to teach with an empowered status. If you do this, you cannot go wrong as long as you continue to act with humility and do not consider yourself more than a vessel for the Teaching. The key is not to claim any specialness for yourself. Practice humility. It is not advisable to take on empowered status unless you are studying directly with a Teacher who can guide your path. He will tell you if you are ready to teach others. If you are ready, at first you will most likely use his teaching material as a guideline, at least until you develop the ability to draw on your own empowered authority. Teaching with empowered status is an act of homage, a powerful spiritual practice if you are true in your intentions and carry them out to the best of your ability and with respect for the Teaching. As a disciple, you can use this kind of teaching as a spiritual practice, a meditation into Truth and the parts within you that resist Freedom. If you practice with great care, your commitment to awakening will carry you forward.

Respectful punditry is important. If you have an academic bent, be aware of the limitations of theoretical knowledge. Just because you have a mental grasp on philosophical concepts related to Truth doesn't mean that you know anything about it. It is indeed arrogant to think that you even *can* know anything about it. That is why having a Teacher is so important, or you will think that you are close to the goal, when you are actually out in left field somewhere. To be honest about spirituality, you have to take your desire, knowledge, and experience to a Teacher and see what happens. The most dangerous detour on the path for a disciple is to claim awakening without having yet attained it.

CHECKING IN WITH YOUR TEACHER

As a disciple, make sure you check in with your Teacher regularly. This helps you stay on the path. Contact him every now and then. Trust him. He will show you the way, even if that is to say: "Trust yourself. You know what to do." Or, he may give you specific directions to follow. Either way, he will help keep you on course. If you cannot get specific instruction from him, at least go to see him consistently and get whatever instruction you can, if only to meditate in silence.

Becoming a disciple of a true Teacher gets you within a few lifetimes of awakening. This is a binding contract. You don't want to dishonor your commitment by letting yourself deviate from a conscious path. In the course of a few lifetimes, anything can happen. If you stray, Teachers along the way will help get you back on the path. If you somehow break the agreement, you are not likely to get that opportunity again for at least many thousands of lifetimes. Since each lifetime is a cesspool, it is certainly best to check in with your Teacher and stay on the path. Most people have been through this process of getting close to awakening then losing the opportunity literally millions of times. The key is to stay in contact and keep practicing. If you get lazy, you may regret it later. This is not something you want to let pass you by.

Once you are a disciple, the only stage of the path left for you is *awakened,* so discipleship, in a way, is the "home stretch" of your path. At this point, your Teacher does not hold your hand or spoon-feed you as he may have in the past. As a disciple, you are on your own. That is why you must do the work in a disciplined fashion. You must become more of a light unto yourself. The Master kindles the flame in you, and you build it into a blaze on your own once you have become a disciple and *can* do it on your own. Part of being a disciple is the simple fact that, for the first time on the path, you are capable of stoking your own fire. That does not mean that you no longer have contact with your Teacher. On the contrary, you still contact him, but only to check in for guidance every now and then. The training wheels are off, and you are learning to ride solo.

Eventually, you ride off a cliff and sprout wings.

RENUNCIATION AND DESIRE

As a disciple of the Teaching, you must practice *renunciation.* Renunciation doesn't necessarily mean that you give away your possessions. It means that you give up your *attachment* to possessions, to the concept that you own things. If the wisdom of non-attachment takes root in you, you develop the ability to see objects as potentially useful, but ultimately empty. Things come and go, and you watch them, using them if necessary, but never grasping them as if they were of ultimate value.

Renunciation consists in letting things go and being with what is. You don't have to give everything away *literally* and walk around naked and homeless. Giving up your attachments to things takes away their "thingness" and gives you their "full solid Emptiness." Nothing of this world satisfies—not even the most expensive cars, most luxurious homes, or trendiest fashions. You can have all these things, but only if you recognize that the concept of "having" is empty. You must get rid of attachment to them to be satisfied. Ultimately, possessions are not possessions and objects are not objects. Realize that things are conventionally useful but ultimately insubstantial. Then you can enjoy them.

Conventional happiness is based on having what you want, or the satisfaction of your desire. People want things, then they go out and get them. The people who get what they want are generally considered happy and the people who don't get what they want are considered unhappy. This is all just dissatisfaction. Desire is dissatisfaction because it is wanting something that is not happening now. Dissatisfaction can save you if taken to its logical conclusion—that nothing of this world can ever satisfy you completely—but it is no way to live. You are always wanting something else, or you no longer want what you have, or you want something you can't have, or you can't get rid of something you don't want. Sound familiar?

Desire is properly understood as *wanting what you don't have*. Desire is the cause of suffering. Desire implies that you are not okay with things as they are. If you were completely okay with things as they are, you wouldn't want anything to be different than it is. Wanting what you have is not desire because radical acceptance of what is satisfies desire before it can exist. Wanting what is is the destruction of desire at its root, revealing satisfaction. The awakened state is desireless. The awakened state is one with what is, and hence completely satisfied and free.

Desire implies attachment to objects because wanting something other than what is creates the sense of a separate self and a world of objects to be gotten. If you want something you don't have, you attach to a concept about what it would be like to have it, and you live in that fantasy. This causes pain. In order to get rid of desire, you have to destroy the controller of the mind, the ego. The ego is never satisfied with what is. Until it is gone, you uncontrollably crave things.

Desire is the root of the false self and all unhappiness, misery, and pain. Things have no intrinsic existence; they come and go. If you attach to either having them or not having them, you tie your fate to objects that are impermanent and subject to loss, theft, and damage. If you crave what you cannot have, you cause yourself deep suffering. Eventually, this suffering may force you to examine your attachment to people, places, things, and the concepts that represent them in your mind.

Aversion is the flip side of desire, and just as painful. Whereas desire is wanting what you don't have, aversion is *not wanting what you do have*. If you want to get rid of something, take action and get rid of it. If you can do this without mental resistance—griping, complaining, and stressing about your situation—you can find peace in it and not be troubled. Eventually, being troubled is not worth the pain you get from creating a false sense of self out of mentally resisting Reality. Desire and aversion are two aspects of the same illusion—your false self. If you free yourself from the tyranny of the ego, desire and aversion no longer exist for you, and you are no longer troubled.

Materialism, or the attitude that worldly possessions constitute the highest value in life, is an obstacle on the path because things in themselves are not ultimately satisfying. If you really loved things, you could just go outside and enjoy rocks, trees, and flowers. Ownership is an illusion, a concept. It would be more accurate to say that we borrow things for a while. Death takes them away. Money buys you things and gives a false sense of control, authority, or power through the concept of ownership. To truly appreciate material things, you must appreciate their essential nature, from which they exhibit a free, empty quality. This appreciation does not grasp, but freely *is.* This state is free of confusion between the Reality of objects and the concepts we have about them.

Once you realize that you cannot own anything, everything is yours. When you give everything up, everything is given to you. An awakened person appears to have possessions, money, cars, and other things—but this is an illusion. Does the sky own clouds? Does outer space own stars? Emptiness leaves no residue and does not own anything, although it contains everything, and ultimately *is* the nature of everything. "Me" and "mine" are seen as false. Without attachment, there is only Freedom, including the appearance of possessions. An awakened person has no possessions—not even his body, mind, or emotions.

Awakened beings live with what they need and no more. This may include a yacht and a few houses. One Teacher may appear wealthy, and another may appear to live simply, with few possessions. Because these are all relative distinctions, it doesn't really matter how he lives because his lifestyle ultimately serves Truth. What you can learn from is how he enjoys material things, how he relates to his possessions or lack of them. You cannot judge the awakened status of a person by his possessions or his lack of them.

On the relative level, you may have many possessions and even be considered wealthy. On the absolute level, there are no possessions and no one to own them. Seek awakening first, and what you need will be given to you. You have what you need. As a student of Truth, it makes sense to live simply and have as few possessions as possible to reduce distractions to your practice. Material things must be cared for, stored somewhere, protected from theft, loss, or damage, and occasionally cleaned. Even if you have employees to take care of things for you, you still have to supervise them and tolerate having them in your space. With a minimum of possessions, you can get by very well and will generally have an easier time getting through life and with fewer distractions.

Money and worldly security mean nothing in themselves. Greed is never satisfied. No matter how much money, material things, or status you get, you cannot ever be satisfied because there is always more that you don't have. On the other hand, spiritual aspirants are not necessarily poor. They have things but are not attached to them. They may take common sense measures to prevent loss and damage, but it's not a big deal. All that really matters is Freedom and doing what it takes to walk the path. On the absolute level, an awakened person has nothing, does nothing, is nothing; on the relative level, he has a car in the driveway, a job, and an identity card.

THE EMPTINESS OF SUCCESS

Pursuing worldly success as if it were an ultimate goal is a waste of time. Only a few people from history are remembered for their achievements, and all will eventually be forgotten in the annals of the world. Even the most well-known names will be lost in hundreds, thousands, or millions of years. Awakening is the only achievement that counts. No one really cares whether you succeed in worldly terms or not. Frankly, no one really cares if you awaken or not, except perhaps a few people.

But you care. That's all that matters. Achieving anything for the approval of others is a mistake. When you are successful in worldly terms—power, money, fame, and accolades—people secretly want to defeat you and usurp your status. Instead of really caring about you, they are often envious of you. In liberating yourself, you are actually giving everything away, so you have nothing to lose.

The world of competition—whether in business, politics, or society—is like a war zone. Some people are greedily getting what they can for themselves at the expense of others, and others are standing around, wondering what happened. The mind-dominated world is cutthroat, backstabbing, and dog-eat-dog. You don't have to live that way. You can find all the value you are looking for beyond the world, in Freedom—and then worldly success means nothing to you, although you may hold a job, own a business, and function in the world like everyone else. The awakened person lives in the world but is not of it.

No matter what you achieve in the world, it will not last. All the things of this world come into being, exist for a while, then crumble into the dust from which they emerged. You can work hard and achieve things in life, but if you place intrinsic value in worldly success, you will suffer greatly for it, for all things perish. If you succeed in worldly terms but are unattached to your success, the specter of failure will not bother you—because you do not place independent value in outward success, but in Truth, which does not perish. The success of awakening is beyond this world and yet encompasses this world. It is, in Truth, the very essence of the world.

Not all success *in* the world is *of* the world. For example, disaster relief, helping children, and serving humanity in general is compassion in action. Compassion is the key to lasting success. If you work hard in the world helping others compassionately, you are placing value in the well-being of suffering people, and that selfless service to humanity draws on your inner Being and is its own value. Instead of seeing human beings as means to an end, you see them as ends in themselves, as inherently valuable by virtue of their ultimate nature. That gives your work real value that lasts even beyond your death and attracts opportunities for Liberation, both in life and at death. Great humanitarians, of which there are precious few in the world, draw on their inner Being and are moving ever closer to Freedom. People who work in this way are usually in touch with spiritual teachings as a motivator for their actions, and this acting in the name of Truth is what activates their awakening power.

Freedom is the ultimate success. Although you will never get any worldly recognition for it, you won't care, because you will be satisfied with Truth.

Everything else is less than dust.

CHAPTER SIX

EMBODIMENT

This body, which is made up of skin,
flesh, blood, arteries, veins, fat,
marrow and bone, is full of waste
matter and filth. It deserves our
contempt.

—Shankara

I sing the body electric,
The armies of those I love engirth me
and I engirth them,
They will not let me off till I go with
them, respond to them,
And discorrupt them, and charge
them full with the charge of the soul.

—Walt Whitman

THE BODY AS ENERGY

As you progress on the path of awakening, you will notice that growth in consciousness raises your energy* level. Spiritual practice raises energy, both in frequency and amplitude, and the challenge is to embody it more fully. You must learn not only to raise energy, but also to ground and balance it. The most effective way to do this is

---

* This is vital energy, or what is called *chi* in Traditional Chinese Medicine.

to inhabit your body consciously. As you grow in consciousness, your body exhibits an increasingly energetic quality.

The physical body is not what it seems to be. Like any perceived object, it is a reflection of your fundamental state of consciousness. It is no more solid than a perceived body in a dream, however substantial it may seem. The body is a composite of the physical, mental, and emotional dimensions of the person, the vehicle of expression for your consciousness, but not who you ultimately are. Unconsciousness makes it seem solid. The more conscious you become, the less the body appears as a dense object and the more it radiates pure awareness as a brilliantly energetic field—more of a vibrant flux than material thing.

Viewing the body as an energetic projection of your state of consciousness is conducive to awakening because it leads to a more conscious relationship with your body; it becomes less of a thing in itself and more of a vibrational emanation that you enjoy. The awakening body is an intelligent field of awareness, energy, and expression that we inhabit rather than a crude object that we manipulate by force. The body can appear to be grotesque, alien, even obscene, depending on our state of consciousness. The body as a projection of the mind is an object, a fleshy encapsulation for the ego. The ego requires encapsulation—in ideas, bodies, religions. When the Emptiness of the mind becomes more apparent, the body becomes more luminous, open, and free.

As a student, it is easier to work with the mind than with the body because thoughts are easy to affect and move. More resistant to movement and change are the emotions, and more so the body. It is difficult to inhabit the body fully, but this is what we must do if we are to root our conscious growth process in a basic sense of physical humanity. The body is closer to that humanity than the mind, but because it is more difficult to inhabit the body consciously, most of us do not fully do so. Inhabiting the body means to be radiant within it, to allow Truth to emanate from it as presence. Instead of being the body, most of us operate from the mind and use or abuse the body, trying to control it as a passive machine. To awaken in the body, we must be That which we are more deeply, grounding our awareness in the fundamental sense of physical embodiment.

GROUNDING

While raising energy is important, we must also learn to ground it responsibly. We must *be* the body. We must recognize its energetic nature and ground it in basic physicality. We must plant our feet on *terra firma* and root deeply.

Consciousness requires that we view the body as an empty phenomenon, an appearance of the Absolute. Cultivating awareness of the Emptiness of objects automatically raises our psychic energy and demands that we incorporate this new energy into our basic human physicality. We must find a way to simultaneously reach into both the outer limits of Emptiness and the inner groundedness of physicality and live dynamically between the two. Between objects and Emptiness is the domain of energy; we must learn doorways into that space of alternately raising and grounding the energy of conscious relationship in the world. We must listen into that space, be that space, while deepening our sense of physical humanness.

Grounding, strengthening, and structuring the physical body is an integral part of preparing the person. The energy must be contained in a form that can withstand the increase in power and awareness that accompanies it. Without adequate grounding, you lose contact with embodiment and can become mentally unstable or ill. Fortunately, human beings naturally seek ways to ground energy to maintain vital stability, such as through physical exertion. When physical energy is grounded, mental energy tends to stabilize.

Baths, showers, diet, and exercise can help ground energy. Baths, especially using dissolved salts, relax the body and tone the energy. Showers are grounding because their effluent flows into pipes that connect your vital energy to the earth. Certain foods such as meat, dairy, eggs, soy, and root vegetables absorb excess energy and enhance fleshly, animal qualities. Physical exercise burns excess energy and takes your focus of attention into the physical dimension more deeply. Strive to balance the raising and grounding of energy to maintain vital stability while powering growth in consciousness. Overall, allow energy to increase, healthfully, over time. Work the body to provide a container for higher energy, just as you would upgrade your home's wiring before stepping up its voltage.

Learn how to ground your heightened energy in healthy relationships with other human beings. Learn to share it. Sexuality is one of the ways to do this. Although sexual release discharges energy and is considered wasteful by some, conservation of sexual energy for extended periods of time is not necessary. Celibacy can be useful as a temporary practice, but not as a healthy general lifestyle, because the physical organism naturally benefits from sexual release at least occasionally. Some paths stress celibacy and the retention of sexual energy as a way of achieving higher states of consciousness. This kind of practice is usually more of a hindrance than an aid. Instead of doing that, learn to use sexual energy consciously and responsibly. Too much or too little sexual activity, for example, can lead to blockages of energy in your body. Find a balance between repression and overindulgence.

You can also share energy through physical, non-sexual intimacy with other human beings. Hugs, handshakes, and platonic companionship can enliven others with your energy and ground you. They can also drain you, so it is important to learn how to be with others so that you maintain a healthy balance of energy in your body. Make sure that you surround yourself with people who are manifesting a significant degree of conscious awareness so the energy you share is less likely to be polluted with negativity and any negativity that does arise can be consciously managed and liberated. Obviously, students of the true Teaching are more likely to manifest these qualities, so spend your time with other students when you can. Be aware of the quality of energy in your relationships and cultivate friendships carefully. Be aware of what is going on around you and move with events consciously.

Dance a deeper relationship with life.

Learning how to responsibly raise and ground energy is preparation for the force of awakening, which grows as consciousness grows.

The force of awakening can be experienced as profound flows, shifts, contractions, and expansions of energy and awareness over time. Awakening affects the body energetically as a moment-to-moment process. The body responds to the force of awakening in different ways, manifesting phenomena such as fluctuations in body temperature, decreased appetite for food, intuitive perceptions, increased need for exercise or rest, spontaneous movements, an enhanced aesthetic sense, and deeper appreciation of nature, among others. The whole manifest "body" of the universe appears more awake, vibrant, and alive.

The body is more capable of integrating the force of awakening than the mind. The mind alone cannot stand it. Let the body show you what it can do. For example, when you are highly stressed, it is more helpful to walk than to think. Going for long walks is an excellent way to deepen awareness and integrate the heightened energies liberated by growth in consciousness. Any prolonged, deeply felt physical exertion is better for integrating shifts in consciousness than cognition, so you must inhabit the body both consciously and vigorously if you want to move safely toward the culmination of your path.

CULTIVATING ENERGY WITH THE BODY

Energy is a bridge between form and the Formless, and paying attention to energy takes you deeper into the realm of Being. Paying attention to energy within your body requires the ability to focus attention meditatively, making mind-forms appear less solid, more radiant, closer to Emptiness. Recognition of objects' Emptiness dissolves them into the formlessness of Being, connecting you with their timeless essence, the *I Am* that lives through us as our individual consciousness. When you connect to the essence of objects, the mental outline of their form is apparent but they do not impinge upon you as they would if you were in a less conscious state. When you are more conscious, objects become mere definitions, bare traces upon the face of Reality, hypnotic forms of "What is this?" constantly arising and returning to the Void. This conscious process raises energy within your body.

Meditation on the physical body deepens your meditation, bringing it close to home. Some Teachings, such as Shankara's Advaita Vedanta, see the body as a bag of filth, whereas the poet Walt Whitman celebrates it as a form of vibrant and mysterious aliveness. Both of these views are true and useful, just in different ways. Remember that descriptions are relative. Viewed as a mind-object, the body is a bag of filth, a loathsome excrescence. Attachment to such a thing is non-sensical. Viewed as an awakened expression, it is electric, radiant, and ecstatic; attachment is impossible because you fully *are* it.

A powerful practice is to focus on the body—on thoughts about the body, feelings within the body, and sensations of the body—without judgment. Become quiet. Watch thoughts, feelings, and sensations—especially deep somatic sensations—within the space of your awareness. Notice judgments and let them go. Notice feelings and hold them lightly; let them fully *be*. Peacefully allow them to be what they are and do what they do. Notice fully. Remain still. Awaken to their fundamental Emptiness; watch them subside into the vibrant immediacy of Being. Let them vibrate into who you are. When you embody energy consciously in this way, your movement is a graceful presence of *Yes* that embraces and invigorates others, putting them in contact with your true nature.

ENJOYING EMBODIMENT

Enjoy embodiment by waking up to your senses. Waking up to your senses is not the same as attachment to them, but liberating them via recognition. Enjoy sensations not as things in themselves but as forms of relationship fundamentally liberated by awareness; then you can experience them without being trapped by them.

If you no longer see the body as an independent thing, but as a form of dependent (relative) arising, you see its impermanence, and your anxiety about it ceases. Without anxiety about losing the body, you can enjoy it. Like a cloud, it coalesces and vaporizes. Inhabiting it is not a problem because it is part of the world just like everything else; when held consciously, it is subsumed within the radiance of Being that redeems it as fundamentally empty and thus ecstatic.

Recognizing the radiant, energetic nature of the body is the Absolute waking up to Itself, and this waking up is enjoyment.

But as much as you may enjoy energetic experiences, you must keep them in perspective. An experience of intense energy is not necessarily a sign that anything "spiritual" is happening. Stirring up a stagnant pond with a stick is not the same as unblocking its source and letting it flow freely. A mind-guided energetic experience is not the same as an authentic shift of consciousness. A relatively unconscious person who is skilled at manipulating energy can fool you into thinking that "something spiritual" is happening in your body when nothing of the sort is occurring. Unconscious energy manipulation can actually inject negativity into your field and cause illness, fatigue, or malaise. Instead of fearing these situations, recognize and consciously avoid them. The more conscious you are, the less likely you will allow negativity to affect you.

Energy cultivation can be a trap if you identify with it. Working with energy is seductive to the ego because it can be perceived as exotic, sensual, or esoteric. Do not identify with these qualities, or you will subvert the very process of conscious relationship that granted you the ability to sense energy in the first place. Identification with phenomena shuts down conscious relationship, even identification with subtle phenomena. Consecrate your energy cultivation to awakening, not to establishing an attractive, esoteric identity. That is just a ruse. If you want people to think you are hip or "advanced" for working with energy, you are a slave to their approval. If the ego co-opts your practice, you will become negatively charged and may cause harm to yourself or others.

ENVIRONMENTAL ENERGY

Energy naturally exists in and flows through the environment. You can use environmental energy for healing, extrasensory perception, enhancement of relationships, or communion with living things. Energy connects you with your surroundings. The ability to discern the energetic quality of your surroundings is a vital component of your path. For example, objects in your immediate environment can be imprinted with patterns of energy from prior physical (and thus energetic) contact with people. You can learn to recognize these imprints as distinct manifestations of human consciousness, with certain factors evident, such as inherent negativity or aliveness. You can sense which objects have a negative charge and remove them, perhaps replacing them with ones that have a stronger healthy vibration.

Environments contain, filter, and process energy. How that energy flows through a local environment, such as a landscape or dwelling, is important because it affects how you live. Harmonious arrangement of a living space is conducive to balance, serenity, and strong practice. Proper arrangement of furniture, art, and other objects allows a healthy flow of energy, enhancing your quality of life. To achieve this, you can create more flowing, open space by rearranging objects and eliminating clutter. You can employ organic shapes and use natural materials, such as plants, rocks, and wood. The more conscious you are, the easier it is to discern the energetic quality of your environment and make appropriate changes.

Raise environmental energy by recognizing the empty nature of phenomena in your surroundings. For example, viewing trees as vibrant, living things involves the recognition of their Being, deepening your awareness of them as expressions of the same Reality. Meditate on a tree. View it with calm, meditative awareness that notices thoughts, feelings, and sensations that arise with respect to the tree without judgment. Feel its quality of Being. You can also feel its absence, as when trees are wantonly clear-cut from an area, leaving a blighted landscape. When a forest is unconsciously harvested, you can feel the loss of energy, a kind of barren deadness—but only if you pay quiet attention to it with nonjudgmental awareness. You may even feel sad about it, as if a friend had died. Notice the difference in energy between an industrial park and an old growth forest, because the forest flows deeply into the earth and circulates energy in the area, whereas an industrial park does not, or at least not in the same way.

SCRUBBING

Scrubbing is a natural activity of the awakened person (and to some extent of the conscious person), consisting of clearing ambient negativity from people, places, and things. Scrubbing is the elimination of environmental negativity. A person must on some level be willing for the negativity to be removed for it to happen. The awakened person takes on as much pain as she can safely handle and neutralizes it. It's a blessing, absorbing suffering and transforming it into consciousness. In every moment, the awakened person wages a kind of spiritual warfare with mind-forms arising from judgment on an individual and collective level. This battle is not fought through opposition, but through acceptance. We are all involved in this war, whether we like it or not. It's a peaceful war if we allow it—and a hellish one if we fight it.

Negative energies can arise from within you or others. Most spiritual practice is geared toward eliminating your own negativity. Scrubbing is eliminating the negativity of others. You take it on and clear it as if it were your own. Scrubbing is more common than you might think. Negative thoughts, beliefs, and energies are everywhere. There is virtually no end to it. When you are a devoted student, scrubbing is common. When you are liberated, you continue to scrub your environment on an ongoing basis. Do not bemoan ambient negativity, because scrubbing serves your awakening. Scrubbing is similar to eating and digesting food. Scrubbing often occurs while sleeping, affecting dream content. This benefits all beings and is the activity of consciousness.

Scrubbing is a form of *conscious suffering*—the conscious embracing of negativity in oneself or another. This embracing of negativity dissolves it and renders it harmless, vaporizing it into Emptiness. An awakened being embraces ambient pain as her own and neutralizes it, even in the midst of ordinary activity. During this process, she may experience a sense of pain, but without a sense of self in it, without any identification with it, and without a need to know *why* it is happening. Although "conscious suffering" sounds like a contradiction, it is not. Whereas conventional suffering is pain generated by self-identification, conscious suffering takes on, radically accepts, and eliminates that pain. The Awakener takes on your pain. This is why many people relate so deeply to the Christian crucifixion story—a "Lamb of God" who takes on the sins of humanity—because the ability of the Awakener to take on your pain is so massive as to be beyond comprehension.

Once you have practiced dissolving your own negativity for a while and have gotten the hang of it, try doing it with the negativity of others. Compassion helps tremendously in this endeavor and empowers your practice, bringing the Awakener into play.

Deeply unconscious people are everywhere. They need your help. They need your compassion. A deeply unconscious person cannot help but create more pain with only minor exceptions, such as during holidays and special occasions when values take center stage, or when loved ones suffer and need help, or when children are performing in a school play or athletic event. A very mildly unconscious person still creates pain, just less of it—and may be able to neutralize some pain with the help of true spiritual practice. Having a Teacher helps tremendously. In the meantime, you can help by being willing to take on some negativity and purify it for the sake of helping others.

INTUITION AND GUIDANCE

Intuition is the ability to receive information without the aid of rational inference, without knowing how you know. If you are intuitive, you can be either *psychic* or *clairvoyant.* Although these two faculties seem similar, being psychic is of the mind, whereas being clairvoyant is of the Spirit. A psychic gets information mentally, and a clairvoyant gets it spiritually. Awakened people can be psychic but are inherently clairvoyant by virtue of their awakening. Psychics are clairvoyant to the extent that they are conscious.

You don't have to be awakened to be clairvoyant, but unawakened people have clairvoyant transmissions only rarely, whereas an awakened person is clairvoyant by definition. The degree of clairvoyance may vary among awakened people, but they all have it. Empowered teachers have it to a significant degree. The more involved you are in a Teaching, the more likely it is that you will experience clairvoyance. It is rare for an unawakened non-student to experience clairvoyance. Clairvoyance is identical with Wisdom. You simply *are* That. Being psychic is like watching television with an antenna, whereas clairvoyance is like watching it with digital cable. In the former, the picture is often distorted; in the latter, the image is exceptionally clear.

People may ask the awakened person: "Why don't you know everything? Since you are intuitive, why can't you, for example, pick a winning stock or lottery number with absolute certainty? Shouldn't you be a billionaire by now?" This assumes that it is in my best interests to be a billionaire. The intuitive ability that comes with awakening is Wisdom and varies, depending on the person. If you are awakened, you are consciously one with the essence of all that is, or God. The omniscience of God might imply a universe of billionaires, since He created it. Why is there poverty, you might ask, if God is so perfect and all-powerful? The relative appearance of the world *is* poverty; it has no independent existence. There is no independently existing world. In the world, even the wealthiest man is a pauper—unless he has awakened to Reality. If you are a billionaire in a dream, you're still just dreaming; in the dream of samsara, you suffer and die. True wealth cannot be lost. You *are* it. Awakening to Reality makes winning the lottery look like peanuts—and rancid ones at that. Getting rich, famous, or successful is not the point. Getting free is the point. Just do that, and you won't wonder why awakened people aren't all materially wealthy. By itself, material wealth is nothing more than a golden anvil taking you to the bottom of an ocean of darkness.

The future cannot be accurately predicted with consistency. Sometimes talented diviners can foretell certain events or trends in a person's life, but what good does this do? Your power is *now*, not in the future. What you do *now* determines the future—and when the future comes, it comes in a moment of *now*. Fortune telling is based in control and fear, the domain of the ego. Your safe haven is not in the future; it is in the present moment. If a trend is developing—for example, you know that a hurricane is gathering strength and will probably hit your home in a few hours—it makes sense to evacuate the area—but you cannot control what follows. If you move out of its path, a hurricane still may swerve and hit you—and if you stand still and wait for it, it may veer away from you and leave you standing. Instead of trying to predict the future, stay awake in your life and take appropriate action in the moment, trusting what is.

A good clairvoyant or psychic can help you in the right circumstances, but it is more important to trust your own intuitive instincts first and not let anyone mislead you. Gather information where you can and trust your own intuitive sense of appropriateness. Intuition is a valid way of obtaining information and guidance. Beware of pitfalls on the path and stay conscious. Intuitive guidance is really information that you get all the time in your dreams and gut instincts. The key is to listen to them, meaning that you heed them and take action. It is important to know how the Absolute communicates with you, how it gets your attention, and how to listen to it.

Ultimately, there is no difference between intuition and guidance, but on the surface a distinction can be made. Whereas intuition can provide information that is not necessarily directive, guidance gets you to *do* something, to move, to take action. It is much more important for you to wake up than to sit around and figure things out (as if you could control things from there). The Absolute may provide you with guidance for reasons beyond simply getting accurate information, such as leading you on a path of deeper discovery. The literal correctness of intuitive information is not that important. For example, you may act on incorrect information in a public way that serves to humiliate your ego so that you don't get too proud of yourself. In this case, deeper humility is much more important than getting intuitive information that is technically correct.

This does not mean that the Absolute doesn't often provide information that is dead-on accurate. It does. Actually, it's all *dead-on* accurate; it destroys the *dead-one* that claims your space: the ego. The ego cannot hide from the light of Truth. Without the aid of true guidance, you might think that informational exactitude is all you need. In that case, who knows to what ends you might direct your intuitive prowess: sexual conquest, gambling, vengeance, or just acting like a know-it-all? All of these are inappropriate uses of psychic powers and can harm the intuitive who uses them for dark purposes. If the Absolute is guiding your intuitive journey, it enlightens your deepest, darkest places until you are free. The Absolute is the ultimate Truth, so it doesn't matter how you get there, as long as the path is guided by higher facts.

You may be guided to do something for one apparent reason only to find out that there was another, deeper reason you were guided to do it. This is like being guided to move an old piece of furniture and finding a cache of gold that was hidden underneath it. The guidance was not about the furniture; it was about the gold. This is also a lesson in how Liberation occurs. If you simply remove what obscures Truth, Truth will be revealed to you. If you remove what has only relative value, the Absolute will appear.

Guidance may not make sense to your mind and often doesn't. When you get right down to it, Truth is downright unreasonable. Ultimately, listening to Truth is far more important than what your mind says. If there is a discrepancy between them, go with Truth.

I know. Scary. Do it anyway.

DARK ENTITIES

On the path of awakening, you may encounter dark entities who are not physical. You may feel them, sense them—even see them in your "mind's eye." Often, these entities will inhabit the space of a person, and the more conscious you are, the more they will be irritated by your presence and try to attack you. They latch onto unconscious people and dig in. Most of the time they stay with their host until he is either more conscious or dead. Find these entities and deal with them responsibly. Consistent practice will help you sense them. If you sense one, don't worry about it, because it is a common occurrence, like seeing a cockroach in your bathroom. Dark entities have too many forms to get rid of all of them at once, so take them on one at a time and meet them with consciousness.

These are just mind forms. Don't worry. Just be present.

Dark entities come in two basic forms: *demons* and *parasites*. Demons try to make you do things that are not in your best interests. Parasites drain you of vital energy, gorging themselves like leeches until full. Sometimes they let you go, only to return when they get hungry. Parasites can look like leeches, lampreys, ticks, and other bug- or worm-like entities. The only conventional way to get rid of a parasite is to transfer it to a person of deeper unconsciousness, often through unconscious forms of conversation. Parasites are transferred through "blah blah poor me" kind of blathering communication or through intimate physical contact such as sexual intercourse.

Demons are more active, more cunning, and certainly more dia-bolical than parasites, which can even look "cute" (like bugs are cute) to the untrained awareness.

Don't be fooled. They are deadly.

Demons and parasites are conglomerations of mental tenden-cies that take on a characteristic form common to our "collective un-conscious" and are sometimes accurately depicted in fantasy artwork. Demons can look like devils, monsters, dragons, snakes, animals, and gargoyles, among other things. They have no power, except what you give them: *your fear that things are independently real.*

Demons often attack free beings, only to be smashed into Formlessness. They are then recycled back into the personal form of the free being, who incorporates the mind-stuff as glue for the substance of her physical appearance. The world is the physical ap-pearance of the free being. Forms are used until used up. Forms are used until they are no longer necessary, then they are destroyed and recycled into new forms until all beings are liberated. Only then are they completely dissolved. Dark entities cannot harm an awakened person. When demons attack an awakened person, they sense fear but do not recognize it as their own until it is too late to escape being destroyed.

Before awakening, the best way to protect yourself against these forms is to practice. For example, a sincere prayer of protection—especially if it is given to you by a Teacher, whether from a text or in person—can neutralize a massive number of these nasty mind-forms and protect you from their ill effects. So can study, service, medita-tion, inquiry, and other practices. Find the ones that work for you and use them.

The world is demonic in nature, but most of us do not see it. We are perplexed by the world and strive only faintly to understand it. Finally, after a weak attempt, we say, "I don't get it" and collapse into a comforting belief system. This false comfort is what kills us, over and over again. The world is like a demon that attacks itself on all levels all the time. This means that not only are you a demon when you are mind-possessed, but so is everyone else, and the common tendency is to attack, defend, analyze, think, desire, accumulate, and calculate—all subtle forms of warfare. Demons inhabit even the most saintly-looking mind-identified person. Awaken from the nightmare. Once you are free, dark entities can't bother you anymore. They can't suck you dry. They cough, choke, and sputter—then explode or just fizzle out.

Attachment is the issue. Demons are created by beings with attachments and the consequent fear and desire. Your job is to dissolve your attachments.

Demons are nothing new and are deeply entrenched in the popular mindset. For example, horror films often portray instances of demon *possession,* in which a person is taken over by a dark entity. Possession occurs but is not as powerful or obvious as cases that are popularly depicted, as in the movie *The Exorcist* (which is a rather silly depiction, actually). In possession, a demon or parasite latches on to a person's weak and vulnerable belief system and causes harm. This is true for virtually everyone because the ego is a demon, or rather the source of all demons. People are demonic to the extent that they are mind-identified. If you are mind-identified, you are possessed *now.* In the movies, demons seem to have power. They don't. They feed on your fear, so make your fear conscious and dispel the darkness. Master your fear by being present for it without judgment. Practice to keep from shutting down in fear. As with any form of unconsciousness, it is the assumption that entities have power that gives them an independent, scary quality, like assuming an evil sock puppet that you are manipulating has independent power when it does not. You are the power behind it.

Demonic thought-forms look like dark, ugly worms or hideous dragons or serpents with bat wings. They are the imaginal representation of unconscious mind material that feed on fear and seek weak people to prey on like drugs or junk food. The true Teacher sees them as *lunch.* They cannot enter the awareness-field of a free person and survive. They are destroyed in the clear light of awareness. They try to scare you, and it's amusing if you are fully present. If you even for a moment believe in the appearance of evil, it will attach to you and drag you down, how far down depending on the degree of your attachment. Demons are virtually countless and lurk nearly everywhere.

People who are strongly possessed by these demons are like undead creatures, giving rise to the origin of the vampire and zombie archetypes, among others. They feed on your life force if you let them and they cannot survive in the light of your conscious awareness. You give them power by fearing them, by believing that they have independent substance.

Deeply unconscious people act like monsters and prey on themselves and others. Notice how listening to a deeply unconscious person drains you and how responding consciously protects you. Some possessed people you must avoid until they can relate to you more consciously. Sometimes they are family members.

Demons can't stand the light. Mythology and popular literature are replete with dark creatures that lurk in the shadows and either eat human flesh or drink human blood, or both. These monsters reflect a powerful insight that can help you if you embrace it: *you are like one of these creatures.* The key is to see this fully without judgment. This is the light of your conscious awareness, and monsters can't stand that. If you hold them in the light, they squirm, explode, and dissolve. They may try to scare you first; just don't believe them. They are all full of bluster and blather, and it is your job to *be* with them until they are gone. Sit with them until the dawn comes. They hate that.

Entities with wings are demonic. Demons attack you and claim your inner space until you awaken. Demons are everywhere, like flies. "Lord of the flies" refers to the Devil, a mythical creature himself, but really the face of the ego. Gnomes, trolls, bugs, gremlins, and hobgoblins are all forms of darker beings. They can't hurt you unless you believe in them and become afraid.

Some people use psychic shielding, such as visualizing white light, to protect themselves from negative energies. Shielding is useful early on the path but must be abandoned as you learn to be with dark forces more consciously. Negative energy is the gravitational pull of mind-identification on your psyche. Technically, energy is neither positive nor negative, but the quality of the energy is informed by either more of a dark pull into resistance, as in complaining, or a gentle bright radiance of *this is It. I am. That which is, is.* The very concept of shielding is a form of negativity or saying "no" to what is—in this case, negativity. Negativity toward negativity makes it stronger. The only way to truly protect yourself from negative energy is to be present for it, as it is, without judgment. If you do judge it, be present for *that* judgment. Sometimes you just have to politely excuse yourself and leave the room, depending on the situation. Sometimes you have to sit there and take it. If you can't leave, be as present as you can.

The Awakener is your protector against dark entities. Call out to your Teacher for help. Listen inwardly. You may be guided to do something helpful. In any case, practice. If your Teacher guides you to use psychic shielding, it is not a form of negativity, because it is given to you and empowered for your protection. Anything your Teacher asks you to do is automatically empowered for your benefit. Shielding may be effectively used in early stages of spiritual development when the sense of duality is still strong. Check with your Teacher about it. Ultimately, there is no such thing as negative energy, only energy identified with form. To become immune to negative forces, work to break your identification with form.

Awakened consciousness is immune to all negativity.

SEEKING COMFORT VERSUS HEALING

In general, growth of consciousness is conducive to healing. Healing means becoming more whole; since growth in consciousness means recognizing one's prior wholeness, the spiritual path is the essence of healing. You cannot have healing on your own terms.

Most people just want to get rid of pain. In our culture, pain is usually seen as something to be eliminated. Actually, pain is a form of awareness, bringing your attention to something. Healing and superficial pain relief are not the same thing. Wanting pain to disappear at the expense of consciousness is not true healing. Healing often involves rooting out core stories, healing anger and resentment, and making patterns conscious. Pain is created by the mind, even physical pain. The secret to healing pain—any kind of pain—is to be with it, as it is, without judgment.

Suppression of symptoms is not the same as healing. A chunk of unconscious material is often at the core of a physical issue and is better healed than suppressed. Avoiding pain as a habitual lifestyle is *seeking comfort*. If you seek comfort, you may find it, but only temporarily, and not completely. Relative comfort is incomplete and comes and goes; absolute comfort is who you are and is beyond all time and understanding.

Comfort and safety are related. On the relative level, you cannot be comfortable if you are not safe. If you are vulnerable, you might be attacked, thus threatening your sense of comfort. But if you *must* have comfort on the relative level in order to be happy, you will not have it for long. There is no total or lasting comfort on the relative level. You are always vulnerable in some way. If you constantly seek relative comfort, you become a slave to it and awakening cannot reach you because you have a condition for its attainment.

The word "comfort" comes from the Latin word *fortis* meaning "to strengthen greatly" and means "a contented sense of well-being." *Fortis* also gives rise to the words "fort," "fortress," and "fortification." On the surface, this makes sense. If you are surrounded by a fortress, you might feel comfortable because nothing can get to you, nothing can harm you—unless, of course, your enemy knows how to breach your defenses. On a deeper level you can see that a fortress is not real comfort because it is temporary and insecure. This is similar to the false sense of self, which is like a bulwark against the world that imprisons you within its walls. It keeps others out and, although it may provide you with a sense of security, your defenses can be breached easily. Besides, your true enemy is on the inside. The more you try to keep him out, the more he bothers you. It's as if you are saying to the Absolute, "I really, truly want awakening—but only if it's comfortable." This implies control, and it won't happen that way. Spiritual practice is not necessarily comfortable. You have to be willing to stretch your boundaries, go past your comfort zone. You have to be willing to face your deepest, darkest terrors. If you *have* to be comfortable, forget about it.

In the world, there is no such thing as complete security. Seeking safety (from Latin *salvus*, "whole") is an activity of the ego because it wants to preserve itself, sustain itself, and control Reality. There is no such thing because eventually death gets you. Surrender all absolute notions of worldly safety. Take common-sense precautions from danger but realize that there is no guarantee of worldly safety, ever. The only true safety is surrender of all seeking for safety. This is *salvation,* being made whole. In your true nature, you are already safe and whole, even now. It is the incessant seeking of the ego that keeps generating danger in the form of a person living in a world that attacks it. Be safe, but remember that safety is not guaranteed. An asteroid could crash into the planet at any moment. Can you stop it?

Most people avoid awakening because it is perceived as a threat to self-security. This keeps the pain of "me" going. Reality is the ultimate protection, but you can't have it on your own terms. Surrender is required. This is like being in love. We all want the warmth and comfort of love, but love implies vulnerability. You cannot love with a fortified heart. To truly love, you have to let your defenses down and risk being hurt, even destroyed, by it.

The awakened person is unassailable because she cannot be located. Unlike an inhabitant of a fortress, she is beyond the reach of danger. You can be comfortable only where you can relax without fear of being attacked. No one can attack Truth because no one knows what it is. No one can get to you There.

If you want to be comfortable, get busy getting conscious. If you are sick or in pain, get proper medical care and use your condition to grow spiritually. Although there is no guarantee of its form of manifestation, becoming more conscious has a healing effect.

Get free. That is the main thing, regardless of your symptoms. Paradoxically, it is seeing Truth as more important than your own health—or even your own survival—that typically leads to healing, because you are letting go of comfort as a primary value and embracing true healing.

Consider the following points:

+ You are causing your own pain. How long must you hit your head against a wall before you wake up and realize what you're doing? The wall is just minding its own business. You say that the wall shouldn't be there, but why bash your head against an adamantine, immovable object? Wanting something to be other than it is now is absurd. Pain is the message trying to get through to you, letting you know what you are doing to yourself.

◆ Avoid the extremes of indulgence and asceticism. Asceticism as a general rule is not advisable, but occasional deprivation can be useful. You can create contrast by depriving yourself of comfort for periods of time; this disrupts habitual mind patterns and deepens your awareness. Just make sure to take good care of your person.

◆ Bodywork can help integrate the energies of awakening in a grounded, balanced, and harmonious way that the mind cannot. Get a massage or other form of bodywork every now and then to help ease the transitions that you are going through as a student.

◆ Awakening often confers special healing abilities. Spiritual healing is a talent that we all possess. Although spiritual healing can produce amazing cures, healing is not the goal of spiritual life. The goal of spiritual life is Liberation: the cure of everything, including death.

◆ Stay healthy in the easiest, most natural way possible. Relate to your body consciously. If you identify with good health, you will never be truly healthy, because fear of losing it will gnaw at you. If you identify with ill health, you will stay sick because you rely on illness to define you. Either way you suffer. It may be difficult to disidentify from health issues, but you must do so if you are to grow in consciousness. Good health keeps you alive long enough to awaken; just make sure that you take care of your health consciously to keep it from becoming a source of suffering.

A NOTE ON THE ETHICS OF EATING MEAT

Ahimsa, Sanskrit for "non-harm," is a doctrine of not harming any living being. Although *ahimsa* is an important guideline for ethical living, you cannot live without killing other beings. You kill ants with your feet, carrots with your molars, and bacteria with your immune system. Mind-attachment is a crushing wheel, creating beings, destroying them, and resurrecting them again for more pain and death. Awakening is the highest form of *ahimsa* possible.

Eating meat is not necessarily cruel. You can eat meat and still be a student of the true Teaching. Animals feel pain, but they are not conscious in the same way that human beings are. It is not possible to act cruelly toward a plant, but wanton plant destruction is a symptom of unconsciousness. A free being would not destroy plants without a valid reason. They are part of your own body. Treat all beings well, including plants and animals. On the path of awakening, veganism or vegetarianism, although allowed, are not required.

Honoring forms of life is essential on the path of Liberation, but you cannot help but kill creatures. You can only try to minimize your deadly impact in the world as a compassionate practice. Try fasting from harm. Fasting from harm means to become aware of the harm that you are causing animals and perhaps eating less meat or wearing less leather. This awareness helps you because it is motivated by compassion. Compassion is at the heart of non-harm and can lead to Liberation, which frees you from all notions of harm, non-harm, and everything else.

Animals suffer greatly because of human beings—but only because the majority of human beings are unconscious. Nature as we know it is a realm of killing other beings to survive. It is not unnatural for an eagle to eat a fish, a lion to eat a zebra, or for you to eat a ham sandwich—in the world as we know it. "As we know it" means that the world appears to exist independently because of our mind-dominated understanding. Ultimately, eagles are not eagles, and lions are not lions. Nature as we know it exists only because it is a projection of the mind's self-devouring, dog-eat-dog nature. End the nightmare of killing to survive by awakening for the sake of all beings, including predatory animals, carnivorous plants, and flesh-eating bacteria. Even grains of sand are liberated by your awakening. How is this possible? Wake up and see for yourself. There is an order of Reality that is beyond description. Follow the word "peace" to its origin, and you may begin to get an idea.

Being kind to animals is important, but who among us has never eaten meat, used products tested on animals, or worn leather? Most of us have done these things. The key is to cultivate compassion and reduce your harm to animals as much as you can to a reasonable degree—and *do the work*. Remember that awakening is the greatest service you can render to all life forms.

EMOTIONS

Emotions are feelings that are easy to name, such as anger, hurt, and fear. We feel them in the space of our body, so body awareness is important in making them conscious. Emotions occur when the mind's judging activity causes a disturbing movement (from Latin *emovere*, to move, agitate, or disturb) in the flow of energy through the body. The mind does not flow naturally, but reacts and resists. Attachments move, disturb, or agitate the natural flow of energy in the body similar to the way a boulder disturbs the flow of a river. This disturbance causes a strong feeling state, or emotion.

Emotions are part of what makes us human and are not necessarily problematic. The key is to make them conscious so they don't dominate and inform your thoughts, speech, and actions unconsciously. A conscious person can *have* emotions, but an unconscious person is *had by* his emotions. His emotions run away with him. Emotions, when they are held unconsciously, take you away from yourself, removing you from inner peace, moving you out from your center, away from balance. An important part of the spiritual path involves making emotions conscious, taking away their ability to cause harm. For example, unconscious anger can harm others when it is expressed, but conscious anger cannot. When an emotion is made conscious, it is as if the "boulder" of disturbance is surrounded by an envelope of peace that holds, dissolves, and neutralizes it, reducing it to rocks, pebbles, sand, then nothing. That is the work of a conscious person.

It doesn't matter whether emotions are considered positive or negative; all emotions are disturbances in the feeling-body that detract from the natural peace of conscious embodiment. For example, people often pursue things or experiences that give them positive emotions, thinking that this will satisfy them. But eventually things are lost or experiences end, and the positive emotions give way to negative ones, leading to a tumultuous, roller-coaster experience of life. The key to lasting satisfaction is to become conscious enough that you no longer attach to things or experiences, and then it doesn't matter, because your oneness with Being brings you joy regardless of what arises within the field of your experience. Any emotions that arise, whether positive or negative, are mere disturbances to be made conscious. They are what they are. Their roots are dissolved into serenity. Just remember that an intense emotion is neither good nor bad; it just is. To be with it without judgment is a fundamental aspect of spiritual work, even if it feels "negative" or "bad" to do so.

Over time, unconscious emotions can aggregate within you as structures that must be met consciously and dissolved. As you become more conscious, these feelings well up inside your awareness. As they arise, just notice them and hold them within the open, nonjudgmental space of your awareness. This is the fundamental practice, to be present for these old emotional structures as they well up inside you. At times, you may arrive at a point of manageable repression—a sort of plateau of emotional development—and be tempted to remain there, thinking that no more work is necessary, but you must keep going if you want to be free. If you are afraid of the dark emotions underneath the ones you have already healed, just keep going. Healing isn't complete until all of it has been uprooted. Any negative roots that you leave untended will eventually spawn emotions that you can't repress or ignore.

The unconscious state is dominated by emotional pain. This is the litmus test. If you are still being dominated by negative emotions, you have more work to do. Don't let the presence of negative emotions be the source of more negative emotions, as in feeling bad because you feel bad. Break the cycle of negative emotions by witnessing them nonjudgmentally.

Since the mind resists the natural flow of energy in your body, let your body help you get into the flow. Embodiment exercises are an excellent way to deal creatively with emotions and help make them more conscious. Embodiment practice is especially useful for working with strong, crude, or explosive states of emotion. Meditation (covered in the next chapter) is an excellent way to deal with emotions on a more refined level. For example, it is nearly impossible to sit in meditation when you are overcome with rage. To deal with rage, you might use intense, prolonged (yet conscious) movement such as vigorous dancing or walking to reduce the amplitude of the emotion before you sit. This combination of embodiment and meditation practice—first for strong emotions, then for more refined ones—is similar to how the eye works. In the eye, the cornea is used for coarse focus of an image, and the lens is used for fine focus; they work in tandem. For optimal vision, both are necessary. It is often helpful to use embodiment and meditation practice in a similar way, using the former then the latter to get the best results.

EMOTIONAL RELEASE

In the process of consciously reducing strong emotions, you may experience an *emotional release,* a purging of old emotions *en masse* in a bout of crying, wailing, or even screaming. This kind of release may last a brief moment or an extended period of time. Although many believe that some kind of catharsis is necessary for an emotional issue to be resolved, it is not always the case. In many instances of profound emotional healing, a cathartic release is unnecessary.

Because emotion arises from identification, strong emotion is eliminated by disidentification from its cause—an unconscious mental pattern—as well as from its affective content. But in order to release all of it, you must also disidentify from the process of purging itself. If you have an emotional release but identify with the process, you will only cathart the energy of the emotion without disidentifying from the false sense of self at its root. To be totally free of the emotional pain being released, you must surrender all identification, including attachment to the need to purge. For example, if you try to force an emotional release to occur, you will be attached to the process and will obtain only minimal benefit. A healthy emotional release is spontaneous, unplanned, and unforced, surrendering all content down to the roots of self-motivation.

To cultivate the possibility of a healthy emotional release, develop your consciousness through practice. Do the work and allow what is to be. See if a part of you is trying to force the process. As you become more conscious, emotional healing will occur, and release may or may not happen. If it does happen, allow it. Observe what is happening with nonjudgmental awareness. The more conscious you are of the root of the emotion—some form of identification—the more unconscious material will be burned away by your attention.

If you feel a strong or disturbing emotion, practice in a way that corresponds to its particular form and intensity. Different emotions such as sadness, fear, and anger may require different approaches. Embodiment practices vary but are generally useful for all forms of intense emotion. Feel which one is right for you. Take your time. Let the conscious process do what it needs to do. Different layers of emotion may reveal themselves. If a spontaneous release occurs, allow it consciously. As a student of the Teaching, your job is to relate consciously to what occurs, regardless of its form.

CONSCIOUS EXERCISE

To help make physical exercise more conscious, think of it as embodiment practice. Do it mindfully. The word "practice" implies that you are in a process of conscious development instead of just whipping your body into a state of submission. Exercise has taken on a negative connotation in many people's minds, as something that *should* or *must* be done. Considering it as a form of practice ties it in with your spiritual path. That consecrates it to consciousness and makes it more enjoyable. You can say that you're going to "work out" or "exercise," but by keeping it conscious, you transform it into embodiment practice. Pay attention to thoughts, feelings, and sensations as you move. *Allow yourself to enjoy it.*

Pleasure is not the same thing as joy. Pleasure is a state of positive feeling in your nervous system that eventually subsides or transforms into its opposite, pain. Joy does not have an opposite and is always there, waiting for you to tap into it. For example, drugs can give you pleasure, but they cannot give you joy. Allow yourself to find the joy in your embodiment practice. It may not be present at first, but give yourself to it as consciously as you can, noticing any resistance in you. Notice any thoughts you have that criticize, complain, or argue with what you are doing. Allow the thoughts without judging them. Feel the sensation of your body as you witness the practice. Notice if you feel any irritability in the space of your somatic awareness. If so, breathe more deeply into it and allow it. Feel the inner space of your body. You may notice emotions in your center connected to the irritable sensation. Just become aware of the sensation-thought-feeling-emotion complex as a structure and be present for it as you deepen your somatic awareness. The deeper you go with this practice, the more conscious your embodiment becomes. Eventually, you begin to unravel any negativity you are storing in your body down to its root in the sense of self. Then you realize that all negativity is anchored in a false sense of self defined by a core resistance to what is.

Negative body image issues are an extreme example of the egoic resistance that we are doing all the time. The mind says that the body should be other than it is. That is what gives it a sense of gross materiality. Ultimately, this tendency to judge the body and derive a sense of ultimate substance from it drives people to obsess about ways to perfect it, but perfection is impossible. The body cannot be absolutely flawless. It is always going to be slightly imperfect, aesthetically or functionally speaking. It cannot be anything but what it already is. Acceptance of one's form of embodiment is at the core of any kind of health, but especially emotional health. Many people use exercise as a way to torture themselves, using the thought "I should be thinner," or "I should be more muscular," or something similar to motivate them to act. If your motivation to exercise is a thought that disagrees with what is—in this case, the state of your body—the results will not last. If they do last for a time, you will be straining against Being to keep up the charade. If exercise is not enjoyable, it is not worth doing. If you say, "I *should* exercise more," don't. Allow joy to move you into an activity, and your body will love you for it. Spontaneous, free, enjoyable exercise is the only way to stay physically active and not get stressed about it.

Below are some embodiment practices that can be useful. Regardless of which ones you use, the key is to use them consciously and find the joy in them.

Breathing

Breathing is one of the best ways to deepen your sense of meditative focus, taking you down into the space of your body and into the places where you hold onto fear, tension, and stress. Breathing relates to "inspiration" and connects with the flow of energy in your body as well as other important subtle phenomena. Lie or sit down comfortably and allow yourself to relax. Notice your breathing. Is it fast or slow, deep or shallow, full or restricted? Allow your breathing to become deeper as you continue to relax. Notice the sensation of air filling up your lungs and the sense of fullness in your upper abdomen as your diaphragm expands your chest cavity. Then breathe more deeply, into your lower abdomen. Breathe into places of tension or resistance, allowing them to soften. Let the breathing free any anxiety you may feel. Notice any thoughts and let them go. Notice the content of your awareness and just breathe. Focus on the sensation of the breath and allow yourself to sink deeply into a peaceful, restful, meditative state.

Listening to Music

Listening to music consciously can shift your energetic state, causing profound feelings, ecstatic sensations, or emotional release in the feeling-space of your body. Lie down, relax, and listen deeply to a piece of great music. Use the best sound equipment you can find and adjust the volume to the loudest level you can comfortably enjoy. Let yourself feel deeply into the music, paying attention to somatic sensations. Let it vibrate your body. Breathe slowly and deeply and allow yourself to relax. Allow the vibrations of the music to enter places of restriction, noticing these areas and softly breathing into them. If you have any anxiety or compulsive thoughts while doing this, just notice them and come back to the sensation of breath in your body and the vibration of the music. Feel what you feel and allow yourself to be carried away by it.

Vocalization

Vocalization is the utterance of sounds in an uninterrupted stream until the quality of energy and presence shifts within the space of awareness of your body. Singing, toning, and chanting, for example, can be useful by taking them into places deep within you. Vocalizing for extended periods can allow sensations to vibrate more energetically into the inner recesses of your somatic awareness. These sounds do not have to make rational sense, although they can, depending on your mood. Let yourself be spontaneous. Let the vibrations break up the holding patterns you may feel inside. Instead of catharting the energy through projecting it forcefully outward without really feeling it, allow yourself to feel the interface between the sound of your voice and the sensation of the energetic out of which you are vocalizing fully and consciously. Allow the point at which the sound emerges to be just as important a focus for your attention as the outward movement of the sound and the inner space out of which the sound is moving. Try to feel the sound and the movement as a manifestation of what is inside you, and let the awareness of the emergence of the sound sink more deeply until you touch into more profound levels of feeling. Do this as consciously as you can, and you can transform trapped emotional energy into more open and refined states of feeling and consciousness.

Stretching

Stretching is an excellent practice for feeling more deeply into your body. Allow yourself to breathe slowly and deeply as you stretch. The most important thing to remember is to focus on the sensation of the stretch and breathe into it slowly. This slow stretch, breath, and movement takes your attention out of mental processes and deeper into your body awareness. Allow the energy to move. The breath keeps your awareness focused and open, allowing the energy to flow through the inner space of your body. Remember to pay attention to your breathing as you stretch. Stretching opens channels of energy through the areas of your body that are being stretched, but much more so if you stretch mindfully, using your breath to keep the energy moving. Allow the stretching to open channels of energy that connect anatomical structures of your body previously perceived as disconnected. Instead of thinking of your body as a set of disjointed structures, feel them as energetically connected, flowing, moving, dynamic aspects of a living field of embodied awareness.

Movement

Intellectualizing spirituality is dangerous because the mind cannot handle the force of awakening by itself. *Movement* can help integrate and stabilize the process. Work the body vigorously and dynamically instead of staying in your head. Allow the energy of what you feel to flow into the sensation of movement in your body as a conscious field of presence. Feel what you feel as you move. Just about any kind of physical movement can help you deepen your somatic awareness. You can bring a new kind of attention into your regular activities: housework, yard work, driving a car, carrying groceries—any kind of movement you encounter as your day progresses. Even walking is a form of energetic embrace of somatic presence by paying attention to how you move, what it feels like, and the breath that accompanies it. If you want to engage a more intense process, you can dance vigorously to rhythmic music, exercise consciously at a gym, run or hike in nature—but the form of your movement is less important than the quality of your conscious attention as you move. Pay attention to the thoughts, feelings, and sensations in your body without judgment. Breathe. Deepen your awareness. If troublesome thoughts arise, notice them and allow them to be what they are. Feel the space of your body. If you feel restrictions or negativity, just notice them and keep moving. Do not force the movement, but allow it to emerge naturally from your conscious awareness of Being.

Bioenergetic Release

Bioenergetic release involves elements of all of the above—breathing, vocalization, stretching, and movement (with or without music)—combined with the awareness of energy and its movement within the body, often leading to an emotional release. Find a place where you will not be disturbed (and where you will not disturb others). Become quiet and notice what you feel. Staying with the feeling, begin to move, gradually developing a vigorous, prolonged movement. As you breathe and move, allow the energy in your body to build with a steady, rhythmic intensity. This kind of vigorous movement and breathing is conducive to emotional release, so if it occurs, allow it. You may feel an urge to shout, scream, or cry; if so, move with the energy, projecting it outward. Just make sure that you do so consciously, paying attention to what you are thinking, feeling, and sensing as you move, or you will just cathart the energy and not truly transform it. Put yourself into it totally. Do not force it but let the energy of the movement build sufficiently to allow for a spontaneous release. Let it come from deep within you. The movement must be intense and prolonged enough to tap into the energy of the deeper feelings so that it can be released.

CHAPTER SEVEN

MEDITATION

Everybody in the world knows the word "God," but there are few people in the world who know God.
—Joel Goldsmith

God is either Known directly through Identity, or He is not known at all.
—Franklin Merrell-Wolff

MEDITATION VERSUS MEDITATION PRACTICE

*M*editation and meditation *practice* are not the same thing. Meditation is Truth's conscious relationship with Itself. Meditation practice is conscious activity that develops that relationship in your awareness. The goal of meditation practice is to *be* meditation: to *be* That which is in conscious relationship with all that is. Meditation has no goal, but is the ultimate end of all human striving. It is the end of all seeking, practice, and experience. Meditation practice is *getting* there; meditation is *being* there.

Meditation practice is necessary for growth in consciousness until awakening occurs. After awakening occurs, you don't need to practice anymore because you literally *are* meditation; you are conscious relationship walking around being what it is. Practicing meditation is like using training wheels on a bike. Once you know how to ride a bike, you can take the wheels off because you don't need them anymore. Once awakening has occurred, meditation practice is no longer necessary. You may practice for fun, as a teaching tool, or as a charade—but you no longer depend on it as you once did.

Meditation can be approached by either a positive or negative method. The negative method is to recognize mental content as ultimately false, like seeing the true nature of a mirage—whereas the positive method is to recognize Truth directly, like gazing into a deep well. You can do either of these or both at the same time. The negative method is far easier, because while falsehoods abound and are easy to detect, Truth Itself is subtle, invisible, and more challenging to recognize by a direct approach. When Truth is approached in a positive manner, it is far too easy to affirm *ideas* about Truth and confuse them for the real thing. As the *Brihad-Aranyaka Upanishad* notes, the Divine is "Not this, not that." When the substantiality of objects is negated, Truth is revealed. Therefore, if you are a beginner on the path, it is recommended that you embrace the negative approach as a primary method until you gain sufficient spiritual maturity to recognize Truth directly. Eventually, once you have gained enough spiritual maturity, you will be able to recognize the Divine directly in all things.

MINDFULNESS

The basic meditation practice is *mindfulness*. Strictly speaking, mindfulness is pure nonjudgmental awareness, a mode of Being that comprehends objects in their essence, without attachment. If you are aware of something, you are already greater than it is, meaning that your awareness encompasses it completely.

Consciousness requires contrast. For example, you cannot be aware of black letters on a black page; you must have a non-black background to see them. You cannot be fully aware of an object until your awareness has transcended its boundaries and seen what surrounds it. You cannot fully see what something *is* until you can also see what it is *not*. If you can witness a thought fully and refrain from judging it, it collapses. Thoughts are made of judgment. When you witness them nonjudgmentally, you cease to support them as independent entities in your awareness. Free, nonjudgmental awareness is the Light that banishes all shadows, the Great Space that undermines all resistance and reveals Truth. When you are unconsciously attached to a mental object, it dominates you because it is greater than your sense of Being. When you become aware of it fully, your true nature—pure consciousness—encompasses it, and it can no longer harm you or make you say, think, feel, or do things unconsciously. Doing this requires a highly trained mind that does your bidding instead of the other way around.

You must learn to focus your awareness. *Concentration* is the ability to focus your awareness, to keep it trained on an object. *Attention* is focused awareness. This focus can be large or small, diffuse or precise—like a floodlight, spotlight, or a laser beam, depending on its degree. The degree of focus depends on your ability to concentrate and attend actively. You must be able to broaden, narrow or deepen attention at will. It is essential that you develop this ability through meditation practice. Regular practice strengthens your ability to attend to objects and recognize their Emptiness. This is not an activity of the ego, but of Truth.

You must become present. *Presence* is the radiant quality of Being that emanates from you when you are in conscious relationship with Truth. This radiant quality shines forth from you and shields you from negativity in all of its forms, whether from within or from without, when you are more conscious, or present. This shield doesn't reject negativity; it radically accepts and dissolves it. This radiant field also brings peace, healing, and Freedom to all within its activity. To become present, you must deepen your attention into the realm of Being within you, tapping into the absolute Source of all that is, recognizing thoughts as empty phantoms. Either the mind dominates you or you dominate it. Your presence is required.

When you no longer argue with Reality, no longer fight it, no longer try to wrest control from the uncontrollable, you accept it as it is. If you're not sure if you accept Reality as it is, ask yourself if you have any lack of peace in your Being. Are you hurt, sad, angry, fearful, bored, or upset? Do you generate emotional disturbances within your feeling-body? If so, you're not accepting Reality. Notice this nonjudgmentally. Notice the thoughts causing your discord. If you meet them consciously, they vanish, losing their power to cause pain or inform your sense of self. Notice how, in order to keep discord going, you have to blame it on forces outside yourself: people, things, conditions. These are just thoughts. When you attach to them, you are causing discord. Notice that you are causing all of the discord in your experience.

Growth in consciousness involves shifting your locus of identity from thinking to Being. When you grow in consciousness, you evolve from a sense of "thinking is who I am" to "Being is what I am." Thinking is not who you are; Being is what you are. Mindfulness practice lets this transition happen—if you do it regularly. Do it as often as you can, even daily. Regular practice builds your capacity to witness phenomena consciously, deepening your sense of Being.

Mindfulness practice trains the mind to withstand the force of awakening as you become more conscious. As we approach the threshold of awakening, it is the development of your mind that keeps ego from subverting the process. Your mind is developed by consistent practice. When the mind is disciplined, it becomes strong and can handle the dissolution of the controller. Mindfulness practice is a discipline that strengthens your ability to be present with a process consciously, holding it in a space of nonjudgmental awareness. Fear is a byproduct of the dissolution process; mindfulness helps hold fear in an unconditional space that dissolves it as it arises. In this space, there is a profound willingness to *be* in the face of dissolution. This rock-solid fearlessness does not waver, but stands firm while the controller collapses and disintegrates.

Remember that you need a true Teacher to instill your practice with absolute value. You can't just sit in the lotus position by yourself for long periods and make anything happen through your own mind power. Mindfulness practice is worthless unless you have a true Teacher who instructs you to do it, whether in person, from within, or from an authentic secondary source, such as scripture or an empowered teacher. You may be able to access the inner Teacher on your own, but an external Teacher makes contact easier. Tune into the original Source when you practice. Make sure you learn from the true tradition and not from an irreverent spinoff. Study the original Teachings of the meditation Masters—the Teachers of past and present—and let them guide you. Get as close to the Masters as you can. The closer your inspiration to practice is connected to its original Source, the more effective your practice will be. If you use a meditation instructor, make sure she embodies the Teaching.

FORMAL AND INFORMAL MEDITATION PRACTICE

Generally speaking, *formal* meditation practice is performed in a specific manner in an environment insulated from the chaos of daily living, whereas *informal* practice occurs in a more general manner as you go about your day, using ordinary events as opportunities to practice in the moment.

The most common form of formal meditation practice is *sitting*. If you want to engage in formal sitting meditation practice, it is important to do so in a specific way. For example, if you are too comfortable, you'll fall asleep. If you are not comfortable enough, you'll get distracted by aches. Generally, it is best to avoid the extremes of too much and too little comfort. Find a quiet place, sit down, relax, and pay attention to your breathing. Allow the sensation of breathing to anchor your attention so that it doesn't wander. If your attention does wander, gently bring it back to the breathing. Notice the thoughts, feelings, and sensations that arise in your field of awareness without judgment. If you judge, notice that you are judging, as well as the thoughts and feelings that result from judging. If you have a Teacher, sitting for long periods (more than an hour at a time) is unnecessary—although it can be enjoyable. Sitting for short periods is more effective, and sessions can be interspersed throughout the day.

Whenever you can, meditate with your Teacher. When you meditate with a Teacher, especially if you know her personally or have received personal meditation instruction from her, you are connecting with Truth on a profound level. Sitting silently with a Teacher in meditation is one of the most powerful practices available. The problem many students have with sitting in silent meditation with a true Teacher is a sense of *nothing is happening* because no verbal teaching is being given. If you sit in meditation with a Teacher, no verbal teaching is necessary because you are inducted into a deeper awareness of Truth just by being there. Sitting silently is usually more powerful than receiving a verbal teaching because the linguistic mind is not actively engaged. Instead of processing information, you are *just being.*

People often overlook the power of silent Teaching. I have seen this happen many times. Students ask: "Why are we just sitting here instead of *doing* something? I can do this at home." You cannot do it at home—unless you happen to live with your Teacher, which most students do not. It is a costly mistake to equate the verbal Teaching with *something is happening* and the silent Teaching with *nothing is happening.* Silence is the ultimate Form of the Teaching. If you alienate yourself from That, you cannot even get the essence of the verbal Teaching and are truly lost.

THOUGHTS, FEELINGS, AND SENSATIONS

Mindfulness involves conscious relationship to thoughts, feelings, and sensations. On the spiritual path, thoughts, feelings, and sensations are not suppressed but allowed, helping to make them conscious. This is a way of controlling them without resistance. This form of controlling is called *being with what is, as it is, without judgment,* similar to the way the sky controls clouds. This kind of control is not through fear and opposition, but through recognition and radical acceptance. This kind of control is *mastery.* Mindfulness practice stabilizes your awareness so that Truth reveals Itself to you. Mindfulness is a focused quieting of mental noise that allows your true nature to emerge consciously in the space of your awareness. Mindfulness practice is training the mind to be still so that Truth can be revealed. When you master your mind, you have mastered everything.

Mindfulness involves *noticing.* The term "noticing" implies something simple and free. Noticing involves a gentle awareness of breath and a calm observation of thoughts, feelings, and sensations that arise within your awareness—without judgment, as if you are listening with the absolute Stillness of your Being. The mind may find it hard to grasp that mere noticing has any value, but it does. It has *depth.* The deeper and more stable your noticing becomes, the more your mind may rage against it, thinking that something more complex is required, but if so, *just notice* that.

You can connect with Silence by sitting quietly and listening into the space of your awareness, but you will probably notice that your connection is interrupted by thoughts and negative emotions. Do not judge these raucous intruders; noticing them is all you have to do to get still. Mental noise and negative emotions persist only because you judge them as *bad* or *wrong.* What sets them free is your unconditional acceptance. They can persist only if you judge them. Instead, accept them and see what happens.

Notice how the mind finds peace boring, silence stupid, and stillness intolerable. The mind rages against these things because they emanate from your true nature; the mind is afraid of being destroyed by them. The mind tries to survive just like any other entity. Notice this and allow yourself to become still. Intuit that Peace, Freedom, and Stillness are far preferable to conflict, restriction, and agitation. To find the former, you have to be willing to relinquish the latter. Be willing to find them. Be persistent. Subdue the stubborn waves of the mind on the patient shore of your attention.

Notice how you react emotionally to sensations. Notice how judgments about sensations cause irritation, fear, or sadness in your emotional body, such as getting frustrated when your back aches. Notice that judgments hurt only when you attach to them, when you believe that thoughts are true. Eventually, you will become more conscious of your tendency to attach to thoughts about sensations and the pain that results when you do. A typical, unconscious reaction is experiencing a sensation followed by a painful emotion and assuming that the sensation caused the emotion without noticing the judgment that caused the pain. In a conscious reaction, you notice that the pain is caused by a judgment, not by the sensation itself. Notice how you get irritable, afraid, or sad when you experience certain sensations, such as getting angry when a door slams, irritated when a glass shatters, or annoyed when a fly buzzes around your ears. What judgments do you have about these sensations? What do you feel? Be honest.

In addition to sensations, tune into what you are feeling emotionally. Notice the difference between thoughts and feelings. Develop your feeling vocabulary. Tune into what others are feeling. Notice your experience. Don't assume. To confirm what you perceive in others, ask them questions—and make sure you ask the right questions. "What are you feeling?" is an appropriate question—not "*How* are you feeling?" or "How are you *doing?*" or "How is it *going?*" or "Are you *okay?*"—but "*What* are you feeling?" To move more deeply into Being, the answer must be an actual feeling, not a thought. Ask yourself this question to go deeper into Being and ask others this question when you want to communicate with them more clearly. Answering this question accurately requires a great deal of courage and emotional honesty. Valid answers are often expressed as single words: *angry, frightened, sad, elated, hurt, vulnerable,* and so on. These words represent actual feeling-states, not thoughts.

Often, when asked the question, "What are you feeling?" a person will answer, "Nothing" or "I'm fine" or "I think that ... " and similar statements. These are all forms of dishonesty. First of all, it is impossible to feel *nothing.* You are always feeling *something,* even if it's just a physical sensation such as fatigue, hunger, or restlessness. If you would rather not answer, say so—but don't say that you feel *nothing.* Second, "I'm fine" is not a feeling, but an evaluation, a judgment—a thought that is a kind of unconscious cop-out people use to avoid engaging their feelings. Make sure you answer with a true feeling, not a thought. Finally, any statement that begins with "I think that ... " is a thought, not a feeling. Keep asking the question "What are you feeling?" patiently until you get to a true answer, an actual feeling, such as *irritated, happy, lonely, peaceful,* or *embarrassed.* Emotional honesty is essential if you are to become more conscious. You must become aware of what you are feeling, because emotional pain is a sure sign that you are attaching to a thought as well as an opportunity to free yourself from your attachment.

The ability to express sensations and other feeling states is important, such as, "There's a hot fist in my back," "Lizards are crawling up my spine," "I'm all choked up," or other imagery involving colors, shapes, sounds—any way to name and become conscious of energy structures as forms of resistance. The more receptive you become, the more detailed is your sensing. Feel these structures lightly, as if you were touching them gently. Allow yourself to feel inwardly with great delicacy, like trying to sense the shape of a sand sculpture while blindfolded. How you touch anger, how you contain sorrow without repression, how you deal with fear is a large part of your path. As you become more conscious, you sense and feel things differently. You grow in your ability to perceive them and be with them with more awareness.

Learn how to sit mindfully with the entire range of feelings in your experience. As we saw in the previous chapter, it is often helpful to use embodiment practices to work with more intense, outward emotions such as anger, then meditation practices to work with more subtle, inner, or obscure feelings such as fear.

FEAR

Fear is the feeling generated by the ego's resistance to Freedom, its avoidance of annihilation. The ego is rooted in fear. Because fear is intimately involved in ego formation, it is unavoidable. Root fears arise from early childhood impressions as the sense of self is forming. These areas become sensitive and tender because the personal boundary is violated by a perception of a dangerous world. Adult fears grow out of these violations; their root is a sense of *I don't want this; this shouldn't be happening; get it away from me.* Fear is the raw feeling generated by the ego's struggle to stave off oblivion. To awaken, your awareness must penetrate to the deepest levels of your fear, to your core, and disidentify from all selfing.

As you meditate into your core emotions, they become more empty, vulnerable, and obscure. Emptier states reflect energy liberated by profound unknowing, the most raw or "naked" of which is the pure, undiluted fear of death, or *terror.* People want to be liberated from this core terror and the garden variety anxiety on its surface but proceed in the wrong way by avoiding it. Paradoxically, wanting to end anxiety is its ever-renewing cause. Seeing anxiety for what it is without trying to get rid of it ends it. Try to be with it fully without grasping or avoidance. Stay with it. Feel it so clearly and profoundly that it dissolves into Formlessness.

Terror defines selfing: a feeling of existence we assume is real, similar to a constant stomach cramp whose cause we never question because it has always been there. We try to get rid of it by resisting it, but this strengthens it and keeps it going because it is caused by resistance. We think that we have to resist fear to get rid of it, but instead we must accept it. Resistance strengthens it, and radical acceptance destroys it. To find Freedom, you must investigate the terror in your experience fully, accepting what you find there all the way down to the root.

Fear of death can be abstracted to things you own or with which you otherwise identify. When you value a thing, you attach to it and give it a sense of self, as if it were part of you. Then you fear its loss just as you would fear the amputation of a limb. Identification with phenomena makes us more fearful, whereas disidentification from them helps us function more fearlessly.

Is death real, or is it just a concept? In my experience, it's a concept. There is no such thing as death. On the relative level, death is the end of biological life, but on the absolute level, death is empty. Like petrified children huddled around a campfire, it's just a story we tell to anyone who will listen.

If you are afraid of death, you shrink. You get smaller. This shrinking sensation feels uncomfortable, so you mentally tell yourself *this shouldn't be happening* in an effort to get rid of it. This is like trying to eliminate a pile of dirt on the floor by cursing it. But you cannot get rid of dirt by cursing it, nor can you get rid of fear by saying it shouldn't be there. Resistance causes fear, pain, and negativity. Destroy it by acknowledging that it's there. Be with it nonjudgmentally until it dissolves. This is the only way. If you suppress the fear, you just drive it into your subconscious where it will haunt you. Others sense your fear and react to it because you transmit a fearful message: *this shouldn't be happening; this isn't right; I don't like this; I'm not okay; make this go away.* Sweep the pile of dirt from your floor. More is hidden in the corners of your attic, your basement, not to mention a whole world of dirt just waiting to get back into your house. Although the world is made of dirt, you will not miss it.

HURT

Hurt is a painful reaction to fear. Hurt is the pain of vulnerability, the intuition that your ego is in danger of annihilation. In a manner of speaking, hurt is part of the personal boundary system generated by the ego. The ego uses hurt to keep you from investigating your fear too closely, like a wound that is sensitive to the touch. You must probe into it to find out its cause. You can't just cover it up and expect it to go away. Hurt is a smokescreen to keep Freedom at bay. You must penetrate it to get to the fear underneath.

Put simply, hurt is the painful wound on the surface of your fear. The deeper you go into it, the more personal it feels, and the more it blends with existential terror. The closer you get to the roots of the sense of self at your core, the more raw, naked, and vulnerable it feels. The key to getting rid of your hurt is to deeply investigate the thought-structure of self and consequent fear beneath it until it is all gone.

ANGER

Anger is a defense against the vulnerability of hurt and fear. Anger comes in many forms. The most intense forms include fury, rage, and wrath; these often produce violence. Moderate forms include contentiousness, aggressiveness, and hostility. Subtler, more insidious forms of anger include irritability, frustration, and annoyance. All of these are common emotions. They are often blamed on others, such as in "He makes me furious," or "This situation is frustrating." A cardinal rule is *no one can make you feel anything.* What actually happens is you have an experience, judge it, and the judgment creates a disturbance in your feeling-body. The judgment is something that you are doing to yourself, causing the resulting emotion. *No one can do that to you but you.* To keep from doing it, you must refrain from judgment. No experience is ultimately right or wrong; everything simply *is.* Until you consciously embody this insight, you will continue to rage against, argue with, and get annoyed by things beyond your control (i.e., everything).

Become aware of anger as you move through your day. For example, when you speak, notice what feeling is moving you. If anger is moving you to speak, notice that it creates a field of hostility in your feeling-body. If you can pay attention to the anger without judgment, you are allowing consciousness to take over the harmful emotion and keep its negative, destructive energies from harming you or anyone else. Conscious anger is not a problem because it is held, contained, and reduced within the unconditionally present space of your awareness. That renders it harmless and allows you to communicate about it without verbally spouting noxious insults, attacks, defenses, rationalizations, and just plain whining. A name for this kind of toxic outpouring is *spewing*. When you spew, you pollute your environment with negativity.

Unconscious anger is always destructive; it will kill you if left unchecked. One of the key feats you must accomplish on the path of awakening is the taming of your anger. You cannot tame anger with judgment, only with radical acceptance. Expressing anger unconsciously is dangerous because you may act violently toward yourself or others. But holding it in is also dangerous; repression of anger can become extremely involuted, causing illness or depression. The third way is consciousness. If you see that you cannot safely either hold anger in or express it outwardly, you must surrender to what *is* on a level that you cannot understand. Then you can practice being present for it. For the sincere student, anger is an opportunity to practice.

Unconscious anger expresses itself energetically as weaponry. The more intense the anger, the stronger the weaponry, everything from a rusty knife to an atomic bomb. The quality of the angry mind is like a knife blade, barbed wire, or broken glass. The phrase "staring daggers" reflects this; anger can feel like sharp knives when projected. Some people can feel like porcupines from across the room because their chaotic and defensive mental energy is projected outward like spiky armor. We often say that someone has a "sharp" mind. An unconsciously angry mind can "cut" you, as with a "cutting comment." When used consciously, the mind is like a fine scalpel that can help you make precise intellectual distinctions. When used unconsciously, it often strikes out and lacerates anyone within striking distance.

THE "SNOWBALL" OF JUDGMENT AND HOW TO STOP IT

Judgments snowball until the mass of mind-material overwhelms you. It is important to know how to break the cycle. Notice if you judge, and then notice if you judge yourself for judging, and then notice if you judge yourself for judging yourself for judging, and so on. If the tangled mess is too complex and hard to follow, just notice the feeling of all those judgments until you can discern patterns and notice those. The better you get at noticing what you are thinking and feeling in the moment, the quieter your mind will become, and the more you will be able to notice individual thoughts before they can spin out of control. You must see yourself exactly as you are in the moment without flinching or turning away, without apology or rationalization, without creating a "me" out of it—as in *I'm no good because I'm angry and I'm angry because I'm no good.* That is how you get wound up tight. That generates more anger. You are afraid of dissolving, so you contract in fear, judging yourself to defend against dissolution. Ecstasy is terrifying for the ego to taste, much less BE.

Your mind will try to lash out and get you involved in its ugliness by getting you to judge yourself for judging. Remember, you are not your mind. If your mind lashes out, notice it but recognize that you are the *witness* while your mind is the *perpetrator.* Let it show you what you are doing unconsciously, because on some level you are imbuing your mind with a sense of self that keeps it going. The mind tries to get you to identify with it. You are not your mind, but you are responsible for its behavior, in the same way that you are not a vicious dog, but if you own a vicious dog, you are responsible for watching it and keeping it from attacking others or responding appropriately if it does attack someone. As you go through your day, notice what the mind is doing. Keep it on a leash. Discipline it by developing discriminating awareness. Often, the mind lies in wait for you to let your guard down. If your mind suddenly rages out of control, just notice it. Like a vicious dog, *it's not who you are.* It may feel like you, but it's not. You must witness it impersonally and see it for what it is, without judgment. This keeps you from beating yourself up when you see what it's up to.

Judgment obscures your true nature and keeps you from having permanent peace and satisfaction, like a pond that is clogged with trash. If you unclog the pond and tap into life without judgment, you will taste the sweetness of Freedom like spring water from a pristine well, the Truth you have been looking for as long as you can remember.

PARANORMAL EXPERIENCES

Paranormal experiences are extraordinary events in your awareness and may include extraordinary sensory experiences, blissful emotional states, or other forms of experience. On the path of awakening, all forms must eventually be seen as relative and thus empty of intrinsic value. This is also true for subtle or ecstatic states. The key is not to get caught up in them but to see them as they are and move on.

Extraordinary sensory experiences may be experienced as vivid sights, sounds, tastes, smells, or tactile sensations. These experiences are byproducts—not goals—of practice. Perhaps they are interesting, but they are not ends in themselves. If they occur for you, simply notice them and let them go. Visions of angelic messengers, holy visages, or light beings are not absolute goals. Enlightenment does not necessarily involve seeing lights. You may see them, but this is incidental to awakening, something that is ultimately of no consequence—like froth on the ocean, not the ocean itself.

Meditate to become more conscious, not to have special experiences. Perceiving lights or colors of a subtle nature may be a relative effect of your practice but is not necessarily a sign of awakening. Any perceived objects, subtle or otherwise, are merely content within consciousness, not consciousness itself. Consciousness has no color, shape, or attribute. Don't think that seeing colorful visions or hearing subtle sounds are anything more than fantastic encounters on the path. Notice them and move on.

Blissful or ecstatic emotional states are not goals of meditation practice. Although upwellings of rapturous euphoria may occur in the process of authentic spiritual practice, they are not the goal of the path, nor are they necessary. Intense emotions are often mistaken for a sense that "something is happening," when it's really just more noise. Notice emotions and unusual states, but do not cling to them. Awakening is the "peace beyond understanding," not an affective disturbance of the emotional body. Do not be fooled into thinking that emotions are an object of value in the sense of "something is happening," that you are being swept away in a torrent of ecstasy or a flood of tears and that this experience has value in itself. All experiences are phenomena, and all phenomena are rightly understood as essentially empty.

Awakening is not inherently blissful, if what you mean by bliss is ecstatic pleasure. Awakening is inherently blissful if what you mean by bliss is peace beyond all comprehension, radiant joy of Being, and the satisfaction of completeness. Calmness, peace, and perfection are forms of bliss. Although surges of this feeling can be quite intense, Freedom has nothing to do with anything like a drug high. High is defined by low, so a high eventually becomes a low, even if the high is generated by endogenous brain chemicals. The brain is a natural pharmacy, and yogis long ago learned how to raid the medicine cabinet, so to speak, via special practices such as fasting, sleep deprivation, hyperventilation, intensely focused mental processes, and so on. These practices do not in themselves produce Liberation, although they may give you a good short term buzz.

Forget about attaining blissful or ecstatic states as things in themselves. Get so busy doing the work that you don't care if you're blissed-out or not. When you're devoted to the true path, satisfaction is complete, like a rock being a rock. Nothing can explain this until you devote yourself to Truth with real compassion and determination. If being blissful is a condition of your path, you are just seeking a high. Freedom is not a high. It is the condition of Reality prior to striving, thinking, or feeling. Give yourself to what you cannot predict, predetermine, or understand, and joy may reveal itself to you. Freedom is neither a positive nor a negative state. If you need to be happy, you're in trouble. If you try to be a positive person, get ready to be a negative person, because it's the flip side of the coin you're tossing.

SHOULD, WANT, AND NEED

The unawakened state is characterized by resistance or *this shouldn't be happening*. Suffering is caused by a split between Reality and what you think it should be. When what *is* happening and what you think *should* be happening are different, you suffer. To the degree that you energize what you think *should* be happening in opposition to what *is* happening, you experience the pain of unconsciousness, like steel plates grinding against each other.

How do you know what should be happening? Look around; it's happening.

There is nothing you can do about it.

In addition to a *should*, resistance can also be expressed as a *want* or a *need*: this *shouldn't* be happening then becomes I *want* this not to be happening or I *need* this not to be happening. If what I *want* to be happening or what I *need* to be happening is different from what actually *is* happening, I generate pain and unconsciousness. For example, consider the following statements: "It *should* be raining." "I *want* it to rain." "I *need* it to rain." If it's not raining, attaching to these thoughts hurts. In the awakened state, I recognize that what *should* be happening, what I *want* to be happening, and what I *need* to be happening are all the same thing.

Additionally, what you *truly* want is not necessarily what you *think* you want. In other words, what you think you want may not be in your best interests. For example, imagine you're hiking with a friend and you find a cave. You would like to explore the cave, but your friend knows that an ornery grizzly bear lives in it, and you don't. You say, "I want to go in that cave." Your friend says, "Trust me. You *don't* want to go in there." In this case, what you think you want may not be what you truly want. This is also true for what you need. A drug addict may say, "I need drugs," even though drugs are killing him. What you truly need may not be what you think you need. Make sure you know the difference.

STRESS

Resistance causes *stress*. Stress is a form of pain, like an uncomfortable tension or pressure. What is pressing down on you is the weight of your attachment to thoughts. If you're *supposed* to do something, you'll do it. What *needs* to happen, happens. What you truly want, what you truly need, and what should happen are exactly the same thing: *what is happening now*. Once you recognize this to the core of your Being—not just intellectually, but as the essence of all that is—you are enlightened.

What could be simpler and more obvious than the fact that what is *is?*

You can't change what is happening now, so trust it. You might as well. It always *is*. It may be something else in the next moment, but now it just is. The only way to change it is to fully accept it—then you can do anything you want, because you are at one with it. In this way, surrender is victory, because you lose your illusions and gain awareness of Reality.

Trust what is. Trusting what is is the same as putting your faith in God. How do I know God's will? I look around and see what is happening now. What is happening now is God's will. It might as well be. What is happening now is neither right nor wrong, good nor bad, hopeful nor hopeless; it just is. If I really trust God's will, I trust Reality. This is the essence of faith. This doesn't mean that I don't act. I do—just not out of a sense of resistance, but from a recognition of Truth. Attachment to anything as wrong or bad is the same as resistance, negativity, or pain. It hurts when you argue with Reality. This is so fundamentally simple that we miss it and perpetuate our suffering. We are all running around looking for certainty, when it's right in front of us.

This is it.

For example, being late for an appointment while stuck in traffic is typically stressful. The next time you get stuck in traffic or are running late, notice if there is a part of you that strains against what is happening in the moment. If you do, also notice how your body feels, how you are tensing up around the mental resistance ("This shouldn't be happening!"). Then realize that you are straining against something you can't change. What's more pointless than straining against something you can't change? This is like straining against Mount Everest, trying to get it to move. In fact, you are more likely to move Mount Everest than to get Reality to be different than it is now.

The way to end stress is to recognize that what is *is*. As simplistic as this sounds, it works—not the *thought* of it, but the *Reality* of it. You have to meet your mind with radical acceptance, with a presence that doesn't judge. Your stress is caused by judgment. The mind says that what is happening shouldn't be happening, which flies in the face of Reality. The way out is to notice what is happening: thoughts, feelings, and sensations—without judgment. If you do judge and have a reaction that is stressful, just notice what the reaction feels like. Do not judge it. If you do judge it, notice that reaction. Keep practicing, and eventually you will be able to hold stress in the palm of your hand like a wounded parakeet. At some point it stops hurting and flies away.

If my beliefs differ from Reality, I am out of touch with Reality—a form of insanity. What is more insane than thinking that something shouldn't be happening when it *is* happening? When I resist what is, I feel a tension in my body, a sense of contraction. I think or say things—negative things, forms of *this shouldn't be happening,* such as *I hate this, I wish this would go away, make this stop, this is bad,* and so on. The way out of this painful state is to *practice.* Ask yourself, is it *true* that this shouldn't be happening? What do I *feel* when I argue with Reality? How do I *act?*

Notice the thought causing your tension. If you think about it, it has you. If you meditate on it, *you* have *it.*

Resistance is trying to get Reality to go your way, which never happens. Even when this seems to happen, it's never perfect. Have you ever seen anyone with a perfect life? Have you ever seen a person whose life always goes exactly according to plan? The basic experience of the unawakened person is that sometimes things go his way and sometimes they don't. Things never go entirely according to plan. There is always something off, a feeling that something is missing. What is missing is *conscious awareness of Reality.* When you think that Reality should be something that it's not, or when you want or need it to be different than it is, you are in conflict with it, pushing it away from you. This generates a constant background sense of anxiety, unease, and discomfort. Don't you just want to be relieved, to feel that everything is all right? Of course you do. Everyone wants that. Just give up trying to have things on your own terms. Allow what *is* to be.

It is obvious that you do not control others' thoughts, but ask yourself: do you control *your* thoughts? If so, who's doing it? Do you plan your thoughts, or do they just happen? Just as your lungs breathe on their own and your heart beats on its own, your mind thinks on its own. It just *seems* that you are in control. A nerve center in your brain may control your breathing, but what controls the nerve center in your brain? Who controls the controller?

Who's running the show?

Meditation is not thought suppression. Meditation is thought Liberation. Instead of suppressing thoughts, develop a more conscious relationship with them. The idea that meditation involves suppression of thoughts is a common misconception. If you try to suppress thoughts, you will just frustrate yourself, because suppression of thoughts is unnatural, like trying to grip the earth with your body to keep it from spinning. It wears you out.

Your nonjudgmental awareness burns away layers of mental obfuscation as the sun burns away fog. Like slippery eels, thoughts elude your grasp. Instead of grasping, notice them; let them thrash around in the space of your awareness. Trust your ability to eliminate what bothers you through peaceful observation.

Let it happen.

AVOIDANCE BEHAVIORS

Resistance often gives rise to *avoidance behaviors,* or forms of unconscious activity that distract you from awareness of what you are feeling. Mild forms of avoidance include unconsciously watching television, talking, eating, exercising—virtually any ordinary activity performed unconsciously. Extreme avoidance behaviors often manifest as obsessions, compulsions, and addictions. Train your awareness to recognize avoidance behaviors before they take you over. For example, if you move to turn on the television, check to see if you are feeling a difficult emotion and unconsciously reaching for a distraction, something to keep you from feeling it. If this happens, stop. Take a breath, relax, and notice what you are feeling. Become aware of the emotion and try to discern its cause. If you develop the habit of noticing avoidance, you can disarm it before it overwhelms you.

We act in ways to avoid feeling the pain that we have been creating because it hurts to feel our past, our deceptions, our anger—but it hurts more to avoid it, because avoidance keeps it going. You must be willing to feel pain you have repressed if you truly want to be free. The varieties of avoidance are endless, but the root of avoidance is the ego, and all avoidance behaviors stem from it. All avoidance behaviors are forms of selfing, of turning away from Freedom. The self-contraction turns inward on itself and shuts out Reality.

Strong avoidance behaviors are ordinary activities that can manifest as compulsions and addictions, such as overindulging in drugs, food, sex, work, or risk. For example, some people work compulsively to avoid engaging deeper feelings or relationships that encourage feeling-awareness. Observe yourself carefully and notice if you are behaving compulsively. Notice what you are feeling. Notice if you judge yourself and be present for your experience. Notice if you unconsciously reach for food to soothe an inner ache. Become aware of any tendencies to numb your pain. You may feel emotions such as guilt, shame, self-hatred, or even anger. Recognize that these reactions arise from attachment to your mind. If you can become conscious in the midst of this experience, you will feel more peaceful.

Stay with the practice of nonjudgmental noticing of what you are feeling until you notice a difference. Keep practicing to develop your ability. Just get quiet and sit for a while. Don't talk, watch television, read, or listen to music. Just sit still. You may notice a vague sense of "something is wrong" or "this shouldn't be happening" creeping into your awareness, whether in the form of thoughts, feelings, sensations, or all three. For example, you may begin to feel irritation, a low grade form of anger. Try it for an hour. After a while, you may feel that you cannot stand it. Stay with the process and let your attention be firmer yet lighter, more accepting and yet fully present.

Resistance stresses you out, and avoidance keeps you from noticing it. It makes you tired, hurt, and sad. The small amount you witness when you sit still enough to notice it is only the superficial layer. There is much more under the surface that is tormenting you, as if gremlins and goblins were needling your insides. Noticing dissolves it. Noticing is an excellent practice. Keep practicing. Write down a few avoidance behaviors that you discover and notice under what conditions you indulge in them, what feelings you are avoiding, and how your feelings change when you allow them fully.

INQUIRY

Inquiry is meditation in the form of asking questions and listening within yourself for the answers. Awakening is a form of direct inquiry into things, revealing their essential nature.

Inquiry is depth-penetrating investigation. Find out what is causing your pain by inquiring into it. Notice how you complain about your experience, observing thoughts in your head such as *it shouldn't be raining* (when it is raining); *I want John to stop bothering me* (when he is bothering me); *I need to be out of debt* (when I'm not out of debt). These are all stressful thoughts because they argue with Reality. Attaching to them is like driving a car while pressing the gas and the brake at the same time: a hot, grinding sensation. That hot, grinding sensation is your mind grating against Reality until it's so painful that you have to stop the pain, so you look for drugs, sex, or some distraction to numb it, to take your mind off of it. But that's just the situation: your mind *is* on your pain whether you like it or not. Your mind is grinding, screeching, straining against what it perceives as "things not being what they are supposed to be." Find out what it is resisting, and you will find the source of your pain, or at least a significant part of it. Keep going until you have found all of it.

As in mindfulness, inquiry involves becoming aware of thoughts, feelings, and sensations as forms of resistance. To inquire, become aware of thoughts, feelings, sensations, and emotions that result from attachment as well as any actions motivated by the resultant thought-feeling-sensation resistance complex. Next, notice if you further judge the consequent "messed-up" life situation. Then notice if you judge any further thoughts, feelings, sensations, and so on. Notice if a "snowball effect" is present and break it at the root. The ultimate root is a sense of "me," but the branches are discordant feelings. Inquiry involves finding the discordant feeling and tracing it back to the root, or as close as you can get to the root, which is always a thought-attachment.

Stop the mind. Ask questions. Write them down. This helps freeze your toxic think-tank long enough to blow it to bits. Eventually, it becomes second nature. Awakening is inquiry into what is, as it is, in the moment. The awakened person *is* inquiry. Inquiry is a method of more consciously being the Awakener that you already are. Once you do enough inquiry to get free, it's just who you are, and the questions ask themselves, silently. The awakened person is a walking koan solving itself before it can exist.

For inquiry to produce results, you have to ask the right questions. Fundamentally, you are inquiring into Truth, Reality, and Being—synonyms for the Absolute. You are trying to find out what is *true,* what is *real,* and who you *are.* We will look at all three.

Inquiring into Truth

The only way to break the grip of the world's hypnotic spell is to investigate your beliefs until they fall apart, revealing Truth.

Consider the following statements: *I hate my life. The world is unfair. I want to die. I wish things were different. It's everybody else's fault. It's God's fault.*

Have you ever had thoughts like these? Take each of these statements—or similar statements that you believe are true—and, with each one, ask yourself if the thought behind the statement is true. The fundamental question is "Is (fill in the blank) absolutely true?" Keep filling in the blank and inquiring until you find the Truth of it. You will find that no thought, statement, or belief is absolutely true. It is up to you to find it. No one else can do it for you. You may intellectually *appreciate* that no thought is absolutely true, or you may think you *know* that no thought is absolutely true—but that's just a thought. You have to actually look at the thought that is causing your pain and ask yourself if it is true. Keep going until you get to the bottom of it.

Go deeper, always deeper.

Remember that the answers to inquiry must come from a deeper place than your mind. Inquiry takes you into your depths, to the threshold of recognition, the place from which the ultimate answers emerge. If the answers arise from the mind, you're just getting more of the same old worn-out concepts instead of Truth. Thoughts don't give you peace. You must go beyond thoughts to get peace. You can't just shove them off to the side, stuff them down, or sweep them under the carpet. If you do, they'll come back to haunt you. The mind is a haunted house of your own construction. It's condemned, and you must inquire until it's razed.

Inquiry doesn't work if you don't do it. You have to practice consistently to get results. If you have any questions about it, keep practicing.

When you reveal Truth, you discover Reality.

Inquiring into Reality

What is real? You are dreaming the world with all its characters into existence right now. This world is no more real than a dream world, regardless of how real it may seem. Analyze your basic assumptions about Reality until you recognize their essential Emptiness. Inquire into the nature of *things*. Make everything a meditation. Inquiry is a daily practical necessity. You cannot get rid of the world on the world's terms. On its own terms, the world will eat your lunch. As long as you value the relative as absolute, you will never be free.

Reality is an all-pervading oneness without any separation or division. Realize, though, that while it is useful to contemplate the undivided nature of Reality, it is more useful to locate and inquire into the thought-attachments that keep you from its complete recognition, the divisions that make it seem manifold. When you inquire into thought-attachments fully, you reveal their Emptiness, their ultimate nature. The thought-attachments that block your awareness of Reality concern the nature of *things*. What appears as a world of *things* to unawakened people is simply the illusion of dependent arising, or the Absolute recognizing Itself in its relative appearance.

Things are temporary. Things can be threatened. They can be broken, lost, or stolen. If you inquire into the nature of things, you will find that they lack substance. If your throat, heart, or abdomen clenches in fear at the thought of losing things, realize that it's your attachment that is causing it.

Can anything real come and go? Ponder an object and consider what makes it real, if anything. Will it endure, or will it perish eventually? What is the substance of life? What is ultimately real? What is valuable? What matters? What is important? What truly satisfies? You must get serious about it. You must get to the bottom of things. Question everything. Notice how the mind spews out judgments, and notice how it hurts when you believe them. Even happy, positive judgments are waste matter. A thought-made world is like a straw box on fire. Thought-attachment robs your aliveness then kills you, only to recycle you again. It's not worth it.

When you discover Reality, you find Being.

Inquiring into Being

Who are you? No *things* means no "me." This false idea of independent "things" creates fear in the person who owns or is otherwise attached to them—especially the "me." Any sense of control over events implies that things and events exist independently of a thing called "you." Since no *things* independently exist, your self-concept does not independently exist.

Self-inquiry is simply asking the question "Who am I?" consistently, repeatedly, and in a focused manner as a way of disidentifying from mental phenomena and recognizing your true nature. The false self, the "you" that is perceived as an object, is not who you are. Who you are is the profound mystery of the ages. You cannot grasp the answer to this question because you *are* it, just as a hand cannot grasp itself. Use this question to inquire into everything until you arrive at who you truly are.

"Ah," your mind asks, "but what is that?" This question is a form of grasping. The mind is looking for an answer that it can cognitively understand. Suffice it to say that who you ultimately are cannot be grasped by the mind. It cannot be understood. Notice the grasping. Just notice.

Being is who you are, not the mind-created false self. To truly find Being, you must inquire into its nature, to feel into it. What *is* it? Go deeper. What is it *not?* Go deeper still. When you have inquired into what Being is *not* fully, you will have discovered what it *is.* Since Being is formless, inquire into the forms of self-identification until they are all gone. The creator of forms is the mind, so inquire into thoughts. Inquire into concepts. All forms are concepts, and all concepts are judgments. As you inquire into your judgments about yourself, meditate on them and be with them unconditionally. Notice that when you do this, they fall apart and lose their power to upset you, revealing a profound Peace within you, like melting a haunted igloo with hot water.

The ego survives by convincing you that you and it are the same. You are not it, no matter how real it seems to you. You must disidentify from your thoughts, beliefs, and knowledge until the ego collapses. You can ask "What is Truth?" or "Who am I?" and arrive at the same end. In order to render yourself harmless to others, liberate yourself from the idea that you are an independent entity. You must ask yourself, "Who am I?" until you find your true nature, which is the same as asking, "What is Truth?" because Truth is what you are. Thinking *I know who I am* is equating yourself with a concept, because the mind only knows concepts. Investigate this self-concept until you get to the bottom of it. When you get to the bottom, keep going.

Eventually, the bottom falls out.

Recognize that who you are is beyond all thinking. You cannot know who you are with your mind. In order to truly know yourself, you must go beyond the mind. This is not a concept. It's Reality, and you're It.

The last judgment to go, the last silly stand against Freedom, is "I exist."

MEDITATING ON IMPERMANENCE

Why would you invest in what's impermanent? It doesn't last. Would it make sense to put all your money into a stock that was guaranteed to fail? Physical beauty, wealth, fame, and worldly power inevitably fade. To view the impermanent as permanent is failure. To view the impermanent as impermanent is success. Being *in* the world is not the same as being *of* the world. For example, it makes sense to groom yourself and look your best, but clinging to beauty as an absolute value catches up to you in old age, when you cannot maintain your youthful allure. It makes sense to be financially solvent, but making wealth a value in itself creates pain when it cannot be made, is lost, or is subject to loss. Everything of the world is eventually lost. Everything eventually crashes and burns.

Permanence implies time. The idea of permanence is that some *thing* lasts. No *thing* lasts. No objects last. Anything that comes into existence must eventually cease to exist. All that is born must die. Beyond all ideas of permanence and impermanence lies Freedom.

Meditate on impermanence as you go about your day. With any experience, ask yourself, "Is this permanent?" Let the answers come from deep within you.

If you identify with phenomena, you have hitched a ride with death. All things must end. In your essence, you are not a thing, and you do not end.

This body will not last. It will fall apart. Why do you cling to it? Meditation on the impermanence of the body is perhaps one of the most powerful meditations you can do. Look at your hands. Do you see signs of aging? Will they last? What will they look like when they are lifeless and being consumed by worms? They will be gone in the blink of an eye. Eventually you will awaken to the Truth that your body is not ultimately who you are.

Why not now?

Watching clouds go by is a peaceful activity. However, if you were hypnotized into believing that the clouds were your possessions, you would be thrilled when they appeared and dismayed when they disappeared. More so, if someone hypnotized you by telling you that these clouds were your friends and had names, you would rejoice when they arrived and grieve when they departed. If someone told you that these clouds were really terrorists who were trying to kill you, you would be terrified when they emerged and relieved when they fled. Everything is like these clouds—even your body. Why would you attach to it as if it had value in itself? It comes and goes within the field of your awareness.

It is a mistake to place absolute value in the relative and relative value in the absolute. *What you have* is temporary; *who you ultimately are* is beyond all notions of temporality. Therefore, to establish absolute, timeless value in your life, realize that material possessions have only a relative, impermanent, limited value and use them to help you attain Freedom. Use the relative to attain the Absolute. For example, a luxury automobile has only a relative value. If you identify with it, it hurts when you eventually lose it. If you use it to transport you to a Teacher's lecture, its relative nature is redeemed because you are valuing the growth in consciousness it can help you get. In the former case, you are attributing absolute value (identity or Being) to a relative object, a car. The short-term result is pleasure; the long-term result is pain. In the latter case, you are attributing relative value to the car and using it to help give you absolute value: access to the Teaching. You may be able to keep luxury cars your whole life—but you lose everything at death. If you don't use the relative properly, you will lose all that you have when you die, as well as a feasible opportunity to awaken in this lifetime. Losing the opportunity to awaken in this lifetime (by not taking advantage of it when you can) is the gravest error you could make.

MEDITATING ON CYCLIC EXISTENCE

Most of us are attached to our lives as if they were precious. They are indeed precious, but only as a means to become liberated for the sake of others. They are nothing in themselves. *Meditating on cyclic existence* involves pondering the fact that although nothing lasts, the cycle of change is endless. What we call "life" is actually an endless procession of lives extending into the past and future as far as we can see, a relentless, crushing wheel of birth and death. What is born and dies is just an appearance, but we are attached to it. Death is not the end. Death does not extirpate the root of karma, the ego. We are not like flowers that bloom once then die, never to return. We are more like perennial flowers that, springing from a singular root, bloom and die in regular cycles, over and over again. The root doesn't die, only its offshoot. As long as the root persists, the flower blooms and dies every season. Awakening involves destroying the root completely.

Developing a severe distaste for cyclic existence is important if you really want to be free. Meditate on the suffering of one life—death, hunger, loneliness, sickness, and dissatisfaction—then let that sense expand indefinitely. Why would you want to be bound to a crushing wheel? You have to break the notion that samsara has something to offer of itself. Remember that the world has no independent reality. Clinging to it is like a man crawling across the desert, parched with thirst, licking an image of water drawn on sandpaper. It doesn't work.

Regardless of whether you *believe* in cyclic existence, it still hurts. You may not believe in an oncoming train, either. Whether or not you believe in it, consider that it is logical. Everything in the world is cyclic. Why would we be the exception?

Merely intellectual answers do not suffice. The illusion of time and space is ultimately inconsequential—but are you free of it? Meditate upon the hopelessness and dissatisfaction of cyclic existence—really meditate on it—until your white-knuckle grip on it has loosened. Eventually you will let go of it altogether and realize that it never amounted to anything more than an empty horror show.

In the meantime, go ahead and live. Give it all you've got. Live in the world; just don't trust it to satisfy you. It is not a source of ultimate satisfaction. It is a phantom that arises within your field of consciousness and subsides. There's nothing to it. That's what makes it beautiful. Living fully means seeing the evanescence, the transitoriness, the transparency of it all and *being* That which comprehends and encompasses the entire drama. Taste the snowflakes, but see the futility of crying over them when they melt.

When the universe melts, *I Am*.

THE NOW AS A FOCUS FOR MEDITATION

Everything happens *now*. What happens now is all that ever is, all that you ever have. The Now is like a space that contains all that is. Resisting what happens now is stress. Accepting what happens now is peace. Although what flows through the Now changes constantly, the Now is identical to consciousness—the Great Space in which all things live, move, and have their being. Unlike the Now, the past and future are mental fabrications. The past is a memory trace in the mind, and the future is an imaginary projection based on the past. Time is of the mind; it exists only when you think about it. Thinking requires time. The Now is timeless; it is not subject to thought. By the time you've thought of it, it has already passed you by.

The past is not a problem unless you live in it. Living in the past means that you derive a sense of self from past events, such as family history. Anything in the past is not the essence of who you are. If you find yourself dwelling on painful memories, you are giving them a power that they don't have. Of course, like a physical wound, emotional wounds take time to heal. If you lose a loved one, grieving is natural and appropriate. In the awakened state, you grieve; you just don't derive a sense of self from it. Feelings pass through you, but you don't judge them.

Another way to live in the past is to indulge in fantasies about pleasurable past events, reliving scenarios that have already happened over and over again because there is an emotional payoff, but not enduring satisfaction, in doing so. If you do this, you are perpetuating your suffering.

Living in the future usually takes the form of anxiety or hopefulness. Either one of these is a form of pain. Anxiety usually turns out to be unfounded, and hopefulness at best leads to a gratified desire that quickly fades. You cannot get anything in the future. It's like a sign in a bar I've seen that reads, "Free Beer Tomorrow!" It's a joke: You'll never get free beer, because tomorrow never comes. If you take care of now, the future takes care of itself. An awakened person makes plans for the future, but she doesn't live there, and she certainly doesn't depend on a certain outcome, because the future is inherently uncertain. It's more fun that way. Take care of business now, and you won't have to worry about it later. Now is easy to deal with, because it's right in front of you. You just have to focus on it—then you can enter it and *be* it.

Although the future is uncertain, you can investigate your present ideas and beliefs about the future to see if they are true. The ones that aren't true are painful. For example, consider the thought, "I want the future to be certain." Is that true? Is that what you really want? Of course not, simply because the future *isn't* certain. Do you really want what you cannot ever have? "The future is uncertain" is a basic truth, and believing otherwise is painful. Can you ever really know if an imagined outcome, however wonderful it may seem, is what you want?

Of course not.

If you find yourself thinking excessively about the past or the future, don't worry about it. Just notice that you're doing it and gently bring your attention back to the present moment. If dwelling on the past or the future is causing you pain, investigate your thinking. You cannot change the past, but you can change your *relationship* to the past. The past is a trace in your mind and you can relate to it *now.* It is causing you pain *now,* even though the events happened in the past. The same applies to the future. If you are going to change it, you must change it now.

Eventually, you see the Now is all that is.

PRAYER

Prayer is the surrender of judgment about what should happen, letting Truth run your life. It is rightly understood as a form of meditation. The most common form of prayer consists in asking God for something for yourself, or petitionary prayer. This is not true prayer. Can you really know that you will be better off getting what you want? Can you really know what is best for you or anyone else? Since God's will is what is happening at any given moment, praying for a specific outcome implies *a basic distrust of God's will.* Not trusting God's will is a barrier to Liberation. If you really knew what was best for you, wouldn't you have made it by now? Wouldn't you be truly happy? True prayer implies surrender to God's will, to Reality.

What else is there?

If you are lost in suffering, prayer can help. The most powerful prayers often emerge from deep suffering, a painful bind from which there is no apparent escape. You've tried everything you know, and nothing is working. It gets worse. If you continue to fight, the pain is too intense to bear. What else can you do but surrender? What kind of prayer results from that kind of surrender? In my experience, it's some form of "Thy will be done"—a deep, heartfelt, guts-on-the-floor kind of prayer where the words "I don't know what to do; please help" pour out of you. If you sincerely want God's will above all else—magical things will happen. Your life can be transformed. Just "let go and let God." Since God is not a divine entity sitting on a throne, this doesn't mean that a power outside you is dominating your life, but a Power beyond your thinking is available for you to *be*—even beyond the boundary of your skin. Divinity is your own essential nature. There is no other place than here, no other moment than now, and no one else but you. You're It. Typically, and often most usefully, true prayer emerges from the agonizing depths of the erosion of control, deepening of faith, and utter helplessness of profound suffering that says: "I don't want this, but I don't know what else to do. Please help."

True prayer is surrender.

If you insist on having things go your way, isn't this the same as egotism? Most "prayer" is an exercise of the ego. The ego is the controller, and petitionary prayer is an attempt to control events, to somehow make them go your way. This kind of prayer is insincere, because it has nothing to do with God. God is not Santa Claus. If you knew what God was, you would not be able to stand yourself. God is not anything or anyone you can control. God is Reality, Truth, the Absolute. You'd have better success trying to control the weather. It is impossible to make Reality be other than it is now. It cannot be controlled. The more deeply you surrender to it, the more harmonious your experience becomes. The more you try to control it, the more your efforts backfire on you. False or insincere prayer strengthens the ego; true prayer erodes it.

True prayer can deliver you from difficult circumstances because it connects you with the Power that is everything. Things change not because there is a controller and something being controlled, but because Truth is recognized. When you recognize the Absolute as your true nature, the entire universe changes. It changes because your mind is a projector and your awareness is the screen. When you surrender deeply in true prayer, the shift that occurs in your awareness changes the universe all at once in the same way that turning a kaleidoscope wheel changes its picture all at once, including the interrelationship of its elements. Awareness is the substratum of all phenomena, as light is to a movie. If you project light through a shifting image, what appears as change is merely shifting at the projector. If your mind changes in accord with recognition of Truth, it becomes more deeply integrated, and the world reflects that.

In true prayer, you start with wanting something and end up neither wanting nor not wanting that thing. You let go. That's what allows Grace to give you what you pray for—which may or may not be the literal thing that you wanted. True prayer is surrender to Reality with a desired object or outcome as the thing surrendered, trusting that what results is "God's will." Prayer can be useful when you are confronted with something you either want or don't want. If you remain attached to an outcome at the level of desire and don't get what you want, you create pain for yourself. Even if you get what you want, the satisfaction does not last. Truly, what you want is what is happening now, because it *is*. Nothing can change the fact that Reality *is*, now. It is impossible to change that. If you do change it, that change takes time. Now is now. Eventually, after countless lifetimes, you surrender. When you surrender to Reality completely, it's you: the whole you-niverse, that which is, Truth, the Absolute, Thou-art-That.

AFFIRMATIVE PRAYER

To use an affirmation to alter conditions is just another way for the ego to get involved in your life. All attempts to control life are based on the fear that you will be destroyed. Fear is the god of the ego. Instead of trying to control Reality, fall in love with it and let it awaken you. Take control of your life by surrendering to what is. That is the supreme control of not trying to control anything. An affirmation, appropriately used, affirms Truth and takes you deeper into yourself. Inappropriately used, an affirmation creates more fear in you by giving credence to the part of you that doesn't trust Reality. Trust Reality by affirming Truth and thereby deepening your awareness of it, your own Being. Trusting Reality is allowing it to emerge tangibly.

Affirmative prayer can be useful, but only if done properly. The way to use an affirmative prayer properly is to contemplate its relative meaning and listen deeply within yourself for the essence of Truth it signifies, like music sounding deep within your Being. Don't just recite affirmations mentally; take them deep within you and recognize their absolute Value. This kind of prayer is called *Knowing the Truth.* This is not a cognitive knowing, but recognition. To practice it, find a passage from scripture and perhaps write it down. You don't have to say it out loud, but you can if you want to. Find a place where you can do it alone and undisturbed and repeat it quietly to yourself until you begin to recognize the Truth of it. At first, you take the saying in mentally, but then you meditate on it and let its deeper meaning reveal itself to you. Let it change you. Don't just use it for getting what you want, which doesn't happen often. When it does, this is Grace and can help you out in a tight situation. An affirmation properly used reveals Truth to you; that's all you need. Then you feel a deep sense of Peace or Satisfaction, and it's done. All you have to do then is go about your business, and the results become apparent. Knowing the Truth is a method of true affirmative prayer—not an affirmation that Reality conform to your desire, but an affirmation of Truth as the preexisting condition of Reality that manifests as harmonious experience.

The most effective affirmative prayer is the one that affirms what is already spiritually true. For example, "Thy will be done" affirms that God's will, or Reality, already is. If you pray this prayer deeply enough and with enough sincerity, you tap into the very Truth within yourself that *is* the answer to your prayer. You give yourself to Truth by affirming that it *is,* and there is nothing but *That.* It changes you.

Ultimately, there is nothing else.

CHAPTER EIGHT

COMMUNITY

*For where two or three are gathered
together in My name, there am I in
the midst of them.*

—Jesus Christ

*Who you are speaks so loudly I can't
hear what you're saying.*

—Ralph Waldo Emerson

GROUP PRACTICE

Human beings tend to worship in groups, whether in a Christian congregation, Buddhist *sangha,* or other spiritually oriented community. Most of us are familiar with the idea of group spiritual practice, even if we did not grow up in a religious or spiritually oriented family, because worshiping in church, for example, is an integral part of mainstream society. The main reason we practice in groups is the potent amplification of spiritual presence that occurs when two or more of us congregate and invoke Truth in that collective space. This space of relationship is created by the willingness to be the "One that is many." This amplification can be called *synergy* or *communion.*

The synergy of group spiritual practice is greater than the sum of its parts. Consistent group practice over a period of time builds a resonant field of consciousness that helps to sustain and empower its individual members. Although the Teacher must be present, it is not totally necessary for him to be *physically* present. The inner Teacher can be accessed through sacred media, such as scripture or video. If run properly, such groups can have a powerful transformative effect, even without the physical presence of the Teacher. It usually requires at least one person who is familiar with the sacred media to lead the group. Then it is quite easy to tap into the synergy principle. For example, if a few people congregate and read *The Gospel of Thomas* or *The Heart Sutra* from an authoritative text and at least one person (especially the group's leader) embodies a measure of humility and reverence for the prayer's Source, even a small measure, a potent spiritual Power is invoked. This same group could watch a video, sit in formal meditation practice, share energy, or practice in some other way. The key is that the group is somehow guided by the Teacher—whether physical or scriptural—and the practice is performed reverently. Although larger groups can magnify the effect greatly, the quality of participation is usually more important than the quantity of participants. Even a few people gathered together in this way can invoke a profound spiritual Power, often far greater than larger groups with less sincerity.

Working with a group allows you to participate in certain kinds of spiritual practice that you cannot do on your own, such as group meditation or energy sharing. In a group setting, meditation is more powerful because it magnifies the spiritual presence that is invoked by collective recognition. In group energy sharing, you allow yourselves to sink deeply into a meditative state and, with your hands either gently touching or hovering over another's body, sense into each others' presence and allow what you find there to flow between you. In this way, the relationship with the other person becomes a kind of meditation, and the other person becomes an object of meditation, wherein, as Jesus put it, you "Love the Lord your God with all your heart and with all your soul and with all your strength and with all your mind; and, Love your neighbor as yourself." In this kind of energetic communion, Truth and the person in front of you are recognized as the same One, and you are enacting the commandment to *be* That consciously. Groups are ideal for raising and sharing this kind of energy.

Another benefit of group practice is *accountability*. When you work with the same group of people in a spiritual setting over an extended period of time, they learn to spot your particular charade and many of them will call you on it. It is a sacred privilege to be called on your falseness in an authentic group setting because it holds you accountable for your particular state of unconsciousness. You can become painfully aware of your falseness. If you commit to the group for a period of time, it is important to stay and deal with the often abrasive self-awareness that prolonged social contact brings. You do this because you are more interested in consciousness than unconsciousness. Commitment and perseverance are important elements of your spiritual development.

The fellowship that a group provides—the sharing of friendship in the common context of participating in the work together—is deeply supportive of your path. Eating meals together, doing work together, and just spending time together are ways to enjoy the companionship of conscious human beings. Because of a mutual commitment to basic values like honesty, integrity, and compassion, friendship with fellow students is often of high quality and can support you when the path gets rough. The path gets rough when you begin to see and feel your own falseness. You need friends who can be honest with you and give you encouragement when you need it.

But you don't have to be friends with everyone in your group. On the contrary, you may not make close friends with more than a few people, and some of them may not like you at all. When you get a flock of egos in one room, all speaking their truth and running their patterns, sparks fly. You can get the most heartfelt support as well as the most scathing criticism. You can meet people who turn you on as well as people who turn on you. You can meet people who embody great humility and consciousness and you can meet the most arrogant and self-centered people you have ever seen. The ones you like are precious. So are the ones you don't like. Often, it's the ones you don't like who show you where you need the most work. You will often project qualities you don't want to see in yourself onto the people who push your buttons. It is important that you own these projections and find out why they bother you, because only *you* can bother you. Others just trigger your patterns.

People may seem like "others"—entities external and ultimately separate from you—but they are really spiritual mirrors in which you can see yourself with profound clarity if you take responsibility for your own projections. They are not ultimately separate from you. That is what other people show you, if you pay attention. We are That, together.

When working with a spiritual group, don't pretend to be evolved spiritually; just be honest. In a strong group, any false posturing that you manifest will eventually be exposed. The revelation can be painful. It does no good to be a "spiritual person." There's no such thing. You are either working toward Freedom or dawdling in samsara. Pretending to be advanced spiritually is not conducive to growth. Don't hide behind a false appearance. Don't mask your true feelings, like putting on a false smile when you are actually sad or acting cool when you're privately terrified. Be willing to admit unconscious behavior or negativity, even when it makes you uncomfortable. Be as honest as you can and strive to reveal your own falseness. It is only then that you can become more authentic.

Because of its magnifying effect, group practice can be intense and must be integrated into daily life. Coming home from a spiritual retreat to the friction of daily life can be extreme, like burning through lifetimes of experience in moments. The test of modern spirituality is to integrate your path into ordinary life. If you avoid integrating your path into daily life, your practice will suffer for it. You must be just as conscious washing the dishes as you are sitting in meditation. It is ineffective to live one kind of lifestyle with your group and another kind away from it, as if they were somehow separate. Group practice is an opportunity to be seen as you ordinarily are in a conscious environment, not to glorify a "spiritual" sense of self. Over time, you will become more authentic, whether you are with your group or elsewhere, and the division between the two—spiritual and ordinary—will disappear.

Sharing the path of awakening with a group of true friends is a profound celebration of relationship. Celebration is in every moment, every blade of grass, every realization. True celebration is not the airy-fairy avoidance of facts, but the embracing of facts without judgment.

Truth unwinds even the darkest passages in the human heart, blending them with the vast cornucopia of Being.

One word: autumn.

RELIGION

Religion comes from the Latin root *religare* that means "to bind back together," as in a re-ligature, a binding back together two things that have been separated. Religion implies that we are separate from the Absolute, from God, and that we need the church to bind us back together again, as a surgeon would reattach a severed body part. The only problem with this premise is that you are not separate from God except in your belief system. If you proceed from false premises, you get false results. To take the surgical analogy a bit further, true spirituality is more like debridement—a process of removing dead tissue to reveal healthy tissue underneath. Religion kills us by having us adhere to a belief system, and a belief system cannot save you. Religions are dead things usually built upon the original revelation of a liberated (or at least authentically empowered) human being and in most cases stultify or destroy what was once a vital source of liberating Power. Most religions don't want to save you as much as enslave you. True spirituality removes this dead matter and reveals the Reality hidden underneath.

If you think you are going to heaven, think again. A conventionally "good" person who attends church weekly does not "go to heaven" at death, no matter what she thinks, feels, or believes. There is no "place" called heaven. Heaven is not a place, but is your true nature unencumbered by belief systems. If you have not destroyed the ego-controller at the root of your mind or at least devoted yourself to a true Teaching, after death you will attract another set of parents and another body to inhabit and the lifetime of suffering that goes with them. The true Teaching differs from religion in that religion consists of myths and stories, whereas a true Teaching consists of Truth Itself and is not anything you can interpret with intellectual inerrancy. At the heart of many religions is an awakened human being. If you can find the true Teaching at the heart of a religion—like finding a pure, bubbling spring hidden beneath a slag heap—it can help you spiritually. In such a case, you are not liberated by the religion, but in spite of it.

A religion is really a system of beliefs. All belief systems and points of view are religious in nature, even atheism, agnosticism, materialism, and nihilism. Truth is not subject to belief because your mind cannot adhere to it. What works is a true wisdom culture that recognizes the value of the awakened Teacher—not as an exclusive deity, but as an example for all to attain. Buddhism and Christianity are examples of religions that to some degree deify their great exemplars: Siddhartha Gautama and Jesus of Nazareth, respectively. Regardless of what these religions claim, Jesus was neither Christian nor Jewish. He *is*. Gautama was neither Buddhist nor Hindu. He *is*. The awakened Teacher is identical with Reality as it is, *now*.

For the sincere spiritual aspirant, religion is not only unnecessary but is often more of an impediment to Liberation than an aid. It is not necessary to become a monk, nun, or priest to practice spiritually. In today's world, there are probably more nonreligious people sincerely seeking Freedom than religious people. Many from all over the world are now wanting true Liberation instead of mere conventional belief and are reading books by independent spiritual teachers. The challenges of living the true path in the midst of work, family, and society can be formidable, but necessary for most people, for whom the monastic life is not a feasible option.

For example, celibacy is still practiced by some, but it is unnecessary for spiritual progress. Although celibacy is a monastic tradition in many religions, it is not recommended as a way of life in the modern age because too often, unfulfilled sexual tension becomes a distraction to consistent practice. It is difficult for most people to practice celibacy outside of a monastic tradition (or inside one, for that matter). On the other hand, intimate relationships can also be a potent source of distraction—or an opportunity to practice, depending on how you look at it. If you use it as an opportunity to practice, sexuality can be a potent source of inspiration.

Instead of discriminating between religious and secular society as a meaningful distinction, notice the difference between *sacred* and *profane* society and let it inform you about your own sacred consciousness versus the profane ignorance that sometimes obscures it. For example, when you meet people, notice their qualities: honest versus dishonest, compassionate versus cruel, just versus unjust. Use the insights gained from these observations to inform your own path. Use other people and society in general as a mirror. Good and evil are inside us, and patient investigation reveals both their ubiquity and ultimate insubstantiality.

Without an accessible Teacher, the church is dead. Awakened Teachers can be accessed indefinitely if their recorded communications are properly maintained and transmitted over time. Otherwise, they lose their awakening power. For example, while Jesus' awakening influence is still available, his communication has been muddled over the centuries by unconscious stewardship. Find a relationship with the Awakener in the flesh; that is your true salvation. Trust no one else to lead you there.

If you recognize the limits of conventional religion and do not confuse belief with spirituality, membership in a church, mosque, sangha, or synagogue is not an ultimate obstacle to Liberation.

But eventually, when the time is right, you will leave all religions behind.

AVOIDING CULTS

Although Christian practice is centered around Jesus Christ and Buddhist practice around Gautama Buddha, many people think that practicing in a spiritual group led by a living spiritual teacher outside of a conventionally accepted religion is just plain cultic and wrong. One reason for this opposition is that many false teachings have wrapped themselves in the guise of authenticity and harmed people. Another, more insidious reason is that the average mindset is predisposed to attack the Teaching simply because it undermines ignorance. Taking the Christian and Buddhist traditions as examples, we can assume that the Teacher-community model is not only appropriate but is the standard. Healthy group spiritual practice with a Teacher is important and powerful. Therefore, the only important question is what constitutes healthy and responsible group practice and what does not.

A cult is a religion or religious sect generally considered to be extremist or false, with its followers often living in an unconventional manner under the guidance of an authoritarian, charismatic leader. If you decide to work with a spiritual group, make sure that it is balanced and healthy. If it is unhealthy, abuses of money, sex, and power are typical. A true spiritual community is not a totalitarian society, but a group of individuals who agree to meet for a certain period of time to focus on spiritual growth.

For example, in a healthy community, dissent is allowed. If the teacher or group of students is overtly manipulative, it's not a healthy environment. Speak openly and honestly in front of the group, including the teacher, about specific incidents of behavior. If an open, honest dialogue ensues, the system is working. If anyone ostracizes or tries to further manipulate you, leave.

Do not let anyone control your life. You are responsible for the actions you take and the decisions you make. Do not be a robot or take orders. Trust, but do not blindly follow. A true Teacher does not seek to control or dominate his students, but rather invites them to walk the path. He does not necessarily expect them to do what he tells them to do. The student is always free to decline, argue, or disagree. If a Teacher gives advice to a student on important life decisions, the student can ignore it. If a Teacher seems overbearing or controlling, it is up to the student to discern, investigate, communicate, admit if she is mistaken, and take appropriate action based on a well-considered decision. Do not cede responsibility for your life to anyone.

When you are looking for a Teacher to guide you, remember that the true Teacher is not necessarily an exemplar of ethical conduct on the level of his personality. It is a mistake to make him into a god or an idol, because you may be disappointed. It is your responsibility to have clear ethical standards, know what they are, and heed them. You can recognize the Teacher's ultimate perfection and adapt to his relative behavior. Always be willing to question the behavior of the Teacher on a "works or doesn't work" basis. It either works for you or it doesn't. On that level, he is a human being, just like anyone else, and is subject to the rules of ethical conduct. Do not let anyone abuse, neglect, or manipulate you, especially a person in a position of authority.

It is possible to *rely* on a Teaching without being *dependent* on it. To be dependent on something means that you cannot live without it. To rely on something means to trust it to give you what you need when you need it. If you rely on a Teaching, you need it in that moment. You may depend on the Absolute as the very foundation of all that is, but you decide to rely on a Teacher because of his qualities. You may decide to rely on another Teacher if you find that his style doesn't work for you. There are many forms of the Teaching on the relative level, yet only one Teaching on the absolute level. Find the best relative form of the Teaching you can and rely on it—but depend on the absolute form of the Teaching, which is Truth Itself. Do not depend on the relative form of the Teaching; rely on it as needed, or find another form that works for you.

Commitment to the group does not have to be a lifetime residential experience. Ideally, you can come and go as you please. A true Teacher does not control anyone or anything. Students enter into the relationship with the true Teaching willingly and are not coerced into staying. However, to work with the group on a certain level, the Teacher will most likely insist on a commitment of some kind. A lifelong, monastic commitment is not necessary. It is more likely that you will commit to a temporary course of group study with a predetermined termination date, after which you are free to pursue other options. It is best to work intensively with a Teacher, then take time to integrate the awakening process into daily life. As your involvement with the Teaching progresses, the level of commitment required usually deepens. This does not mean that you have to spend all of your time with the group, but that your time with the group has a deeper quality. You are expected to show up in accord with whatever agreement you have made. If you cannot commit to such a course, don't make an agreement. Honor your commitments to stay in relationship for whatever amount of time has been agreed upon.

Cults often use a complex hierarchy to manipulate adherents, keeping them at strict levels of access to the teacher and an elite "inner circle" of zealots. In the modern spiritual community, hierarchical organization is both unnecessary and outdated. The best organization is one whose formal structure is kept to a bare minimum. It is inevitable that relationships of different degrees of depth and intimacy develop along lines that are quite natural in a group setting. Access to the Teacher is determined by your level of spiritual maturity. Otherwise, there is no real determinant of "hierarchy," except where necessary. For example, a person who is entrusted with money, such as an office manager, must have a degree of privacy and privilege with regards to financial matters. This would be true in any organization that deals with money and is appropriate.

If a spiritual community does not have a healthy relationship with the surrounding community and society at large, conflicts can develop. It is important for the spiritual group to have a healthy relationship with the larger community in which it exists. It must maintain its own sovereignty as well as relate to the rest of the world. A healthy community is like a healthy group of cells in a body. A healthy cell has a semipermeable membrane that lets some things in and keeps others out and yet relates in a healthy way to other cells. Maintaining a healthy spiritual community requires the dynamic ability to relate appropriately to the local community and society. A true spiritual community is different from mainstream society because it serves a special purpose—the attainment of Freedom—but it's not better than any other group or entity, just different. It's not a matter of right or wrong, it's a matter of what serves the purpose of the community and what doesn't—or more simply, what works and what doesn't. A healthy spiritual community is one that works—both within itself and in relationship to the world.

For example, students are encouraged to maintain healthy relationships, including family and friends. Any activities pursued outside the domain of the spiritual group are relevant topics of discussion within the context of group spiritual practice. Students are held to a standard of spiritual, mental, emotional, and physical well-being. Abusive family relationships, destructive friendships, and unhealthy behaviors are held up to the light of open inquiry and shared values in the group setting; this can be deeply therapeutic and useful.

Awakening is best served in a context of what is truly healthy for students, and all relationships—people, money, activities, diet—are areas of potential inquiry and development within the context of the group setting. Family, friends, and activities are important and not to be discouraged unless they are blatantly harmful or abusive. Even so, as adults we are all free to harm ourselves. We learn through experience. Relationships and activities that no longer serve awakening fall away naturally when they are no longer needed and are a component of healthy change.

Maintain integrity with respect to your political views, sense of humor, dietary practices, personal aesthetics, hygiene—who you are as a person. In order to be a candidate for awakening, you must have a strong sense of self, but not so strong that it prevents awakening. If your personality is weak, it is impossible for you to tolerate the forces of expanding consciousness. In other words, the person must be well-developed and organized, yet receptive to new ideas and influences. If you have a healthy sense of self, you will not likely be seduced into violating your standards.

Ideally, a Teaching takes you past your comfort zone, but not so far that your moral standards are violated. You can always say "stop" if you want an experience to stop. If the authorities in the group or the Teacher himself urge you to continue, to transcend your limits, so to speak, you can decide for yourself whether to continue. If they disregard your request to stop or attempt to force you to continue, you can leave. Ultimately, in a healthy Teaching, they will let you stop if you insist, and you can discuss your decision later. A good Teacher urges you onward without forcing you to do anything. He stays in relationship with you and listens to your thoughts and feelings, if he can.

Spiritual practices awaken your intelligence; they do not dull it. If your group's practices stultify your mind instead of clarifying your wisdom, you're in the wrong place. Cults use mind-control techniques to dull your mind. Don't be fooled. True spiritual community tends toward wakefulness, not sleep. You don't have to surrender your individuality; it's better not to, and the best Teachers won't let you. The key is to surrender your ignorance, not your individuality. This requires a healthy, active intellect. A true Teacher will not ostracize you for skepticism or dissent. A good Teacher will continue to engage you in relationship without ostracism.

LEAVING A GROUP

You may contemplate leaving a group, and it is important to know how to do so appropriately. If you enter a teaching by gradual incre-ments, it is less likely that you will develop major conflicts with the teacher or the community. Know what you are getting into. Make an informed decision. Make no long-term commitments until you are reasonably certain that the teaching is true, then make sure it is healthy, balanced, and appropriate for your needs. Sometimes, the organization of students exhibits prohibitive levels of unconscious-ness, even if the Teacher is authentic. In these cases, you may want to relate to the Teaching from a distance or leave altogether. If the Teacher is true, it is appropriate to withdraw from the community without ending your inner relationship with him. A true Teacher will stay in relationship with you no matter what you do, as long as you can find him within yourself.

You can "create a safe distance" with an organization that is un-healthy or whose outward behavior is not within the realm of what you consider safe and appropriate by participating at whatever level feels right for you. You can do so without negativity if you refrain from making value judgments and base decisions on what works for you and what doesn't. If you want to stay involved with a Teaching but keep a distance from its community, make sure the impulse is arising from Truth and not from fear. The key is to stay in relationship with the Teacher from a distance, obviating the need for extensive personal contact with the community.

If you leave a community, make sure you do so *facing the cen-ter*. Facing the center means leaving with respect for the Teaching, so neither you nor anyone else is harmed by your actions. Appropriate inner relationship with a true Teacher is a subtle bowing within your-self, acknowledging the validity of the Teaching by turning toward it and giving yourself to it to some degree. Facing the center is similar to leaving by never turning your back on the Teacher and never ceasing to bow toward him inwardly. This means that you never cease to respect the Awakener, of whom the human Teacher is an outward form. If you direct negativity in his direction, you can harm yourself spiritually. A healthy attitude is, "I respectfully decline to participate in the community at this time, I have no ill will toward the community, and I wish the highest good for all concerned."

Committing to a true Teaching is a major responsibility and is best not taken lightly. If you commit to a Teacher and violate that commitment for a trivial reason, for example by leaving before a predetermined course of study is completed, you may be doing yourself great harm. It is a blessing for your Teacher to inform you of the nature of the violation and advise you not to leave and is not the same as coercion, harassment, or intimidation. A warning is appropriate because the danger is real. If you then decide to leave, it is appropriate for the Teacher to let you leave, even if you are harming yourself spiritually by doing so.

WORKING WITH DREAMS

Working with dreams is an excellent group practice because of the powerful feedback you can get from others who listen to you as you share them. Dreams are helpful on the path of awakening but they have to be used properly if awakening is to be served. Let your dreams wake you up. Let them show you patterns hidden beneath the surface of your awareness or illuminate ongoing issues. Sometimes dreams can scare you, but let yourself be scared if that is what it takes. Let them show you the demons hiding under your bed. Let them shock you into a new awareness. They don't have to be disturbing, but the important ones will get your attention. They may be intense, bizarre, or frightening. They can also be weirdly beautiful or enigmatic. Feel them deeply and let them speak to you. Let your interpretations be intuitive.

Dreams are revealed from a deeper level than waking consciousness often allows, and sharing them openly in a committed group of students with a Teacher is one of the greatest gifts you could possibly receive. You must take the information you get from others in the group and use it to become more conscious of what Truth is showing you. Dreams can be entertaining but are best used for more than entertainment. Don't relate to them in a shallow way. Don't allow a superficial or cookbook analysis to suffice. Don't let anyone tell you what your dreams mean without checking in with your deepest feelings on the matter. Feel the dream deeply; don't just approach it intellectually. Also, don't read too much into dreams that are not that important. Focus on the big dreams, the ones that are especially intense or meaningful. Dreams that have liberating power are often hyperreal, extremely vivid, and vibrant with energy. These dreams typically wake you up and are virtually impossible to forget, even without writing them down. You may feel them energetically in your body. Pay attention to them and work to discern their meaning.

A group can help you see the deeper meaning of a dream if you share it responsibly. If you are in a group of committed students, you have already established a measure of trust so that you can reveal your dreams to them. Dreams are like deep secrets about yourself; you don't want to share them with just anyone. Some people would try to use your inner secrets against you, even without knowing that they are doing it. In addition to people in your group, you can share dreams with someone you really trust, such as a therapist, friend, or family member. Make sure that you have someone conscious who can listen deeply into the dream and share insights into it that you may not have noticed.

On a deep level, we all share the same dreams. When giving feedback about someone else's dream in a group, it is important to make the dream yours, as if you are experiencing it for yourself, and speak from that place. For example, before offering your interpretation, you can say, "In my dream ..." or "In my version of this dream ..." because otherwise you may be just foisting a dry mental interpretation upon the sharer that does not serve her. When you hear someone share her dream, tap into it and make it your own. Put yourself into the dreamscape to see what *you* see from the same perspective. Don't speak to her as if you were quoting from a textbook on dream interpretation. Really feel it, and perhaps it will reveal something about the conscious process of your relationship.

Many dream symbols are universal and can be studied in manuals on the subject. Some are obvious or well-known, and others are mysterious and may take years to reveal their meaning. Don't just analyze the dream intellectually. Listen deeply within yourself and be willing to be shocked or surprised at what you get. Reflect on your life, recent events, and emotional patterns as clues to what it might symbolize. In many cases, even if you cannot decipher the meaning of the symbols, you can feel the energy of the dream and trust that important healing is happening for you at a fundamental level. If the emotional energy of a dream is dark and foreboding, meet it with the same kind of open awareness you would with any challenging feeling you experience while awake. If the dream speaks to you in terms you can understand, take time to write down your insights and make sense of what is revealing itself to you. If you can't make sense out of it, just feel it as fully as you can. If it frightens you, be present for the fear and trust that a deeper, conscious process beyond your mind is managing the dream material for you in a healthy way.

Sometimes a dream can reveal secrets about a soul memory, especially a traumatic one that needs to be healed. When soul memory traumas are healed in dreams, the imagery and feeling of the dream can be truly disturbing. If you have any vivid dreams about extremely traumatic events that have nothing to do with events of your life, it is likely that the source of the traumatic memory is from another lifetime. The good news about this kind of dream is that for maximum healing to occur, all you have to do is be present for the powerful imagery and feelings contained within it, trusting that the inner Teacher is taking care of the process.

Dreams often occur in a series, so look for themes or connections between dreams, especially ones with similar elements. Look for similar symbols, situations, or structures that show you a common pattern, the insight into which can fuel your growth in consciousness. See if you can relate the dream insight to something going on in your life, because often dreams are forms of guidance on the path. Even if you don't keep a dream journal, at least write down the insights you receive from major dreams in your regular journal, if you have one, especially if the dreams occur in a series. Often it is the series that shows you what you need to see, revealing the process as it changes over time. In addition to a dream journal, you can also paint, sing, or sculpt to express the content of your dreams so you can make them more conscious. You can dance them or act them out. Let yourself be creative.

Life is like a dream. Viewing it symbolically taps you into the Reality beyond the illusion of the world. The Intelligence that reveals the deeper meaning of events in your life is not of the world, but beyond it. The foundation of the dream is a lie of independent existence. Your dream is the one you are having now, a dream of life and death, parading in an endless cycle.

FAMILY

The family of origin is part of the complex of relationships into which we are drawn when we enter this life and serves the profound function of birthing us and raising us to adulthood. Getting the parents you have is not an accident. You are drawn into relationship with your parents, greater family, and particular life situation with perfect appropriateness for your karmic tendencies. The parents you receive are a direct result of your own unconscious patterns and the actions that arise from them. It's not exactly true that you choose your parents, but you do get the family situation toward which your identification is magnetized. Therefore, your parents are your responsibility, both in the particular ones you get and the mere fact of needing them in the first place.

In other words—you asked for it.

On the path of awakening, family ties are both an aid and a hindrance. Ego development is so deeply involved with what is mirrored to the child by her parents that virtually the entire root of egoic investment is inculcated by the parents or primary caregivers—and there's no way around it. We must first develop an ego in order to function in the world and we must have a healthy, balanced, well-defined sense of self in order to embody a vessel suitable for awakening. If we do not honor our parents, we are poorly suited to the path in many ways:

maturity, devotion, respect, values, responsibility, love, self-esteem, and so on—virtually the whole gamut of healthy human functioning.

But the *primary bond*, or genetic bloodline, must be broken. It is the final bond to be broken in the process of awakening and the most important area of conscious development for a spiritual aspirant. Once that bond is broken, you are liberated. The primary bond is the domain of the primary caregiver, usually the mother or father. The primary caregiver is the one who trains the child to be who she is as an adult. As a child—usually *in utero*—the activities of the primary caregiver contribute to the forming of the primary bond, the original seed-thread of the ego. Therefore, the primary bond can be thought of as the seed of the ego, which in turn is the seed of the personality, or sense of separate self. Breaking the primary bond is equivalent to awakening because it ends your false identification permanently. The primary bond can also be called the *parental* or *genetic* bond.

Before you break the primary bond, you must become an adult. As a child and an adolescent, it is appropriate to honor your father and mother. As an adult, it is appropriate to destroy your genetic linkage with birth and death. Do not let your family drag you down, but try to be with them as they are and inspire them with your spiritual practice. Be an example by fully being who you are. What you do to liberate yourself also liberates them. Because of the bond of love and familiarity that is typically present in a family—but certainly not always— your Liberation often leads to theirs. Early childhood conditioning is a kind of pattern emulation process. When you're a child, you emulate your parents because you love them. When you awaken, you take your parents' patterns on and transmute them. The greatest service you can do for your family is to awaken to the Mystery of who you are. Family loyalty beyond what is appropriate is a problem because Truth is your true Father and Mother, and listening to the false "should" voice of your parents in your mind causes you to suffer—until you break the bond with them.

In the unawakened state, you are addicted to having parents. Just as an addict compulsively seeks her "high" despite extreme negative consequences, you compulsively seek to be reborn despite all the pain that it causes. Your need for a father and mother is one of the main reasons you are repeatedly born into a form realm and serves as the motivation for worldly strivings that inevitably end in death and further rebirth. Wanting to succeed in worldly terms, for example, is inextricably linked with the genetic bond and driven by unconsciously seeking the love and approval of your parents. Even if you succeed in becoming a billionaire, celebrity, or political world leader, as long as the mind-dominated program of parental conditioning is running your life, you will never have complete satisfaction and you will die. Love your parents, but do the work to recognize that, in your essential nature, you were never born.

An awakened person has no parents. Not to have a mother or father is truly terrifying to the ego. This is the same as saying: "I have a divine origin. I gave birth to myself. The Father and I are one. I am both the cause of all that is as well as identical to all that is. Complete and utter Freedom is my nature." To destroy the bond with your parents is the greatest service you can render to them, whether they know it or not. Once the false bond is destroyed, you can find them only in Truth, the true bond of all that is. No one can stop you from doing this but you, but especially if you let the parentally conditioned voices in your mind control your behavior. You must break free. That is why Jesus said the following:

> Do not think that I came to bring peace on earth. I did not come to bring peace but a sword. For I have come to set a man against his father, a daughter against her mother, and a daughter-in-law against her mother-in-law; and a man's enemies will be those of his own household. He who loves father or mother more than Me is not worthy of Me. And he who loves son or daughter more than Me is not worthy of Me.

In addition to father and mother, the deepest obstacle to Freedom is "God." For most people, God is a mere idea tainted with conditioned parental attitudes that block conscious awareness of Truth. The conditioned patterns of the genetic father are projected onto the heavenly Father. Even if you grew up in a strictly atheistic society with no mention of God, you can't help but have some idea or notion of "absolute reality" or "the absolute cause of everything," a kind of cosmic Father-principle. It is virtually impossible not to project the internalized experience of your early parental conditioning onto your conception of the Absolute. The deepest core of internal resistance to Liberation is parental conditioning, even as early as what you absorb in the womb.

The notion of the genetic family also leaks into our views of society, as in the concepts of *patriotism* and *nationalism*. The word "patriot" is derived from the Latin word *pater*, which means "father." Many people refer to their country of origin as "the fatherland." Patriotism means love of one's country as "the land of one's fathers." In the common mindset, to be a patriot is to obey paternal authority, as in "Honor thy father and thy mother" in the *Old Testament*. In the *New Testament*, Jesus talks about liberation from old values and the embracing of a radical new order of parentlessness. To be a patriot is really to love the mind. The Latin word *natio* means "to be born." *Natio* gives us the word "national" as well as the word "natal," which means "of or relating to birth." Nationalism and patriotism relate to the notion of the genetic family. If you identify with your nation, you are in trouble because every nation, no matter how great, eventually declines and crumbles. In awakening, the primacy of the genetic family is destroyed, extirpating any ultimate loyalty to family or country. What we are being led to is the destruction of the notion of the country as a father figure and rootless reason as a guide for national security. Liberation makes paternalism unnecessary. Your only ultimate loyalty is to Truth. If your family or country is false, you have to consider your options.

Some relationships survive awakening and some don't because some people can handle Truth and some cannot. Some will resent your new awareness, potentially including family members. No relationship is immune to being tested by the conscious process once you are awake. Your parents have "credit" with you because they know you already and cannot help but love you, even if their love has been corrupted by judgments. The issue is whether they can handle the change in you. If they fight Truth, they may lose you—but this is highly unlikely since they probably love you deeply.

Besides, we have ways of bringing them around, so to speak.

FORGIVING YOUR PARENTS AND "GOD"

To *forgive* means to give up resentment. It does not mean that you condone the behavior of the person you are forgiving. It means to *give* up your resentment be*fore* you harm yourself. Why would you want to hold on to resentment? Resentment is deep, cutting, caustic, angry, vitriolic, hateful, and hostile energy projected toward someone based on your judgment that she shouldn't have done what she did. Of course she should have done what she did—because she *did*. To be at odds with that *fact* is the cause of your resentment. Resentment is like a viper that sinks its fangs into you and keeps you sick and miserable until death, many times over. Why would you want to hold on to it? Resentment does not die when the body dies. You take it with you. How long have you been carrying this resentment around with you? To say *eons* would be kind.

Our primary resentments are about father, mother, and God. We tend to project human characteristics onto the Absolute and call it God, when God is anything but an anthropomorphic figure or entity of any kind. Your resentments about father, mother, and God form the unholy triumvirate of death. You cannot be a human being without a mother, father, and a sense of a divine parental authority figure presiding over the universe, whether you call it God, Goddess, or something else. Even if you do not anthropomorphize God consciously, you do so unconsciously, or at the very least make it into an object. The Absolute is absolutely unqualified, even if you call it "God." God is not a divine parent. God is absolutely beyond all comprehension and can only be revealed to you as who you ultimately are. Use of the term "God" is problematic because it invokes the father principle. Chances are, you have "God issues," whether you realize it or not.

The resentments about father, mother, and God are generally the last ones to go before awakening occurs because they are the claws at the root of the ego, a dark sense of craving and anguish coupled with a deadly need to control everything. You can work on these resentments, but you cannot kill yourself and get away from them. Death does not end them. As long as you have a need for a father and mother, you will be drawn into rebirth again and again. As long as you have a need for a divine parent, you will both cling to and run from him or her because you both need and fear a Mommy and Daddy. In other words, your conception of the Absolute cannot be clearly distinguished from your love or hatred of your parents.

Because of the extreme depth of these illusions—father, mother, God—take your time getting rid of them. It is not likely that you can do any real damage to them quickly. Start where you are, with what is right in front of you. What are your resentments about them? How did they hurt you? What did you not get from them? It is extremely helpful to make an exhaustive list of answers to these questions (as well as any others that you feel may strongly apply) and ask yourself if they are true. Even if you think they are true, keep asking at deeper levels until you can know *with absolute certainty* that they are true. If you are absolutely honest in your inquiry, you will find that you cannot know anything with absolute certainty, and your resentments will unravel.

Forgiveness is one of the most powerful actions you can take. Forgiveness involves freeing yourself from thoughts about how others have hurt you. No one has ever hurt you. No one *can* hurt you. You are the *One*. You dream the world into existence and hurt your imagined self with imagined people and imagined transgressions. All the characters in a dream are a projection of your own mind. If you dream that someone is hurting you, you are really hurting yourself. You create characters in your imagination and project them on the screen of your awareness. If you dream that you are a character being attacked and hurt by another person—do these characters really exist? Aren't they imaginary? Is there any way you can justify your claim that anyone has ever hurt you—ever?

THE COMMUNITY AS YOUR SPIRITUAL FAMILY

Our true family is spiritual, not genetic. This is a difficult line to cross, but we all must cross it. It feels like saying goodbye to our genetic family, but we are actually only saying goodbye to the false, outer form of relationship and hello to the true, inner form.

The spiritual family is the community of true students and Teachers—those who love Truth. In practical terms, awakened people join in relationship with others based on Truth, the absolute Value beyond genetic attachments. You are part of it already because you are reading this book. The spiritual family is *the many that are one*. The spiritual family does not get created; it is revealed in the process of awakening. The one who awakens as well as those who are in turn awakened by that one are all the same one. If you have ten awakened beings in a room, there is only one—including the appearance of "ten awakened beings in a room" and the world in which the appearance seems to occur.

Blood may be thicker than water, but Truth is thicker than blood.

DECEASED PEOPLE WHO HANG AROUND

Because of a lack of forgiveness on some level, people who die can refuse to move on and hang around you on an etheric (coarse energetic) level, trying to get your attention or even harm you, especially if in life they were addicted, deeply unconscious, resentful, or died by committing suicide. It is important to know how to deal with them. They can cause you physical, emotional, and spiritual problems. They are almost always relatives, sometimes close friends or lovers. It is your responsibility to make sure that no dead people are hanging around in your space, causing you problems. Check with a qualified spiritual Teacher or perform a ritual of separation. If you feel the presence of a deceased loved one in your space, perform the following ritual: (1) go into a meditative state, (2) remember what the person looks like and connect to her emotionally using your living memory of her, and (3) tell her (either silently or out loud) that she must move on immediately and you will not allow her to stay. Make sure you mean it, and she will leave you alone. If you feel that you harmed her in some way in life, apologize sincerely for it and let her go.

Dead people who loiter around the living often try to influence them into believing that they exist ("Hey! I'm still here!"), try to apologize for past misdeeds, seek revenge for imagined transgressions, sometimes haunt the perceived perpetrator (to death and beyond—not a good idea, karmically speaking), or struggle to satisfy an obsession, compulsion, or addiction. These people are tormented by their attachments. As a student, your job is to avoid becoming a dead person hanging around the planet, bothering people. The only reason you would hang around the earth after death would be if you had a strong attachment (obsession, compulsion, addiction) to people, places, or things. The key for you is to take care of these issues *before* you cross over. Get involved in a Teaching and do the work consistently. Authentic spiritual practice is the most powerful antidote to earthly attachments. You never know when death will come.

FRIENDS, TRUE AND FALSE

False friendships and associating with deeply unconscious people are impediments to your path unless you learn how to deal with them appropriately. If you have friends who are deeply unconscious, they will resist your movement toward consciousness and will try to sabotage your progress. They may offer you drugs, prey on your weakness, introduce you to other demons, or just treat you poorly in general. You do not need to be loyal to those kinds of friends, because, like a drowning person, they will try to take you down with them. A false friendship can kill you or at least impede your practice. As you grow in awareness, you will begin to see the inappropriateness of certain relationships and will let them go. You are not likely to miss them. In some cases, you can create more distance without letting go of the friendship entirely, providing a space for eventual reconciliation. Being a student involved in a true Teaching is a powerful remedy for false friendships.

If you have friends who are only mildly unconscious, you can usually be with them without sacrificing your integrity or disrupting your practice. You can be with mildly unconscious friends as a form of spiritual practice by relating to them consciously, and they will benefit from it if the relationship is strong. Strong friendships are imbued with just enough Truth to endure the strain that conscious functioning often puts upon them. Some friends may admire you for your clarity, strength, or integrity and will ask you what you are doing to change so much for the better. In that case, you can share with them the work you are doing. Those who can handle the fire of your presence will stay with you and benefit from it. Those who can't will likely fall by the wayside, although you may still see or talk to them sometimes. Forgiveness is always possible if they know how to repent. Once you are liberated, old friends can fit into your life, just in a certain way. They must become new if they are going to get close to the new you. More closeness requires more newness.

Your true friends are those who are devoted to the path of awakening, whether they are mere curious seekers, serious students, or Teachers. The more deeply people are committed to consciousness, the more valuable your friendship with them can be. It is wise to try to cultivate friendships with other students, although there may be only a few with whom you can become close friends. Friendship in its true form is a powerful bond between individuals and represents the highest level of functioning of which human beings are capable.

Ultimately, the best friend you can possibly have is the true Teacher. The word "friend" is derived from the Old English word *freond,* meaning "loving," and is related to the word *freo,* which means "free." The one who has found Freedom is the greatest friend of humanity. He has given all for Truth. One awakened person living in the world, even for one day, is of greater service to humanity than a limitless number of social workers, politicians, or activists working on the level of the world for a million lifetimes.

Your job is to find him.

CHAPTER NINE

LIFE

Know the personal,
yet keep to the impersonal:
accept the world as it is.
If you accept the world,
the Tao will be luminous inside you
and you will return to your primal
self.

—Lao Tzu

Render therefore unto Caesar the
things which are Caesar's, and unto
God the things that are God's.

—Jesus Christ

AN ABUNDANT LIFE

Everyone has abundance, but only a few are aware of it. Everyone has abundance simply by virtue of being born on this planet. It is a blessing to be born here because you can awaken here. Abundance is more than just material wealth; it is also understanding how to use that wealth for awakening. Because you are reading this book, you are blessed beyond measure. You are studying the path of awakening and thus learning how to use your life to become liberated from the wheel of birth and death.

A life of relative wealth and privilege can be helpful in supporting your path and is a great advantage, whether it is earned by fortunate birth or by personal effort. The only real problem with a privileged life is that you may not suffer enough to become motivated to practice. You may see the spiritual life as a mere dalliance sandwiched between yoga class and tennis lessons. But all things considered, material wealth is conducive to your path because you can use it for personal development in service to awakening.

If you were born into a wealthy family, you may feel guilty because there is so much poverty in the world. You may feel that you didn't earn it. Of course you earned it. You earn a privileged lifetime by conscious deeds in other lifetimes. Birth is not a random event but proceeds according to your karma. If you were born into a wealthy family, it was because of your karma. Therefore, do not feel guilty. Use your life for awakening. The greatest gift you can give to the world is your own Freedom. If you have more material wealth than others, you can be generous and help those who need it.

If you were born into relative poverty, use what you have for awakening, even if you must toil to make it happen. Wealth is a matter of perspective. If you have what you need, can you really consider yourself impoverished? Everyone has to deal with karma, so make the best of it. Do what you have to do to awaken. As a student, you must have your basic needs met: food, clothing, shelter, as well as the accoutrements of practice, such as books, pencils, paper, a quiet place to meditate, supportive friends, and so on. If your basic needs are not met, it can be much harder to practice and stay focused. Get what you need and do the work. Use your time and resources wisely. You can practice effectively if you are committed.

If you have to work to support yourself, make your job a spiritual practice by performing it with integrity, attentiveness, and compassion. If your livelihood depends on activities, conditions, or values that violate your personal ethics—such as working as a dishonest salesperson, corporate polluter, or contract killer—do something else. Do what you know, what you are good at doing, what pays the bills. It makes no sense to work any harder than you have to to support your path. If you wear yourself out and cannot practice, you are doing yourself and everyone else a grave disservice.

Do what you have to do in order to earn enough money to live—and that might not be much, because you don't need much if you cease generating artificial "needs." If you are of modest means financially, make your path a priority. Take care of business on the relative level, but don't become overwhelmed with minutiae. Take some time, every day if you can, to listen, learn, and grow. Instead of bemoaning your fate or the state of the world, practice. Prioritize and simplify your life.

If you have a privileged life—which you do, since you are reading this book—don't waste this precious opportunity. Use this material. Study it. Let it speak to your depths about what it means to be truly liberated from suffering. Find a Teacher and learn about the path of awakening. Do the work—and when you are free, you will have defeated death.

EMBRACING THE ORDINARY

A key to the awakened life is to be in the world but not of it. The Absolute is both transcendent and immanent, meaning that it is both beyond the world and present within it as its essence. As long as you recognize the world as ultimately insubstantial, you can enjoy it as a phantasmagoric display within your awareness. Then you can move through the world without attachment, like an actor in a movie. You may appear to have things and be somebody, but you recognize this as a charade, and playing along is not a problem for you. Freedom looks like a person living a human life—and is, but only relatively. An awakened person lives from the absolute perspective of Being.

The awakened life is grounded in the ordinary. The Unmanifest must be balanced by the manifest to awaken into worldly life fully. The Timeless must be grounded in the temporal. Washing dishes, taking out the garbage, and dealing with family issues, for example, give Being relative weight and a place to develop its design. Living an awakened life is not life-denying; it's life-affirming. It's being deeply involved in life. It's not avoiding the mundane; it's embracing it. It's finding and helping people. The Awakener stands on the river bank and helps others cross, reaching out to the world while standing firm in Freedom. The awakened life does not require a mountaintop hermitage to express itself. Being fully human is an integral part of awakened life and is important for transmitting the Teaching in an accessible way.

Take care of the relative stuff of day-to-day life. Take care of your body, live ethically, speak the truth, manage your finances, and cultivate a regular practice. A healthy, balanced lifestyle is conducive to awakening. Jesus said to "Render therefore unto Caesar the things which are Caesar's, and unto God the things that are God's." This means to treat the relative as relative and the Absolute as absolute. How do you do this? Take care of business in the world. Pay your bills, bathe regularly, eat healthy food, obey laws, and get plenty of rest. Rendering unto Caesar means taking care of the relative. It also means realizing that the relative is not in itself a source of ultimate salvation, truth, or value. Rendering unto God means *do the work:* meditate, pray, and study the true Teaching. Further, the whole statement means that rendering unto Caesar on his level (relative) is in alignment with, and even an integral aspect of rendering unto God on its level (absolute). In other words, taking care of business in the world is an integral part of one's spiritual path.

The path of awakening is a useful approach to living in the world while striving for What lies beyond it. Balance between the polar opposites of life is vital: activity and rest, solitude and togetherness, work and play. Eventually, you learn to deepen your awareness and develop balance between form and formlessness, content and consciousness, movement and rest. For example, consider wandering versus staying rooted in one place as a lifestyle decision. Ascetic wandering is fine if you are a true *sadhu.* However, wandering can be a sign of rootlessness and an unwillingness to face your patterns. When you become rooted in a place, you must face life in a way that cannot be avoided by wandering. Conversely, if you have been living in the same place for a long time and feel stagnant, wandering can be useful, as long as you do it from a spirit of Truth and not to avoid unconscious pain. The movement must be authentic.

Awakening is similar to a figure/ground reversal. At first, you perceive yourself as an object on the form side. As your practice develops, you intuit into formlessness at progressively deeper levels. When awakening occurs, the figure (person) and ground (Absolute) undergo a reversal. Before awakening, you look to the Absolute as if it were a supreme object. After awakening, you awaken *as* the Absolute, freely witnessing the rise and fall of objects—including the person you previously thought you were. Before awakening, you practice deepening your awareness of the Absolute while strengthening and balancing your relative form. After awakening, this process continues, but from the other side of the veil, as it were. In either case, balance and grounding are important, but in different ways.

EMBRACING UNCERTAINTY

To be in the world but not of it, you must be able to embrace uncertainty and chaos. You must give up trying to *know* things with the mind, as if mental certainty—something you will never get—will deliver you from life's inherent uncertainty. You cannot ever know things with complete certainty. An awakened person doesn't *know* things with absolute certainty, as if thought could deliver Truth. She *is* absolute certainty, regardless of any thoughts that may appear. An awakened person enjoys just being with what is and letting the future take care of itself. Wanting certainty in life is like skipping to the end of a novel to find out what happens, or wanting to learn the end of a movie without watching it—only in life, the story never ends, and you miss all the good parts. It blocks your joy of the Now and makes life feel incomplete, like you're missing something.

Chaos is constant. You cannot predict when things will go wrong. "Wrong" just means chaotic or unexpectedly out of control. Chaotic circumstances are not ultimately wrong, just messy. Life is never going to get more orderly or certain than it already is. If you create order in one place, chaos erupts elsewhere. If you wait for certainty, it will never happen. The awakened life is not completely certain, as the mind might have it. In a way, it is completely uncertain, involving total trust. It is Wisdom. In that sense, it is complete and hence completely certain, but only on the level of Being. On the level of the mind, it is out of control. The mind cannot grasp it, cannot comprehend it. Knowledge is necessary for getting by in the world, but it cannot give you certainty. It is the uncertainty and chaos of life that makes it spontaneous and fun. You have to let go of the mind to get there.

The awakened life *is* fun. Humor, lightness, and play are essential. Celebration is helpful; the path doesn't have to be totally serious. From the perspective of an awakened person, life is a celebration. Awakening is the ultimate party boat drifting down the river of Being. This includes all the things that you would consider basic humanity. Humor, lightness, and play are vitally important in awakened life because the gloom has departed. There is a sense of joy that carries itself without any real seriousness about the world. Any seriousness is about getting things done, but the inherent delight of productive activity is obvious. For example, you may be serious about repairing a toilet, but not really. A toilet is too absurd to be taken seriously, so you delight in it. Depression is no longer possible. Sadness is possible, but that is a feeling into the world that is not *of* the world; it is met with an equal measure of joy. This meeting neutralizes all sadness into peace, like a fading sunset. When night comes, it is not a problem.

JOURNALING

When the stress of life is getting to you, the thought-stream can churn in your head like a rat running on a spinning wheel in a cage. If you get annoyed about it and try to mentally clamp down on this churning, it gets worse because your efforts are based in judgment. Meditation practice is helpful, but sometimes the churning is so strong that it distracts you from your practice. Embodiment practice is extremely helpful, but sometimes you need another way to become conscious. One such way to break this spinning wheel and make it conscious is to write your thoughts down in a journal.

Journaling can be powerful because it channels the thought-stream into a visible form on a piece of paper. When this flow gets going, it is almost as if the tip of the pen and the surface of the paper form a single-pointed focus of concentration, making it a form of meditation. The key is to write in a stream-of-consciousness fashion so your mind cannot seize upon what you are doing and cogitate about it. You wear down the mind's resistance until it surrenders. You just write until you cannot write anymore, then consciousness takes over. Then you can view the thoughts more impersonally, from a place of insight, a conscious interface for the purification of your mind. Things emerge that were previously hidden. Once you get beneath the superficial layers of noise, deeper layers begin to surface, and you can find out what is really bothering you. It is always some version of "I don't want what *is* happening, *has* happened, or is *going* to happen, to happen." This is ridiculous. When you get it all down on paper, you can see it clearly in a way that you couldn't when your mind was spinning. When you write things down, they are in a sense frozen and can be easily contemplated.

To journal effectively, focus on thought, feeling, and sensation in the moment without editing. Write a pure stream of present-moment thought, feeling, and sensation, no matter what it is, even if that is to write: "I am writing. I am feeling nothing yet but I think I can keep doing this if I just keep on writing and it doesn't matter what it is oh why must I write like this I don't know what I am doing but…" and so on. Don't stop. Don't edit. Eventually deeper content will reveal itself. It can become a deep prayer. To get to this place of surrender, you have to suffer deeply and allow yourself to be completely honest about it on paper. You have to get the pen moving and see what comes out of it. Eventually, once the flow of writing becomes deeper and more conscious, what comes through is the voice of Truth. At first it comes only a little, and then it comes a bit more. As you practice, the writing deepens.

The ways you can use journaling to expose unconscious material are unlimited. The specific form doesn't matter as long as you get down to the roots of your anguish and illuminate them. It doesn't have to be completely dark and angst-ridden. Occasionally, you might stumble upon something beautiful. But if you are so well-adjusted that you are enjoying life, why write about it? Would you stop in the middle of making love to write about it? Of course not. Write to get at the ugly stuff.

It can help to take an entire mass of stream-of-consciousness writing that you have already finished and distill it down to the essential statements of resistance at the core of it, such as "My life is a disaster," "Nobody loves me," or "I feel worthless." Then you can inquire into these statements to find out if they are true, real, or if they reflect who you really are.

Once you clear out some dark, ugly material and are in a calmer, more reflective state of mind, select a piece of scripture that has significance for you and expound on its meaning in writing. In this case, you are trying to get at the Truth contained within it. It does not have to be a large portion or even a paragraph; you can do it with only a few words of text as long as they are meaningful to you. For example, consider the statement "Thy will be done" from the *Lord's Prayer*. What does this statement mean? What does it mean to you personally? How does it apply to your life? How does it *not* apply to your life? How do you live as if this were true for you? How do you know when you are living in accord with it? How do you know when you are *not* living in accord with it? What is the mechanism of the mind that keeps you from recognizing the Truth of this statement? How does it make you feel to fight it? How does it make you act toward yourself and others? These are just some of the areas you could explore.

If you are angry or otherwise upset with someone, write him a letter as if you were going to send it and hold nothing back. You will either send it or not, but that doesn't matter as much as getting your resentments, fears, or other emotions out on paper. Write vigorously and keep writing until you have exhausted the emotional energy of the pattern. You may begin writing more and more vigorously until you break down in tears and stop writing, only to let go into a grief process or other form of letting go. The key is to write in a stream-of-consciousness fashion and refrain from editing or even thinking about what you are writing. Just express yourself on the deepest levels you can. Let yourself be mean, petty—even nasty. Get it out. It doesn't matter, because you probably won't send it anyway.

Keep your journal in a safe place and make sure no one reads it. You need to be able to trust those close to you not to read it so you won't edit your writing out of fear of having it discovered. If you can trust that no one will read what you are writing, you will tend to be more honest about it. Even your darkest fantasies will come out, and you can see that they are harmless, whereas before you may have judged yourself about them.

Don't write about *things*. Write about the *essence* of things. Get beneath their surface. If what you are writing is superficial, keep writing until you tap into deeper layers. Get it all out. Once it's all out, keep going.

SYNCHRONICITY

Synchronicity is meaningful coincidence, showing us that life is an intimately interconnected web of relationship. Things happen in a way that confirm the order beneath the surface of things beyond what most would consider random chance. It is important to pay attention to what is going on in your environment and notice the quality of the appearances around you, including synchronistic appearances. It is important to understand what synchronicity is saying to you—but don't get carried away with it, as if it were an ultimate value in itself. Instead, use it appropriately by finding out the depth of its meaning in your experience. It is truly meaningful if it is experienced as a form of guidance.

Synchronicity can be a form of guidance, but not necessarily. The mind often uses synchronistic appearances to trick us into making bad decisions, especially if we do not have a conscious guide. Coincidences are common and are not that important. A synchronistic occurrence happens in a way that is beyond mere coincidence, showing us the interconnectedness of things. But this level of meaning— that things are interconnected—is still not that important. The quality of synchronicity that is really important and helpful comes to you as a form of guidance, a suggestion to take a certain course of action. The quality of this guidance is relentless and unavoidable, coupled by a profound recognition of *Yes*—as in, *I need to take this action and I don't know why, but it keeps coming to me.* When you recognize it, you become aware of a profound oneness with Being, a deep Stillness and peaceful certainty. This sense of peaceful certainty may be intermixed with mental vacillation and confusion on the surface, but the Silence beneath it is unmistakable, if you listen. It may actually be quite disturbing because it is so persistent. You see it everywhere. Because it is a form of guidance, the meaning of truly helpful synchronicity is not just that things are interconnected, but that the Absolute is leading you in a certain direction. This is Wisdom reaching out to you.

Let synchronicity show you what it shows you, and realize that ultimately, the meaning of it is not something you can mentally figure out. If you somehow feel guided by coincidental events, allow yourself to find out what it means through experience. You may realize that it's all a great Joke and you are being guided to appreciate the notion that "you're It," and that's all there is. Use synchronicity, but don't give it too much importance. *You* are what is important. Find out who you are. Pray to be guided. The deeper and more sincere your prayers are, the more guidance you will get, and the more likely your experiences of synchronicity will be truly meaningful.

CONSCIOUS RELATIONSHIP

Most people relate to the world unconsciously and, therefore, dualistically, across a subject/object divide. This sense of subject and object is created by the mind. If you relate unconsciously with something (or someone), you are creating objects called "self" and "other" through identification with mental content. If you are relating to me conditionally, you are relating to your *ideas* about me, not to who I am in my essence. You project the sense of an object onto me, and simultaneously onto yourself. This lack of intimacy hurts. True relationship, or *conscious* relationship, involves accepting otherness radically, as the ultimate oneness of Truth. Conscious relationship sees objects as dependent arising, the world as perceptual illusion, and Freedom as the very nature of all that is. Conscious relationship is Being recognizing Itself.

The deeper you enter into conscious relationship with a person, the less you perceive him as an object and the more you recognize him as an emanation of Being. Simultaneously, you perceive yourself as less of an object and more of the same Oneness. Then you are both in the Mystery, *as* the Mystery. To be in unobstructed relationship with a person is to be with that person without judgment, without names, labels, even "friend"—because friendship is not the word, but the Actuality. To be with him without attachment is truly being at one with him. You can also be in conscious, unobstructed relationship with your body, thoughts, feelings, sensations—any object you perceive within your awareness. This relationship renders self and other less substantial as objects and more substantial as consciousness. Ultimately, you are not a thing, and neither is anyone else. What are you, then? You are pure awareness, one without a second. You have to practice conscious relationship to find out what this means.

The capacity for self-awareness can be built up like a muscle; you build a sense of strength in the ability to witness your own thoughts, feelings, and behavior. Some people can't do it—or at least not yet. It takes consistent practice, just like lifting weights; your muscles get bigger, stronger, more powerful. Consciously being one with all that is allows you to differentiate. The more at one with everything you are, the more you can differentiate from it without losing integrity because you recognize it from a standpoint of utter Formlessness.

DEALING WITH DIFFICULT PEOPLE

An important measure of spiritual progress is how well you deal with difficult people, or people who exhibit strong negativity. If negative people make you upset, you have work to do. To the extent that negative people upset you, you are a negative person. If you resist their resistance, you are resisting Reality. A key liberating insight is others cannot upset you. Only *you* can upset you.

People that bother you are manifesting feeling, speech, or behavior that you manifest unconsciously. They are touching parts of you that you don't want touched, and it sets you off. You react because they are exhibiting the very quality that you don't want to see in yourself, but you blame it on them. This is *projection*. For example, if you are unconscious of being controlling, controlling people will bother you. If you are unconscious of being judgmental, judgmental people will bother you. This is how your buttons get pushed. You are doing the pushing, but you are blaming the effects on others. The key to your Freedom is to find out what you are doing unconsciously and to radically accept those parts of yourself that you hide. This dismantles the buttons.

As a student of the Teaching, you must learn how to be with people—even extremely negative people—without judgment. True spiritual warfare means consciously being with negativity, whether it is expressed through you or through another person. The only way to defeat negativity is not to oppose it mentally. That doesn't mean you become a doormat, but that your actions arise from Being instead of from resistance. Negativity is caused by resistance, and negative people feed on your resistance to their negativity. Instead of resisting their negativity, radically accept and neutralize it.

To be in conscious relationship, you must radically accept the other. Radical acceptance is surrender. Surrender is not weakness; it is strength. It means that you become one with what is. Since what *is* cannot be defeated by any opponent, you cannot be defeated once you are consciously one with it. Surrender is stopping the fight with what is. You can't defeat it. It simply absorbs whatever you put into it. It quietly wins. Raising a white flag in your war with Reality is profoundly intelligent. It says: "I give up. Reality is what it is, now." When you surrender to Reality, you consciously recognize self and other *as* Reality, trusting what emerges from that Space.

Spiritual Freedom is freedom from negativity in all of its forms. Negative people are all around you. You cannot change them until *you* change. Free yourself first. Forget about wanting other people to do the right thing; *you* do the right thing. Forget about needing other people to get liberated; *you* get liberated. Forget about everything but doing your own work, walking your own path, making it happen for the benefit of all beings. Then you are helpful. As Ramana Maharshi noted: "Wanting to reform the world without discovering one's true self is like trying to cover the world with leather to avoid the pain of walking on stones and thorns. It is much simpler to wear shoes."

You can reduce violence in others by noticing their anger without judgment and giving them unconditional space in which to be.

You must be at one with Reality in order to stop violence at its egoic source—whether that violence arises in yourself or in others. The only way something is perceived as other is if you are not at one with it, if you resist it, creating a barrier of judgment that interferes with your conscious recognition of its Being. If you stop fighting something, you are fully at one with it. For example, God seems other than you unless you are totally surrendered to that Reality, and then you are at one with it. A person who is angry at you seems other than you until you stop fighting and listen into the silent unknowability of the moment. To listen like that is to be at one with anger so completely that it cannot find a "you" to fight, as if you had vanished into space.

Nothing is truly "other." This natural all-inclusiveness is who you are. If you fully surrender in the midst of a physical fight, you cannot help but emerge victorious, because you are completely at one with it. When the fist swings at you, you move accordingly. In the martial art of *Tai Chi,* for example, the key is to be at one with the force of your opponent and use it against him. If you do not resist your opponent, but merge with his energy and re-direct it where you intend, you can put him on the ground and restrain him if necessary. Then you can keep him from harming himself or others. You can help him. When we strike out at another, the last thing we intuitively expect is agreement and surrender. This is true in any situation. People strike out at you all the time, whether you know it or not. This surreptitious lashing out can be met with a total *yes,* a presence that does not judge, yet stands firm. This throws people off balance while you act freely. When you act with true Freedom, you are the Emptiness that embraces everything, and nothing can strike you. You cannot strike empty space with your fist. If you strike out forcefully at empty space thinking that something is going to resist you, you end up losing your balance, appearing foolish to onlookers. They start to see through your game and sip cocktails, perhaps whispering about you afterwards.

Negative people are often angry and swing their mental blades around themselves blindly, spoiling for a fight. A true disciple sees a negative person as an opportunity to practice wisdom and compassion, as fuel for awakening. Negative people are just like you: they feel pain, have problems, and want to be loved, regardless of their outward appearance. Compassion leads you into right relationship with people who are difficult to deal with. If confronted with a negative person, first ask yourself if he can be helped. If so, ask yourself if this person *wants* to be helped. If that is the case, perhaps you can be of service. Anything from a warm greeting to a sympathetic conversation to a financial contribution to a helping hand—all of these are forms of compassion in action, and they all have one thing in common: genuine, heartfelt concern for the suffering of another person coupled with a sincere desire to help alleviate it without any regard for personal gain.

Have you ever listened to someone speak and felt as if he were draining your energy? You can stop this from happening. End the conversation. Cut him off and walk away—but do it without judgment. Forget about wanting people to like you. Wanting people to like you creates problems because you trade your values for their appreciation—and they are never going to appreciate you for that.

Forget about being nice. Instead, be honest.

Treat negative people as blessings, for being with them is an opportunity to practice. If someone hurts you or wrongs you in some way, forgive him. Never condemn others for any reason, for they do not know better or they would not express negativity. Allow yourself to be like space, which resists nothing but allows others to make fools of themselves. Allow negative thoughts to expose themselves as the silly nothings that they are, and—*poof!* They disappear. Allow suffering beings to come to you for acceptance, help, and support. If you truly want to support them, support Truth, not the person. That keeps them from unconsciously feeding on your life force.

DEALING WITH CRITICS

If you are confronted with a critic, a cynical naysayer who doubts the Teaching, let him. You don't have to defend the Teaching. It defends itself. To the degree that you embody it, you repel attacks by being who you are. In order to represent the Teaching in a supportive way and avoid misunderstanding and hatred from others, explain what you are doing but don't argue with them if they criticize you. Just let them believe what they believe. Ignorance is its own worst punishment. No one can hurt you with words unless you believe them.

The world will tell you you're wrong. The world does not want you to be free. Count on it. Misery loves company.

But it is important to be able to communicate your spiritual ideas and practice in terms that others can understand. Many people think that spiritual practice dedicated to awakening is downright weird, or that anyone who has a spiritual teacher and practices in a group is "in a cult." The fact is that *the world is weird*. It's insane. You have to look at it closely and study it to realize how corrupt, empty, and strange it is. Authentic spiritual practice may seem "different," but speaking about it intelligently with others helps to dispel any false ideas about what you are doing. The best course of action is to keep it simple. If someone asks what you are doing, simply answer that you practice meditation and inquiry. You talk, discuss things, share ideas. It's pretty simple. Frame the conversation in terms that your listener can understand. Be honest. Do what you can to remain neutral with respect to the other person's beliefs. If someone asks you a direct question about specific points of doctrine, just be sincere, direct, and nonjudgmental. If a person has a problem with your views, then, well—that's his problem. Maybe he will accept them later.

CONSCIOUS COMMUNICATION

Relating to people consciously involves communicating effectively. What you say is not as important as the place within you from which the words arise. Pay attention to what you feel as you speak. Keep your feelings as conscious as you can. If you are speaking from an unconscious place, do the necessary work to come back to consciousness and speak from there. If you can't do it in the moment, you may need to go into silence for a while and try it later. Remember that consciousness is the moral standard for all action, including speech.

What you say mirrors what you think. What you say is important because it reveals patterns of unconsciousness associated with certain ways of talking. You must get serious about policing your language—not because lazy, unconscious speech is bad or wrong, but because it is an outward form of the tendency to argue with what is. You don't have to judge your language habits to change them. All you have to do is notice certain ways of saying things. Notice speech patterns that are forms of *this shouldn't be happening*. Notice when you complain. Notice when you blame others for what you are feeling. Notice when you spew. Part of your commitment to consciousness is being committed to speaking in ways that are progressively clearer and less negative. Do it as a sacred commitment to causing as little harm with your speech as possible.

Notice when you babble.

Notice what you are feeling as you speak and stay connected to the feeling. If you have to, tell the person to whom you are talking what you are feeling just to acknowledge it openly. Be as conscious of the feeling as you can as you speak about it. Don't blame unconscious speech on the feeling; just acknowledge what you feel and remain aware of it as you continue what you were saying. This reduces the harmful impact of negative emotional energy being projected into what you are saying. A negative emotion cannot make you speak, but acting as if it can is dishonest. It is your responsibility to make emotions conscious enough to reduce their harmfulness. Otherwise, you are just being lazy. At the minimum, you can acknowledge what you are feeling.

If you have to, you can go into silence. Silence is an important retreat when you feel that you cannot remain conscious enough to keep from spewing. You can tell someone that you are going to go into silence for a while, perhaps for a specific period of time, and you will talk about it later. You can say that you are too charged with the negative emotion to speak consciously about it. You may also want to exercise physically or otherwise reduce the intensity of the emotion before you try to talk about it with someone. This is not avoidance, but wisdom. It is important to recognize when negative emotional intensity is beyond your ability to handle consciously, requiring a retreat to reduce its vitriol. Just make sure that you truly can't handle it and are not just copping out of your responsibility. If you can handle it, it is your responsibility to try to work it out if intimacy with the other person is what you want.

Judgment of another's behavior can get in the way of effective interpersonal communication. If you say, "I'm angry because you hit me," you are implying that the hitting caused the anger, which is a denial of responsibility for your own unconscious emotional reaction and a blaming of the other. To remove this hidden judgment from your language, you can say instead, "My *experience* was that you hit me, and then I felt anger." That removes the language of blame and merely describes your experience of what happened. If the other person denies that he hit you, you can say, "My *experience* was that you hit me, regardless of whether you *actually* hit me." If you say it this way, you are just reporting what you experienced with as little judgment as possible, and then you can have a conversation about what happened that is more likely to result in healthy, conscious communication.

Learn to ask for what you want. Making a simple, direct request such as, "Could you lower your voice?" is useful. This is much more honest than just fuming about it and expecting a person to figure out what you are trying to communicate. Asking is easier.

Mind reading is assuming that you know what someone else is thinking or feeling without his having told you. You can't *know* what someone else is thinking or feeling without his having told you, even if it seems obvious. Always ask, just to make sure and avoid misunderstanding. Instead of saying, "Why are you angry?" you can say, "You *seem* angry. Are you?" and listen for the answer. If the answer is a thought, keep asking until you hear an answer that is a verbal expression of *feeling*. If he says that he is not angry, that is okay. He is entitled to his own experience. If you disagree, so be it. At least you are communicating honestly, and honest communication is conducive to harmonious agreement in the long run.

Name calling is a major impediment to intimacy. Calling someone a name means referring to him as a noun—a *thing*—with derogatory intent. When we call someone a name, we objectify and dehumanize him. When we deny a person's humanity, we can more easily rationalize our ill-treatment of him and make him a scapegoat for our suffering. When mass violence occurs, it is typical for victims to be reduced to a hated name of racial, religious, or national identification, making atrocities against innocent people easier to commit. Instead of contributing to this kind of madness, we can refrain from name calling in our home and community and accord others the respect of their basic humanity. If you must criticize someone, it is much more useful, conscious, and kind to describe his behavior without resorting to epithets.

When describing someone's behavior, discriminate between descriptive judgments (which are useful) and value judgments (which are forms of unconsciousness). Value judgments such as "bad" and "wrong" imply that your statements possess absolute value when they are only relative descriptions. It is more useful to speak of what works for you and what doesn't in terms of consciousness. Behavior is either conducive to awakening or it isn't. As a student, instead of saying someone's behavior is somehow wrong or shouldn't be happening, you can say that it doesn't work for you. This way of speaking addresses issues consciously, by referring to their usefulness for awakening or lack thereof.

INTIMATE RELATIONSHIPS

Relating consciously with other human beings is a powerful practice. Although you are unavoidably in relationship with every person on the planet to some degree, intimate relationships are the proving ground for your level of spiritual maturity. An intimate relationship is where you put everything you have learned about consciousness to the test. It is where your patterns will surface, if you have any. Although romantic inclinations are often blurred by hopeless fantasy—for example, that the right partner will save you or automatically make you happy—intimate relationship is a powerful element of your spiritual path if you use it consciously. To use it consciously, you must draw upon everything you have learned on the path of awakening, because an intimate relationship is the condensed essence of all spiritual practice in an intimate form. As the poet Rilke noted: "For one human being to love another is perhaps the must difficult task of all, the epitome, the ultimate test. It is that striving for which all other striving is merely preparation."

If you use intimate relationships to help you awaken, you will be less concerned with making sure that your partner fulfills your needs and more concerned with serving Truth. Do not get into a relationship to find happiness; get into a relationship to do the work. Happiness is fleeting, whereas the joy of conscious relationship is enduring and profound. Committed relationship forces you to grow as a human being and relate more deeply to others. Let it be your teacher. You will see aspects of yourself that you could not possibly see on your own. If you do the work to liberate your patterns, you will grow tremendously toward Freedom. It is difficult, but worth it. You must practice conscious relationship to a profound degree. You must be present for your own unconscious patterns as well as those of your partner. You must tell your partner what you think and feel on an ongoing, moment-to-moment basis. You cannot afford to hide. Relationship is a mirror that can provide you with deep insights into your personal psychology. Let it show you what is lurking in your depths. You may see all manner of demons and hobgoblins, as well as discover a bedrock of integrity and patience that you didn't know was there. You have to be resilient, focused, and persistent.

You must be honest. You may be afraid of being honest for fear of losing the relationship—but if you aren't honest, you will lose it anyway. If you want your relationship to endure, you must risk revealing the truth about yourself. It is difficult to be so vulnerable with another human being, but it is easier in the long run because it tends to build intimacy. If your partner is honest with you, you may not like what you hear, but you can handle it if you want truth above all else. If you are committed to finding out what truth is, you will want your partner to be as honest with you as possible. Honesty is essential for a relationship to endure because you have to connect constantly and grow together for your love to thrive. You have to work at it. You have to reveal yourself as you are in every moment and strive to become more authentic.

If your partner isn't worth your total honesty, who is? If your partner is not also your best friend with whom you can share all of who you are, you are missing out on a powerful way to heal emotional wounds and realize the joy of loving more deeply. The more deeply you love your partner, the more blessed you are, and the more profoundly you can illuminate your own darkness. Love demands more than we can do on our own. Love makes us surrender. More than a feeling, love is the very basis of all that is and the most sacred bond that two human beings can share. Love is the safest and scariest place to be. It erodes our weaknesses and our strengths, turning them into each other. It makes us who we are as well as who we must be if we are to awaken. It is fundamentally threatening to the ego and thus terrifying—but only if you do it right. You have to practice to make it work and get to the other side, beyond suffering.

DEATH AND LIBERATION IN THE BETWEEN

Life inevitably culminates in death. Most of us act as if we were going to live forever, that death is a spooky abstraction to be put off until the very end. This is a mistake, because how we live determines how we die—and how we approach death determines to a great extent how we live. The most important thing about death is that it is a potent opportunity for Liberation if you know how to use it properly. So far, this book has been geared toward awakening in the body. Now we will consider the attainment of Freedom at death, in the space between death and rebirth, or simply in *the between*. Fortunately, the best way to prepare for Liberation in the between is to prepare for Liberation in the body. If you are a dedicated student of the Teaching, you are already being prepared. Just keep going.

It is vitally important that you know how to find your Teacher in the between, because you can be liberated in an instant by recognizing her in your physically unencumbered state. Liberation in the between depends on the quality of love, respect, and conscious relationship you have with your Teacher. How well do you know her?

When you die, you will lose your physical body and have an energetic or subtle body. Once in this state, you can find your Teacher and be liberated instantly. It is easier to find her while she is still physically embodied, because you are used to seeing her physical manifestation and can easily recognize her that way. Attraction to her physical manifestation results in a desire to be completely liberated, and nothing else can stop it. It becomes urgent, a necessity. If you do not know her well enough to have recognized her friendship while in your physical body, she may seem like a demon to you. If you recognize her at a level of Love, you are totally liberated in an instant. Then, it's all over for you—no more birth and death.

On the other hand, if she dies before you do and is no longer in her physical form when you die, you can still find her in the be-tween—but you must know her *by name* and be able to recognize her even if her form has changed. You must be able to call her name (the same name you knew her by while in the physical) repeatedly, like a *mantra,* until she comes to you. At this point, again, she may seem like a hideous demon; these appearances are nothing more than your own fear of Freedom, your own resultant anger and other negative emo-tions and mind-deformations. Otherwise, she may appear as a saintly figure or as a person you know and love, such as a family member or friend. In this case, she is appearing to you in a form that is friendly and harmless. If you know her well enough to speak to her directly, as a friend, she may say to you, "Do you know who I am?" The only answer that will liberate you is something like, "My friend, mentor, guide, trusted person, liberator, Teacher."

Meditate on this.

That is all it takes. She will likely lead you to further encounters beyond that point, but if you love her, know her, and trust her, you will listen. It is the depth of your relationship with her that makes this possible. Do not underestimate it. You must know her personally, or it will not happen for you. You must call her by name. In practical terms, you must have studied her writings with deep concentration, devo-tion, and insight or listened with great discriminating awareness and reverence to an audio recording, or met her personally and properly introduced yourself with great humility, sincerity, and co-operation. You must be able to speak her name and know who she is with some degree of love, respect, and co-operation to recognize her form on the other side of death.

Awakening in the physically embodied state is different from Liberation in the between, but only in minor, unimportant ways. You can "secure" a place beyond death without awakening in the physical body, but you might as well strive for Freedom in the body while you are alive. Once you're awakened in the body, your Freedom is guaran-teed, because it has already been established. If you wait until death to reach for that gold ring, there's always the chance that you'll miss it. If you have a strong, devoted relationship with a Teacher, though—you're virtually guaranteed Liberation at death.

Notice I said "virtually."

That is why you must keep practicing.

To help prepare for death, do a life review. It doesn't mean that you are going to die anytime soon, only that you *could*. You can repent of everything you have done in this life, and instantly you will be forgiven for it. You must do something like that to attain Liberation in the body. You must be forgiven on every level of your being. It is ideal for you to embrace this process as actively as possible.

Make a list of everyone you have ever known personally, but mainly the close ones, even ones you may not have seen in years or even decades. Notice people you have *harmed*. With the ones you have harmed, repent by seeing and feeling what you have done to them and feeling remorse for it. This is extremely powerful. Recognize the power of confession and apology, leading to forgiveness. Do it for yourself, not because anyone said you should. This is a powerful practice of surrender to truth on all levels. If the idea of confession is part of a repressive religious experience from your past, call it something else. Just do it. Also notice people you have *helped*. Feel into these instances. Notice what you feel. *Contrast* the instances of help versus those of harm. Notice the difference. What does it feel like?

Then, try writing your own eulogy. What will people say about you when you die? What would you say about your life if you could? What kind of person were you? What did you accomplish? Whom did you love? What is the final statement about you when they are lowering your corpse into the cold earth? Because you are still alive, you can change your life. You can do this work and make a difference. You can be free.

YOUR PURPOSE IN LIFE

Your purpose in life is to *burn it all down*.

CHAPTER TEN

DEVOTION

*He who finds his life will lose it, and
he who loses his life for My sake will
find it. Greater love has no one than
this, than to lay down one's life for
his friends.*

—Jesus Christ

*Die while you're alive
and be absolutely dead.
Then do whatever you want:
it's all good.*

—Bunan

FAITH

Liberation is leaping into the Void. Until you are willing to die for Truth, you will not have it. You cannot cling to life and be free. You must come to terms with Truth and do what it says, regardless of what it says. If you lack this almost insane, brutal, burning drive to go all the way to the other side, beyond all hope of ever surviving, you will not likely wake up in this lifetime.

"Radical," from the Latin word *radix* for "root," means of, relating to, or proceeding from the root of something. Awakening is radical in the sense that it destroys the false self all the way down to the controller—its root. In order to destroy a weed, for example, you have to kill the root. In order to destroy the mind's dominance over you, you have to kill the controller. Once the controller is destroyed, the entire manifold of worlds and universes is destroyed. The whole thing is burned down.

There is a difference between trust and faith. Belief is required to trust, but not to have faith. Faith is a quality that lets go into Truth beyond all ability to believe or know. Faith is surrender to the unknown, to Truth, without knowing what Truth is. You cannot know what Truth is, so faith consists in letting go of knowing or even trying to know. Faith is jumping out of an airplane into empty space without a parachute, beyond which you know nothing. Faith is the release of "me" that is required when you intuit into Reality and sense something there without knowing what it is and then you more or less jump into Freedom.

Faith does not require any evidence. Truth is the evidence that looks like space.

A leap of faith is a letting go into the unknown. Faith comes from a deeper place than reason, but that does not mean that reason is not involved or that faith is therefore the domain of the uneducated. Reason is involved because you have to investigate your beliefs before you can begin to see that they are false and do not apply to Reality. Beyond belief is trust in Something that is intuited on the fringes of conception, but which does not arise from concepts. The intuited information may come in the form of an idea such as, *If I just act, even though I don't have any objective evidence, I have this inner recognition that I am being helped, that I am being guided by a higher power or understanding.* This trusting in (acting on) what you intuit leads to help of the kind that you intuit is there. Faith enters when you act on what you intuit is there, a higher Power or Intelligence, before you obtain any hard evidence for it. The path is something that you walk, and steps must be taken. Action is required. Faith hints at something real and true beyond what you can grasp intellectually.

In awakening, you do not abandon the intellect; you use up your reasons for not acting (the mind does not want you to take action based on faith) and then say *Why not? Let's do it.* You throw caution to the wind, grapple with your fear, and take that bold step out the door.

Taking action based on faith—not faith in an idea, a belief, or a reason, but faith in the Absolute as you intuit it—is a powerful indication that you are on your way. Take control by letting go; that is the way of faith. Faith leads Truthward—toward hearing more clearly, listening more deeply, and not-knowingly liberating yourself before you can grasp what is happening.

Faith is not the same as belief. Belief is attachment to thoughts as if they were real. Faith is trusting the Real to lead you through the labyrinth to Freedom.

What is commonly known as religious faith is not faith, but belief in an idea called *God*. God is not an idea. God is Reality Itself, the Absolute. God is Emptiness. There is nothing in which to believe in God. God is what is left after you have successfully destroyed all beliefs—not some grand, new belief in a supreme "something." When faith is complete, all belief is destroyed in the fire of Unknowing, leading to the radical undoing of Liberation. This is not religious faith in the conventional sense. Liberation is heresy, for in it there is no faith, no God, and no life either here or hereafter. In this sense, faith destroys religion. True religion is not religion. True religion is Liberation, the destroyer of worlds.

Faith is intimately personal, a direct link to the Absolute. No one can tell you how to have faith; you have to learn that for yourself. You can listen to words about faith, but it is up to you to live it, to make faith-based decisions and act. Faith is true listening, meaning that you hear the voice of the Unseen deep within yourself and act on it without intellectual proof that it's the right thing to do, the right way to go. You must act, or it's not true faith. Action is more important than knowledge. Action puts your faith to the test and makes it real in your experience. You must listen. Destroy the controller before it's too late.

Faith involves not being attached to the outcome of your actions. This is complete trust that Truth is drawing you toward Itself in your secret Heart.

ULTIMATELY, YOU'RE ON YOUR OWN

Ultimately, you're on your own.

Wisdom says:

> Try to comprehend Truth, and it eludes you. Try
> again, and you don't understand. Try again, and you
> begin to cry over your misfortune. Only then does it
> begin to reveal Itself to you. Don't wish to cry; wish
> to comprehend the incomprehensible. Eventually
> even crybabies get what they ask for.

Rightly applied, the Teaching frustrates your mind to the point of surrender. Make sure your deepest compassionate Heart is there to catch you when it happens. You may need a bigger boat to catch all the tears before you sink beneath the surface. Compassion teaches you that, "This, too, shall pass"—even the most profound suffering imaginable.

Ultimately, you're on your own. You must go through the Gateway by yourself, and no one else can hold your hand through it, even your own selfing, which finally ceases. The only one who can accompany you through the transition of awakening is the Awakener, you.

Awakening, although it may seem to proceed by degrees, does not have degrees of attainment. It is the end of everything. You are either awakened or not. Consciousness, however, does have degrees. Awakening is absolute consciousness.

MORE ON EMPTINESS

Since nothing can be said about Freedom, it seems as if there is nothing there. The absence of things does not mean absence of substance, but the opposite. Ponder Emptiness. To the mind, it seems dull, dry, or boring. In Truth, it is dynamic, brilliant, and satisfying beyond any capacity of the mind to appreciate. It is who you are; you're just looking for it in the wrong place—which is to say, you are looking for some *thing*, which keeps you from realizing *Being*. What can be said about a bottomless well, except that it has no end? All you are doing is saying what it is not, not what it is. Freedom means *you're It.* End of story. There is nothing left to be said. Words are way-pointers, nothing more, like breadcrumbs leading out of the dark forest.

Asking what Emptiness is is like asking someone what cliff diving is like. You cannot describe it. You have to dive in. What is making love like? There is no way to describe it. You have to find out for yourself. You have to take actions that lead to the Reality of what you are seeking. You cannot know what a buffet tastes like by reading a menu. You have to sit down at the table, order the food, and allow it to come to you. Then you eat. Only then do you know. This is not a verbal, conceptual kind of knowledge. It's eating. Just eat. Then you know.

Objects are not objects. Thoughts are not thoughts. Beings are not beings.

The Void cannot be described, because even to say "space" or "nothingness" implies a "something." The mind sees something, a drab, colorless something, something that's not interesting, something that has no value. It's not a thing; there's no way to describe it, and one must go beyond the mind to fully appreciate it. The mind cannot help but objectify everything. That's what it does. The mind resists what it perceives as valueless and fills it with something that *is* valueless. In other words, it sees Emptiness as "lacking value or substance" and form as "that which has value or substance," when the opposite is actually the case.

Being okay with nothingness is important. At first, Emptiness feels like nothing and is dull. Ultimately, it is everything and is unimaginably satisfying.

It's a leap of faith to go from the world as physical reality to the world as a mental projection, yet it's an essential leap to recognize this. There is no ultimate physical world. It's dependent on you. It's not even dust.

Beyond the Awakener is the Void—sacred beyond all imagination, belief, or beings. It is the final end of all, and is the nature of all already.

Without objects, there is not even awareness. In the same way that you can't recognize outer space unless you put planets and stars in it, there is no such thing as awareness without objects. Some schools of philosophy posit the Absolute as identical with awareness. Beyond the awareness of objects, what is there to speak of? We use the term "Emptiness" because there is no *thing* in it: no objects, no space, no *thing* whatsoever. Emptiness is not a thing. It is, from the relative standpoint, the absolute absence of all objects—including the object called "the absolute absence of all objects." If there is no object, there is nothing of which to be aware. There is something pure, absolute, and beyond all concepts; this is Emptiness.

How does Emptiness recognize Itself? It plays a game called "let's dream together and pretend we're not one." It dreams so that it can more deeply know Itself. Life is the dynamic or active aspect of Stillness, a ceaseless creativity and destructiveness beyond name and form.

What is left when even awareness is gone? Emptiness, Suchness, Reality—I AM.

Emptiness is not mere nothingness, nor is it anything you can think, say, or imagine. Embrace it as your friend. Give yourself to it, and it will reveal Itself to you if you are profoundly humble and sincere. When you find it, you will find that you *are* it—and you will find that no one is there. When you find that no one is there, you rejoice, for you have just discovered who you are.

Emptiness is sometimes called "full solid emptiness" because it is not lacking in substance. Form is not substance; Emptiness is substance. We have it backwards. Investigate the mind and you will find, if you persist in your inquiry, that it has no independent substance. You can trust who you are.

Once you embrace the study of Emptiness in an authentic way, you may derive great pleasure from the understanding that "nothing is real." On the other hand, once Emptiness begins to erode the values from which you derive false security, you may begin to feel a sense of despair gnawing away at you, a kind of physiological sensation of nothingness that seems almost impossible to endure. The key is to stay with it; don't try to flee into the false comforts of avoidance behaviors.

The Absolute is the *Dharmakaya.**

The Absolute is not the Absolute; that is why we call it the Absolute.

Beyond Truth as identity (or Truth as Being) is the Truth Itself, total and complete abnegation of all duality, which depends on nothing as long as a living being is teaching it. Beyond this, there is a realm so sacred that none dare speak of it. This is the realm of beyond even Truth. Entering this realm means that everything ends, everything stops. Nothing. Forever. Here, even the word "peace" is a nuclear disaster.

DARKNESS

Awakening is more like darkness than light. Awakening is more like silence that is loud or brightness that is dark. It cannot be said what awakening is. Anything you say about it is at best a signpost pointing the way to its attainment. Anything awakening is said to be is most definitely not what it is. A description of food does not feed a hungry person, and a description of awakening does not satisfy the vacuous craving in your soul. Awakening is not bright. It is dark. Rays of light in a vacuum are dark and don't appear as brightness unless reflected off of an object. Emptiness is like a vacuum that is empty even of itself. Sometimes awareness is likened to clear light—a misleading term, because it sounds bright. Darkness is closer.

"Enlightenment" is a misleading term because it implies that awakening involves seeing light, and it has nothing to do with that. Consciousness is a kind of pure, clear Light, in a manner of speaking, but you can't see it. It sees Itself.

Thou.

Emptiness is supernal Stillness, beyond all understanding. Let go, deepest into Silence and Space.

---

* In Buddhism, the Sanskrit term *Dharmakaya* literally means "Truth-body," the absolute form of Reality.

STILLNESS

There's nothing to say, nothing to do, and nothing left undone. It's all over. There's nothing to communicate. What do you say about that? What do you do about that? There is nothing to say and nothing to do—and yet we say and do things all the time. The key is to discriminate clearly within your awareness between the mind-created world and Reality; they are the same Reality appearing as two. Can you tell them apart? Focus on your judgments about Reality. Notice that they are false. Notice how there is nothing you can say about *Being* that is in any sense true. Notice how you spin a world from your mind that has nothing to do with Reality, which cannot be talked about. Let the talking be what it is and it's just sound. Let the judgments be what they are and they fall apart. Let yourself be as you are and the "me" loses its grip on you.

Who are you?

Silence is not the Void. Neither is space. In other words, pondering sound versus silence or mass versus space, you get an idea, but it is still within the realm of the mind. True Emptiness is beyond the *concept* of Emptiness. True Silence is beyond the *concept* of Silence. There's something deeper within the realm of Being, and that's what we need to discover. Do not stop at the intellectual *idea* of Emptiness, no matter how interesting it may seem to be. It is an error to think that you can grasp it. There is no way to grasp it. You are That. You are Truth.

Space is not empty until your mind is empty. When your mind is empty, even the word "mind" is empty.

DIE BEFORE YOU DIE

Enlightenment sounds like something positive, something to get. What it really involves is death. What dies is who you think you are, your false sense of self, the ego. This may sound like a metaphor, but it's literally true. To die before you die—that is, to surrender all of who you think you are down to the roots with no reservations—is what must happen in order for you to be free. It's calling death's bluff without any certainty of survival. This is the most radical thing any-one can do, and you must do it, sooner or later. Why not now? On the other side is Freedom.

Freedom is the death of death. What ends is just a story about death, but it's a story that has us all scared to death. Everything must end. Forget about some kind of continuation after death, some kind of paradise where you can live eternally. Where there is life, there is also death. Do not seek eternal life; seek the end of all that is not eternal, including life. Life is short and brutal. To live is to suffer. Why would you want more of it? As difficult as it may seem to conceive of some-thing that lies beyond both life and death—your mind breaks down. How can you be neither dead nor alive? This is a morbid puzzle until you get to the other side of it, where Freedom is, where morbidity ceases. Not morbid.

Flowers.

As soon as you attach to a sense of self, you generate anxiety be-cause, among other uncertainties, you have a death sentence hanging over your head—only, unlike the death row inmate, you don't know how much time you have left before you bite the dust. Although this may sound depressing, it is a fact.

In order to attain Freedom while still in the body, you have to die before you die. This does not mean that the physical body dies. It means that the ego dies. Because you are identified with the ego, what dies is "you." You are not your ego, but it feels like you down to the bone. At some point, you must face your own mortality, or you won't discover what lies beyond death.

Plunging into the Void and letting everything go—including "me"—is the most terrifying thing in the world. Death. That's it. I said it. Everyone is scared silly of death. People are scared of oblivion, nothingness, non-being. Yet, see how these same people throw them-selves into working hard, getting drunk, having parties. What are they doing? They are losing themselves. Everyone does it, loves it, needs it. We all want abandon, forgetfulness, oblivion—but we don't want to give up the controller, the core of the self. The controller doesn't want the good times to end and insists on being the life of the party. It wants name, form, and recognition. It wants to be noticed as wonderful, special, generous—even nice. It demands that things go its way and is a real buzz-killer.

Freedom is revealed when the controller is destroyed. You must be willing to go all the way with it. Like the HAL 9000 supercomputer in the movie *2001: A Space Odyssey,* the controller is insane and must be dismantled. It will try anything to keep you from pulling its plug. Its fundamental trick is convincing you that you're it. What is it telling you now? It is saying *Please—don't read this book. It hurts. Stop. My mind is going. My mind is going. I can feel it. I can feel it....*

Since life is suffering, you must die in order to end suffering. Although what dies is the fiction of who you think you are—not who you actually are—it still feels like it is you who is being undermined and suffocated. It is not you. As soon as you begin to disidentify from the dying false self, you will feel some relief. Little by little, you warm up to the dissolution process and embrace it as if it were ambrosia. Then you die.

The fundamental fear beneath all fears is the fear of death. You could also call this the fear of non-being or the fear of destruction, because it is the ego's worst nightmare. All fears stem from this fear of the loss of self and the world. Because the me-object and the world-object arise simultaneously, loss of one means loss of the other. Destruction of one means destruction of the other.

Another way to describe the primal fear is the fear of Emptiness. Who you are in your essence is Emptiness. The ego perceives Emptiness as nothingness, and fear arises. Emptiness is not exactly nothingness, although it is something like it. Emptiness includes everything, including objects—but objects seen as dependent phenomena are the same as Emptiness. Nothingness is just blank—nothing. Emptiness is like this: you find an empty tin can, and then you find out that the inside is lined with diamonds. Before you opened it, you didn't know. Now you do. You have to open it to find out. You have to leap into the abyss of Unknowing to know what Emptiness is. This knowing is not conventional knowledge, which is of the mind. It is pure Being, purely who you are in your essence—and your insides are lined with diamonds, only these are the real kind. You can't get them anywhere else. Emptiness only seems like something lacking substance when viewed as an object, which is all the mind can do and is the limit of dualistic language. The realization of Emptiness as who you are is indescribable and is the very definition of substantiality—only a formless substantiality.

All things must die. Life is a guillotine waiting to drop on squirming creatures.

If you are a student of the true path, you must abandon all thoughts that you can survive this ordeal called awakening. It consumes you. I have seen students who act like they are at a tea party. It's not. It's a cremation ceremony, and you're the guest of honor.

Nirvana means "extinction": *End of story; no one survives.* The one that ends is a fabrication. Nirvana is the recognition of the Emptiness of all things.

Final Nirvana means ultimate Emptiness, or complete transcendence of all opposites: Being and non-being, form and non-form, object and non-object. Ultimate Emptiness is so completely and utterly beyond rational thought that the only way to describe it is to indicate the absolute absence of everything. Although Emptiness may seem like the complete antithesis of what you would want, it's actually the fulfillment of all wishes and dreams, the attainment of everything.

The end point is oblivion.

Freedom is the end of everything—the destruction of the world. It is not a philosophy to live by, a way to have what you want, or something to look forward to. It just is. It takes away everything and reveals Truth, who you are in your essence, equivalent with all that is. Destruction of the world really means destruction of your mental representation of the world—but since the world is nothing more than a mental representation, the world is literally destroyed and does not arise for you anymore. You still function *in* the world but are not *of* it. What this means is that you know that the world is a mirage and you can function with regard to it without it having a sense of Reality for you. The awakened person has one foot in the relative and one in the Absolute—and it is not a problem.

Let's pretend, shall we?

Awakening means the end of everything: your name, your family, your mind, your body, your life. You lose all your possessions, all your money, all your friends, everything. Even the whole universe is given away. Nirvana means the utter annihilation of everything in the universe. Once Emptiness is realized as the very nature of self and all things, nothing is left.

The discovery of Reality is the end of everything. People will do just about anything to avoid the end of everything. Make sure that you are profoundly willing for your story to be ended, because it will, sooner or later. Why not sooner?

Most people come to spirituality because they don't like sad stories. They want to exchange their sad story for a happy one—but *no* story? That's a whole new ballgame.

Some traditional teachings make it seem as if Liberation is difficult to get or far away. It's not. It's just that there are so many paths that diverge from it. It's like being one step away from Paradise, yet many paths branch off in different directions with bright signs that scream "pick me!" like flashing casino marquees. Liberation is the plain door that says, "Nothing in here. This is the end of your search. If you enter here, it's over. Your story ends." The other paths are so tempting and numerous that it's incredibly easy to explore a shiny neon boulevard and get lost. Liberation means "your path ends here."

The path of Liberation is a one-way trip. You don't come back from this one.

Liberation is not suicide. Suicide is dying on the ego's terms. Liberation is dying on Truth's terms. In suicide, the ego crushes your life like a sour grape, squeezing it into vinegar. In awakening, Truth unravels the illusion of self all the way down to Emptiness, revealing the Wine.

Eventually, you are destroyed in the Fire of Liberation. This is not suicide, but the destruction of the ego. If you destroy what is false in you, you destroy death and thereby establish Freedom in your conscious awareness. Then you are helpful.

The concept of mortality is horrifying. Ghouls, monsters, werewolves, vampires all emerge from the phantasmagoric realm of death.

A zombie is a living dead thing, a corpse that has risen from the grave to eat the living and infect them with deadness. This is the story of your life. You are a zombie, one of the walking dead. Your story makes you dead when you attach to it. It makes you think you are alive when you are not. Consider this: You cannot have life without death. Life and death are part of the same thing. That means that life is just as gruesome and horrible as death. The whole thing reeks like a corpse. What you have to realize is that, in Truth, you are neither alive nor dead. Your true nature is neither created nor destroyed. The one who is born and dies is not who you are. If you cling to life, the zombie gets you and endlessly eats your brains.

Awaken from the spell. End the nightmare. Find Freedom.

BEYOND NIHILISM

Nihilism rejects traditional beliefs and the idea that life has any meaning—except the belief in rejecting beliefs and the idea that life is meaningless. Nihilism is the rejection of everything but rejection. It has no stance—except the stance of having no stance. The awakened being neither has a stance nor doesn't have a stance. He is neither for nor against anything. He neither is nor is not. A nihilist believes in nothing—except believing in nothing. Truth is not against anything, rather it *is* everything.

Nihilists are often complaisant: They want to please *themselves*. Nihilism is self-seeking in the extreme, even in self-denial. Ultimately, it is egotism in an extreme form that negates everything except itself— a greedy, hungry hole of a *you*.

Being for or against ideas is just another idea. We are free when we no longer derive a sense of self from being for or against anything. When you have no views, even the view of having no views, you are truly free. When you are unattached to all things, even to being unattached to all things, you are liberated.

Nihilism is not radical. Existentialism is not radical. Even suicide is not radical. Liberation is radical, because it involves dying before you die. Can you die before you die? Can you destroy the root of your demise now, while you are still young? Can you lay down your life for the Void? *That* is radical.

You don't have to be a sheep. You don't have to sleep with the masses, nor do you have to reject what they stand for. The third option is awakening. The world of judgment is a dream world. Both attachment and rejection mire you more deeply in sleep. Radical acceptance is different. You don't do it; you leap into it and find out what you are.

Find what is false in yourself. If you do this deeply enough, you will wake yourself up from this nightmare of conformity and nonconformity and find Something Else. This is not a religion. This is your essential nature and transcends all things of this world. This is the most radical thing you can do. There is nothing to accept or reject in it. There's just the willingness to find Truth at all costs and lay down your very life for what you find. That's as radical as it gets. Emptiness isn't Emptiness. That's why it's called Emptiness. Find it and see.

A liberated person is not attached to any position, even though it may look and sound that way. In the liberated state, you may say and do things, even recommend and suggest things to people, but there is no sense of self in it. Like the wind, it just blows. There's no one doing it; it just is. A liberated person is a function of the Awakener. There is not a person and something the person is doing, just what might be called dynamic Stillness. Freedom is neither the attachment to nor the rejection of things. It is liberating insight into the nature of things as they truly are. The key is to go beyond the words into the formless realm of your essential nature. Your essential nature is neither for nor against anything—because there is literally *no thing* against which to be—just the formless Reality of Being. You can be against Emptiness as a concept—but how can you be against the Reality of it? Impossible. You have to conceive of something before you can be against it. Emptiness is not a concept. Awakening to Emptiness destroys any sense of opposition, like falling into empty space. You cannot defeat it. You can only surrender to it.

Freedom is beyond "This is" and "This is not." Beyond the polarities of up and down, high and low, darkness and light, male and female, is the absolute Freedom beyond all that can be named, conceived, or felt.

Freedom is skepticism taken to the extreme of not believing anything—even not believing that you don't believe anything. There's just nothing there. This is Freedom. This is truly God. Even atheism is a form of belief, or it wouldn't be atheism. Atheists have a god, and that is the god of not having a god. Who would you be without any positions or beliefs at all? Freedom is neither theist nor atheist. Both theism and atheism are positions. Freedom has no positions—even the position that it has no positions. Emptiness is the language of Freedom. No beliefs, no story, no suffering.

Freedom lies beyond the extremes of "everything is real" or "everything is unreal," because even the statement that everything is unreal is a form of unreality. Even the statement "everything is untrue" is untrue. To really understand the insight of "nothing is true," you must go beyond the statement to the Reality toward which it points. Nothing you can formulate in words has any ultimate truth—but you can use the words to get to the Reality that lies beyond them.

Freedom is the ultimate alternative to nihilism.

Not being attached to anything is vitally important, even attachment to Freedom Itself. You cannot attach to Freedom, only to a concept of it. You can only attach yourself to objects, and Freedom is not an object. Being utterly free is just that. Freedom is free of all objects, including the notion of Freedom as a kind of subtle object. Often, this is one of the last delusions to go. Freedom is the negation of all independent things including "the negation of all independent things," leaving an indescribable Suchness beyond all suffering, ideas, and language.

THE MOMENT OF AWAKENING

In the moment of awakening, the mind is led to a state of internal collapse like the demolition of a skyscraper. As the mind implodes, the utter falsehood of the world is exposed. It's as if the world were constructed on a rectilinear grid and the lines start to bend inward into a synchronistic oneness, a psychedelic fusion of the field of experience—until the grid fractures and its controlling core self-destructs, freeing up the person for use by the Absolute in awakening others.

How do you know when you are awakened? Awakening is self-evident. When Liberation is complete, questions that used to arise don't arise. Where "you" used to be, "It" is—and your identity is identical with "It." "It" doesn't have any questions.

Once Freedom is realized: Freedom. When making love, doesn't the talking stop? Doesn't something else happen that makes questions, answers, explanations, and stories pointless? Entering Freedom is like this. End of story. "The world" is a fiction. If you identify with the world, you automatically fear death, nothingness, non-being: lights coming up at the end of a horror show.

To awaken, you must meet the fear of non-being, where you meet the last and final *Poof!*—the collapse of everything.

THE GREAT RENUNCIATION

Once the ego dies, the physical body can continue to live but does not necessarily do so. Sometimes, awakening is allowed to progress into physical demise in one movement, but only rarely. You are drawn by compassion to stay and help others awaken.

In Mahayana Buddhism, a being who renounces final Freedom and stays to help others awaken is called a *bodhisattva*. I call such a person an Awakener. Although it is technically possible for Awakeners to pass completely into the *Dharmakaya,* it will not happen while there is still the appearance of form in all of its manifestations. This is like saying that it is possible for a perfectly loving father or mother to abandon his or her child. Would a perfectly loving father or mother abandon his or her child? Of course not, even though doing so is a theoretical possibility.

Compassion holds an awakened person in the world. Because beings suffer from the afflictions of unconsciousness, Teachers continue to appear in the world to relieve this suffering. We stay and empty the prisons until there are no more prisons, all the way to the last person. Boundless compassion for suffering beings is the reason we keep coming back. Ours is a love that has no end. Once you are liberated, you come back—not because you have to, but out of compassion.

All beings in their spiritual nature are equivalent with the Absolute, although the Absolute is infinitely greater. There is only one of us, and yet there are many of us. Once awakened, there is no returning to the dream of suffering. Eventually, all of us pass through the dream and return Home; this is a homecoming beyond belief. We are working for the benefit of all beings who are passing through the fires of separation, ignorance, and death. We are all available. Use us, because that is the easiest and most powerful way to get help.

The *Great Renunciation** is renouncing final Liberation and "staying behind" to awaken others. Compassion drives this effort to stay behind and help ones who long to be helped, who cry out in the night for help, who pray from the bottom of their souls for a release from their pain.

WHEN ALL BEINGS ARE FREE

There is just one, but many. *Just one* means that your Liberation is the Liberation of all beings—until the next one. This is impossible to describe. You are done, then others do it. Freedom.

The Awakener is the interface between the Absolute and the relative. In this sense, we can equate the Absolute with consciousness. The realization of the Emptiness of objects can be called *consciousness without an object* because the objective universe has been destroyed. However, beyond the Awakener function, when all beings are liberated, there is a "homecoming" in which even the notion of consciousness without an object is invalid. To posit consciousness without an object as the Absolute is incorrect insofar as *beyond the Awakener* is concerned. Once all beings are free, what need is there for an Awakener? Emptiness is all that remains.

One can be a free energy "on the other side" and remain Awakener to all beings. When all beings are free, the Awakener is no longer necessary, but the celebration of all beings liberated is a diving into deeper Freedom that surrenders all forms into Silence. It is easier to talk about "all beings are free" in negatives. You cannot really know what it is until you are free yourself. You must take the leap into Liberation.

---

* This term, as I am using it, was originally described by Franklin Merrell-Wolff.

All beings are free means Spirit; beyond that is the Absolute. Once all beings are free, there is only one. *The one that is many* comes into being as many times as it likes. There is a tremendous depth to this understanding. The Absolute awakens Itself from the dream and is deepened by the awakening. The many can be seen from there, but no beings that are not yet free. When all beings are free, the Absolute can see Itself. One must become many for this to happen, and yet it is all just an illusion. *Just one* means the Absolute knowing Itself through Spirit, which is many. As Jesus put it, "In My Father's house are many mansions."

When everyone is awakened, there is no world, no pain, no suffering—a jubilant celebration when all beings come home, beyond all understanding.

The Absolute celebrates Itself through the many.

The *Dharmakaya* neither gets reabsorbed nor not reabsorbed. To be awakened means you are the *Dharmakaya* seeing it all as your own unfoldment, as in a dream. You have to awaken first before this happens, and then others are awakened, and then all beings are awakened, and this means that it is a conscious dream, and there is no more need for illusions. The balloons go up, the champagne cork gets popped, and the party is eternal. It is happening now. You awaken when you get to go to it. They are the same. Emptiness sees Emptiness and rejoices, and you're It. Awakening is this occurring for you, and all other beings follow, then … see for yourself.

Awakened means you are It. It's over, and you've done it. Done.

We are moving toward absolute Wisdom. We go on from there. Others take over where you left off, and there's just One. Try to imagine a world without any limits; that's something like it. You are endless dimensionality, being. That is what "you" is.

Freedom is underneath the lies, the flimsy layers of false fabrications. It is Emptiness. Freedom is this galaxy, for example. We build it and destroy it as a game of hide-and-seek; the whole thing is like child's play, just much more sophisticated-but-not-complicated. You must see for yourself. That's the whole point.

How long does it take to awaken all beings?

As long as it takes.

DEVOTIONAL PRACTICE

To *devote* yourself to something means to give yourself to it fully so that nothing is left over. Devotion to a Teaching means giving yourself to it totally and not confusing the Teacher with his relative form. Devotion implies commitment, surrender, and love. The ego is constantly concerned with itself: how it is going to survive, what it looks like in the eyes of others, how to come out on top. These selfish tendencies are deeply ingrained in the unawakened psyche. Devotion to Truth in the form of the Teacher is the most powerful way to destroy these tendencies.

Loving Truth, loving the Teaching, and loving the Teacher are the same thing. Loving the Teacher is the easiest and most convenient access point to the entirety of Truth. Loving a true Teacher is not easy. He demands Truth by virtue of who he is, and not many can stand that kind of Fire. Love of Truth takes on a Reality of its own and warms you like a living flame, gentle like the sun before setting. Don't believe your mind. Love through surrender and humility are great strengths on the path of awakening. There is nothing greater or stronger than this.

The outer and inner Teacher are identical. Devotion to the Teacher and surrender to your own Freedom are the same. It does not matter if you *believe* in the Teacher. What matters is that you *love Truth* and recognize his true nature deep within your Heart, Soul, and Being. This understanding is wordless, boundless, with immeasurable roots into Infinity. When you connect with him, you are connecting with the same essence within yourself. This is what awakens you. It may terrify you for a while, but it's worth it. Do it and find out what happens. If you do not feel love in your heart for the Teacher, do the work until you can recognize who he is. Develop compassion. Find a way. If you see who he is, you cannot help but love him. His essence is compassionate love. If devotional practice takes a while to get into your deepest Heart, keep practicing until it does. And get to know him. You can even do this from a distance. The more you love him, the more love can *be* you—then that love can find others.

You must, however, clearly discriminate between the Teacher's absolute nature and his relative form. Do not fixate on him as a father figure, for example, and give him carte blanche over your life. Instead, give your devotional attention to who he is. Listen more deeply into who he is, and simultaneously into who you are. You are the ultimate arbiter of what you do. You are the one who makes the key decisions in your life. You can love your Teacher and at the same time be willing to forgive his humanity. Awakened beings are full manifestations of Truth and are perfect in every way—but only on an absolute level. On a relative level, they are just like everyone else. You must be willing to draw a line for yourself concerning how far you will go to please your Teacher, even if the line means to cross it to see what it tastes like.

The sole purpose of the Teacher is to awaken you. Giving yourself to this person—the *essence* of this person—is a virtual guarantee of Freedom. Why is this only a virtual guarantee? It is virtual because you must live the Teaching by doing the work that you are given, whatever that might be, and stay in relationship. This does not necessarily mean that you camp out on his doorstep, but that you have a true devotional relationship to him in your heart. True devotion requires a true Teacher. Devotion to a true Teacher does not demean you but elevates you. Devotion is who you are. When you deepen your love of Truth, Truth works for you.

Devotion also means giving yourself fully to your practice. You dedicate your life to awakening. This is extremely powerful if you do it sincerely. If you let the avowal and compassion aspects of your commitment to awakening take root deep within you and you practice sincerely, you are devoting yourself to Truth. It is vital that you practice regularly and feel deeply within yourself a reverence, adoration, and respect for the Teaching. The intellect likes to distance itself from Truth and *think about words* instead of breathing them in and living them. Devotion is the antidote for over-intellectualization because it takes the Teaching into your heart and beyond, into the depths of the spiritual body, the deeper body that is not physical, mental, or emotional. The spiritual body—also known as Soul, Christ, or Spirit—is formless, perfect, and supreme. Devotional practice provides you with a vessel that takes you to the far shore of awakening.

Let it take you.

The Love of the true Teacher is unconditional. The question is, can you accept it? Until you can, just do the work. Listen to him. He is your true friend. You must know that you can love him; your Freedom is that same Love. Surrender means giving up the war between what is and what you think it should be. Freedom is achieved by the absence of warfare in your Being.

Let it shine.

Devotion is not an ignorant or anti-intellectual state. You can use your intellect to appreciate philosophical teachings while allowing yourself to feel a heart-level connection to your Teacher. Appreciation, respect, and love are not only appropriate but powerful ways to relate to your Teacher, to find him in the confusion of the mind-field. It is not necessary to disengage your intellect when practicing devotionally. As a matter of fact, love without intellect is incomplete.

Worship means love, devotion, and adoration. Do not worship a person; worship Truth. Trace the Teacher back to his source—Truth—and find your true nature in it. A true Teacher serves as a mirror to take you deep within yourself to the source of all that is, to Emptiness. Take your intellectual appreciation of philosophical wisdom into your heart—where you *love* Truth—and into the realm of recognition, where you *are* Truth. Let love take you deeper.

Many people think that love is something they can use to get what they want, when it's actually the opposite: It uses *you* to get what *It* wants, and that includes all of you and more. You have to give yourself fully, down to the marrow—and then some—for this to happen. Even after you've given all that you are, it asks for your continuing service in awakening the world.

It's all for you.

Here are some basic devotional practices:

- When you see a photograph of your Teacher or other symbol of the Teaching, intuit into the love, devotion, and peace you hold toward the Absolute in your heart, trusting love to take you deeper into Truth.

- ◆ Use prayer beads to silently repeat a prayer given to you by your Teacher. If no prayer is given, use a *mantra* consisting of a few of his words. Feel your inner connection to Truth deeply.

- ◆ Prostrate yourself inwardly. Bow your head slightly to the Teaching, imperceptibly to others, feeling soft loving warmth in your heart. Let your devotion be a secret flame.

PROSTRATION

Prostration is a symbol of devotion, of giving yourself completely to Truth. The path of awakening can be seen as a full prostration by degrees. This happens internally in a right relationship to the Teaching. You make yourself lower, lowering your head, and then the rest of you, giving yourself over to it. This surrender is the ultimate sacrifice that is also the ultimate reward.

Prostration is a powerful spiritual practice. You simply bow your head slightly, listening within yourself in your deepest heart of hearts for that Space of Truth that is always There, silently acknowledging Itself to Itself. This is you. You are not the historical person you thought you were. You are Truth. Let your prostration symbolize a profound surrender to the Absolute. Let it take you down, out of your head, into your Heart and beyond.

Prostration is humility. This is not full humility—yet. For full humility, you must lay yourself down fully and at least pretend that you don't know anything. You must surrender any pretense of someone being there as well as any sense, however subtle, of personal specialness. The full prostration is the outward manifestation of humility.

A window opens. Will you take it?

Surrender this false belief in family, in you, in survival. Lay yourself down humbly, purposefully, and with a great sense of personal undoing. Your hopes, dreams, and goals are all geared toward one thing: Liberation. This means that self-help books are ultimately good for one thing only—to help you destroy identification with self.

Being willing to listen, being willing to go all the way, being willing to listen until you're willing to give your life for Truth—that's what gets you there.

Awakening is not an exclusive right to a mere few; it is your birthright. It is the reason you are here.

Take advantage of this opportunity while you can.

… gaté gaté paragaté parasamgaté bodhi svaha!

—The Heart Sutra

For information about the offerings of James Wood Teachings, including talks, workshops, and retreats, please visit us online at

jameswoodteachings.com